COMIC AGONY

T0130792

A L B E R T   B E R M E L

COMIC AGONY

MIXED IMPRESSIONS IN THE MODERN THEATRE

NORTHWESTERN UNIVERSITY PRESS ✳ **EVANSTON, ILLINOIS**

Northwestern University Press
Evanston, Illinois 60208-4210

Copyright © 1993 by Albert Bermel. First published 1993.
First paperback printing 1996. All rights reserved.

Printed in the United States of America

ISBN 0-8101-1410-0

Library of Congress Cataloging-in-Publication Data

Bermel, Albert.
    Comic agony : mixed impressions in the modern theatre /
Albert Bermel.
        p.   cm.
    Includes bibliographical references and index.
    ISBN 0-8101-1071-7 (alk. paper).—ISBN 0-8101-1410-0
(pbk. : alk. paper).
    1. Tragicomedy—History and criticism. 2. Drama—20th
century—History and criticism. I. Title.
PN1902.B47 1993
809.2'523—dc20   93-27280
                                                      CIP

CONTENTS

ACKNOWLEDGMENTS

This book was conceived in the early 1970s, but for assorted reasons, most of them having to do with the real or imagined pressures of other writing, I published earlier versions of the introduction and, subsequently, most of the chapters as separate, orphaned pieces of criticism. I thank the editors of the publications that took them in, including *CommuniCulture*, the *Shaw Review, Modern Drama, Twentieth Century Literature, Exchange* (University of Missouri), *Theater* (Yale), *Theater Three*, the *Eugene O'Neill Review, Alan Ayckbourn: A Casebook*, and *Annals of Scholarship*. I am also lastingly grateful—in no particular order, not even alphabetical—to Helen Merrill's discretionary powers, the director and editors of Northwestern University Press, and so many students, colleagues, and theatre friends with whom I have talked about the plays and the book's theme that I dare not name names for fear of omitting some. I must put in a word of thanks, though, to that gracious and efficacious lady, Ms. Nora Roback, who runs the department of which I have nominally been chairperson. Eric Bentley, the monarch of twentieth-century drama virtuosi and a cherished friend, has been the most provocative challenger I have had the good fortune to confer with by phone and mail and in person. Critics with whom I agree are entitled to sue me for annexing their ideas, although—advance notice—I own insufficient to make it worth their litigious while; and critics with whom I disagree have kindly, if unknowingly, stimulated many of the paragraphs and footnotes that follow, especially the less patient ones. Encouragement and other family perks from Joyce, Neil, and Derek have accelerated the book's overlong incubation.

REDEFINITIONS

The studies in the following chapters arise from the figures each playwright brings onstage and keeps there, or removes from the stage, or leaves absent during an act or scene under consideration. To account for such presences and absences, which determine what is happening before the audience and what is withheld, I use a half-dozen familiar words, nothing as full-blooded as a terminology, in slightly unfamiliar ways. It seems worth starting out with these words and their extended meanings.

Roles and Characters

A role is written; a character is performed. By *role*, I mean everything the playwright asks of an actor: the lines, the stage directions that apply, and any other descriptive material and hints in the text. A role embraces the fewest requirements for the part, but it also implies all that part's imaginable potential. A range of *probabilities* inheres in any role. We may never see them all realized.

By *character*, I mean what an actor elects to do with a role, settling into specific bits of characterization that feel comfortable, shocking, fearsome, funny, or especially convincing. Actors bring to their roles, too, their unique souls and bodies, which they may appear to reinvent, role by role, if they are good at mockery and makeup.

Thus the character of Mrs. Warren in Shaw's play when performed by Uta Hagen draws on Hagen's physical, intellectual, and emotional contributions to the role. These may not coincide with what Shaw had in mind, although they may strike us as an overall improvement on Shaw, in which case they raise possibilities (not only probabilities) unforeseen by the dramatist and his critics. It could also happen that the character, when enacted, will correspond with uncanny accuracy to Shaw's vision of the role, so far as Hagen and we understand it.

Both a role and a character (the role as interpreted) are syntheses or amalgams of what that figure does in a number of scenes. In those scenes the role (and the character) may not add up to a consistent personality. The personality will more likely add up to something inconsistent, for in the successive scenes it unwinds vis-à-vis other roles, and they bring out its differing traits. What we make of Ophelia as a role depends on what we make of her separate scenes with Laertes, Polonius, Hamlet, Gertrude, and Claudius, as well as her soliloquy ("O what a noble mind is here o'erthrown"). But the resolution of Ophelia as a role grows even more complicated when we think of the varied *kinds* of scenes she plays with Hamlet and with Laertes under convulsive circumstances and then mull over the scenes she does not play with Horatio or Fortinbras or Rosencrantz and Guildenstern. The range of probabilities confronting an imaginative performer who will play the character of Ophelia is even broader and more daunting than the probabilities that inhere in the role, but to them we must still add the possibilities.

Character equals role plus the personality and attributes of the actor plus choice of interpretation, the latter being affected by the presence at rehearsals of the director, designer, playwright, and other actors. But—paradox!—because of the foregone probabilities, a role can be larger than the character. After all, for readers of the printed version of the play the role is not mere potential; it is something realized on the stages behind their brows, if not quite actuated.

Action and Story

The *action* comprises what happens to (and between) the roles onstage. This is what the audience actually witnesses. The *story* is much larger and lengthier than the action, for it subsumes all the events that lead up to the start of the action (which the audience only hears about), the action itself, whatever happens offstage during the action, and what happens offstage during act and scene breaks (the audience hears about these happenings but does not witness them).

We learn about the story only in the course of the action. Because we witness the action, we can make our own decisions about it, but because we do not witness the whole story, we have to rely on evidence furnished during the action by the roles. Sometimes we cannot trust the roles. They may (and frequently do) contradict one another. One of the most baffling instances of conflicting evidence in a story crops up in Pirandello's *Right You Are.* Signor Ponza says Signora Ponza is his second wife. His mother-in-law says Signora Ponza is his first wife whom he remarried. At the end we finally meet and hear from the lady in question. Signora Ponza confirms what her husband said and what her mother said, even though the two statements conflict, and she compounds the confusion when she adds, "And for myself, I am nobody."

Plotting and Main Plot and Subplots

By *plotting* I mean the roles playwrights choose to bring onstage for different scenes or subscenes, separately or together, simultaneously or in sequence, and the roles they leave offstage in those same scenes and subscenes. The *main plot* is made up of the roles who take part in the main line of the action. The *subplot* is made up of the roles who take part in secondary lines of the action. It means something other than which performers' names are printed in larger type or whose name sits above the title on the marquee. The distinction between main plot and subplot may sound precise: it isn't.

INTRODUCTION
How Comic? How Agonizing?

We were aware of all the comedy in this. But, as brilliant as we were when we put our heads together, we did not guess until we were fifteen that we were also in the midst of a tragedy.
KURT VONNEGUT, *Slapstick: or, Lonesome No More*

And he died just to give the others something to laugh about, but the others didn't laugh.
JACOV LIND, *Ergo*

An earlier book of mine, *Contradictory Characters*, studied some modern plays in which characters almost willfully damage or destroy their lives. Their self-spiting nature makes them steer toward the rocks along the shores of their lives, shame and ruin, which they dread but which mesmerize them. Like their counterparts in life, they seek happiness, peace of mind, reconciliation with others, or some similarly comforting objective, while they talk and behave in a manner that rules it out for them. Plays that accommodate such figures present us with not only a conflict between the roles but also a conflict *within* some of those roles, generally between what we clumsily call the conscious and the unconscious will.

Some plays—often the same plays—disclose a further conflict, a more deeply seated contradiction, in their very makeup and in how they are meant to be taken. In them, as frequently in life, comic (or farcical) and tragic (or melodramatic) impulses are at odds, so that opposed conceptions of the dramatic material seem to vie for mastery in the one work. The Old Man in Ionesco's *The Chairs* or the hero of Adamov's *Professor Taranne* feels as anguished as does any zany out of a traditional farce, but his fears of looking as foolish as that zany prey upon him in his cursed state of excruciating self-consciousness. Meanwhile, because of the dramatic treatment, we find his plight funny—a bit like that of the old-time zany, except also disturbing. As spectators or readers, we do not feel it is fair to laugh at his fears. Besides, outlandishly amusing scenes that extrude those fears may go forward so shadowed by somberness that they leave us with mixed sensations of pleasure and bleakness, a delight in personality quirks undercut by disquiet. Or disgust. The preparations in Pinter's *The Homecoming* for handing over the oldest son's wife to his father and brothers will let them "put her on the game" in the streets of Soho. In Ionesco's *The Lesson* the capers of the aged teacher and his young pupil will prove to be one stage in a cycle of murders. The playwright in each case keeps a jovial mask bobbing before us but occasionally lets the light glance off it from a distressing angle, as a Noh actor does, until in the last scene he holds it steady. Then we notice a strain around the mask's brow and grinning mouth and, finally, blood leaking at its edges. We laughed at first, if uneasily, and continue to laugh, still uneasily, not because we are heartless but because we respond to what the playwright, director, and actors have arranged for us, a spectacle of comic agony.

As a converse illustration, the inner play of Brecht's *The Caucasian Chalk Circle* (once the "frame" playlet or prologue is past) announces itself in the first three lengthy scenes as Grusha's and Michael's melodrama of adventure, rescue, and pursuit. But the appearance in the last two lengthy scenes of new roles, and particularly the irruption of Azdak, the impudent scrivener turned judge, shifts the work into a peculiar blend of spectacle and exhortation, joy and punishment.

Explainers galore have tried to account for the recent drama's refusal to comply with conventional genres like tragedy and comedy. The explanations, frequently laid out in slogans and sociologese, rely on the symptoms of our century's social turmoil, innovations, and international disenchantments, from computerized, nonstop war to other forms of mass communication; from untruth in advertising to treachery in politics; from the advent of Charlie Chaplin, Albert Einstein, Albert Schweitzer, detective and espionage stories, to the demise of God, Satan, communism, courtesy, restraint, literacy, and Franklin D. Roosevelt, in no special order. My own, undeterministic view is that playwrights during interviews like to chat about the categories and traditions held up to them by criticism for writing and staging a play but do not believe for an instant that the categories and traditions govern their own lonely work. As one outgrowth of playwrights' liberation, comic agony is something other than a mash of opposites: it has the earmarks of a distinctive type of drama; it exhibits a range of related attitudes by playwrights toward their theatre. Our reception of it can hardly correspond to our reception of a purely serious or funny situation, but it will not necessarily lie somewhere between the two.

In what respects does it differ from tragicomedy? During the Renaissance, scholars awarded *tragicomedy* as a classification both to a serious play with a happy resolution, its tragic or melodramatic ending averted, such as one of Shakespeare's several "romances," and equally to a breezy pastoral or a light comedy that ended sadly. Traces of these original meanings cling to the word. At some point in the drama, usually near the end, the tragic or comic mood, the prevailing tone, alters. Unless the playwright transposes with uncommon craft, the result will appear awkward, as if the last part of the work has been tacked on. From subsequent definitions *tragicomedy* has acquired another connotation, that a play given this label keeps switching direction. A funny scene or moment precedes a disastrous or dismal one, which in turn leads into more merriment. This alternating need not happen with mechanical precision. Even if five comic scenes outnumber every two grim scenes in the final tally, the switches back and forth persist through the tragicomic action.

Some writers on the drama, such as John Dryden, could not abide the bastard form:

The end of tragedies or serious plays, says Aristotle, is to beget admiration, compassion, or concernment; but are not mirth and compassion things incompatible? And is it not evident that the poet must of necessity destroy the former by intermingling of the latter? that is, he must ruin the sole end and object of his tragedy, to introduce somewhat that is forced into it, and is not of the body of it. Would you not think that physician mad, who, having prescribed a purge, should immediately order you to take restringents?[1]

Dryden, leaning on Aristotle during what we now deem an age of artistic reason and placidity, intends to keep tragedy untainted, segregated. Samuel Johnson, writing a century later, had something like this switching in mind when he defended the art of Shakespeare and theatrical miscegenation:

The censure which he has incurred by mixing comic and tragic scenes . . . deserves more consideration. . . . Shakespeare's plays are not in the rigorous and critical sense either tragedies or comedies, but compositions of a distinct kind; exhibiting the real state of sublunary nature, which partakes of good and evil, joy and sorrow, mingled with endless variety of proportion and innumerable modes of combination; and expressing the course of the world in which the loss of one is the gain of another. . . .

Shakespeare has united the powers of exciting laughter and sorrow not only in one mind but in one composition. Almost all his plays are divided between serious and ludicrous characters, and, in the successive evolutions of the design, sometimes produce seriousness and sorrow, and sometimes levity and laughter.

That this is a practice contrary to the rules of criticism will be readily allowed.[2]

Johnson's statement is of a different order from Dryden's. It deals with art, not with constraints on art.[3] Johnson, by a tremendous effort of the imagination, clears his vision of "the laws which custom had prescribed," the hard boundaries between tragedies and comedies and other "rules of criticism" that Beaumarchais would later scoff at as "the scarecrow of pedestrian minds."

As critic, Dryden remains the subjective playwright. In keeping tragedies and comedies apart he turns advocate for the unconfused drama he has written himself or will write: in one genre a tragic *Aureng-Zebe* or *All for Love*; in another, a comic *Secret Love* or *Marriage à la Mode*. Johnson, not a playwright, is under no such obligation to personal interests. His criticism can have a partisan tinge, but he is taking Shakespeare's part, not his own, even though he may incidentally be providing reasons for picking his edition of Shakespeare over those of

Theobald, Pope, Warburton, and Hanmer.

We might also frown on Dryden as critic for having summoned the majestic ghost of Aristotle, like scores of dramatic critics before him and plenty after. With a modicum of cunning and touches of guesswork about the incomplete text of the *Poetics* that we have inherited, he recruits Aristotle as his ally. Johnson, however, is playing a comparable game. He takes Shakespeare as his ally, confronting a monumental critic with a monumental playwright. Or, if his preface were a retort to Dryden's essay, which it is not, we might say he is swamping Playwright Dryden with Playwright Shakespeare.

No, the striking difference is that Dryden looks backward, Johnson forward. Today we balk at Dryden's rigidities, whereas the impure qualities Johnson directs us to in Shakespeare seem obvious and obviously apt—and historically established. As Johnson points out, in plays that predated Shakespeare's a serious or pathetic moment may supervene in a comedy's merriment. (And anyway, comic recognition scenes almost always activate the tear ducts, as they were meant to do.) From the other direction, moments of comedy or farce in those early plays make incursions into solemn moods. Northrop Frye ascribes the interruptions to the survival of the satyr-play.[4]

Nearly two centuries after Johnson's preface appeared, Bernard Shaw, in a letter to his biographer, went further in elucidating Shakespeare's art. In *King Lear*, he says, "we find the alternation of tragic and funny dropped for an actual interweaving of the two; so that we have the tragic and the comic simultaneously, each heightening the other with a poignancy otherwise unattainable."[5] In preferring *interweaving* to *alternation* or one of its synonyms, Shaw catches an essential distinction, as I see it, between tragicomedy and comic agony. Since Shaw *tragicomedy* has been redefined with subtle variations, not long ago, for example, in chapter 10 of Eric Bentley's *The Life of the Drama* (1964) and in Karl S. Guthke's *Modern Tragicomedy* (1965). The tragicomic label belongs on a work in which the tragic and the comic alternate, roughly what Johnson meant by "successive evolutions of the design." In comic agony, though, the tragic and comic are interwoven "simultaneously, each heightening the other"; they are threads of contrasting colors in a fabric that is iridescent, neither of the colors and yet derived from both. Bentley implies virtually as much in his essay on tragicomedy when, in his final paragraph, he alludes to "that comedy which is infused with gloom and ends badly, that tragedy which is shot through with a comedy that only makes the outlook still bleaker."[6] An alternative to the interweaving analogy suggests itself: the two-colored eyepieces worn by patrons of 3-D movies and publications. To apprehend the "depth" of the drama, a spectator of comic agony needs to look through the "red" filter of amusement and at the same time through the "blue" filter of suffering. And not only the "depth" of the dramatic images is at stake here, but also their clarity. Viewing through only the "blue" or "red" filter results in blurred vision.

Comic agony, then, is an offshoot of tragicomedy. It has outgrown its ancestor, in certain instances resembling it and in other instances supplanting it, but it retains direct affiliations with the other four genres. The words *comic* and *agony* are of secondary consequence. In tandem they identify a distinctive span of theatre, whether we choose to name it *comic agony* or something else, its identity owed to the "interweaving."

Shaw had spotted much the same interweaving in Ibsen that he subsequently attributed to Shakespeare. In his review of *The Wild Duck* (reprinted in *Our Theatre of the Nineties*), Shaw doubtless overstated his reactions to the play: he claimed he forgot he was in a theatre as he looked on "with horror and pity at a profound tragedy, shaking with laughter all the time at an irresistible comedy."[7] Is that play funny enough to make a spectator, even a deeply appreciative one, shake with laughter? Hardly, unless it's willfully pulled out of shape. But Shaw had made, and would later exploit, an astounding discovery. More accurately, he let himself in on Ibsen's discovery, which colors his later writings on Ibsen as well as his own plays. Shaw realized, then or previously, that something like tragedy can be employed to *conceal* comedy and something like comedy to conceal tragedy. If we were to give this discovery a Stanislavskian formulation for *our* theatre of the nineties, we might say: The tone of the subtext can be at odds with the tone of the text. Shaw saw in *The Wild Duck* that Ibsen had not destroyed the genres, only subverted them. Shaw went on to subvert them differently, and so did many subsequent dramatists. Near the end of our century international theatre, as well as fiction, has featured assortments of comic agony that cut across analytical categories and historical movements. Comic agony goes back at least as far as a number of plays by Euripides, but it has spread wildly in twentieth-century storytelling to become a characteristic form of the artistry of our time, like theatricalism, self-conscious artistry, with which it often joins forces.

Let us suppose that Mr. Uxory telephones Mr. Friend. Uxory sounds beleaguered. His wife has run off with another man. She depleted their joint savings account and left him with their four children. He loves her frantically, wants her back at any cost. If she doesn't return, he declares, he will take his life. Uxory and Friend have known each other since they went to elementary school together, and so, from Friend's point of view, as well as Uxory's, we have the makings of an appalling situation for Uxory.

But what if Mrs. Friend picks up the phone? Since she first met Uxory she has considered him a stuffed shirt and a money-grubber. She could never figure out why her husband remained on close terms with him, nor why Mrs. Uxory, a vivacious and likable woman, stuck with him all these years. Then she learns from Uxory's phone call that he is now in the kitchen wearing an apron and fumbling with pans, spatulas, raw foodstuffs, and recipe cards as he tries for the first time to cook a meal for four wailing children. Here we have the makings of a merry situation, but only from Mrs. Friend's point of view. Uxory still sees himself as a pitiful figure. He still means to put his head in the oven, as soon as he finds out how to turn it on.

A playwright working up this incident might show us Mrs. Friend entering the devastated kitchen. If that playwright contrives to make us look at the situation from Uxory's and simultaneously from Mrs. Friend's point of view, we have the makings of comic agony. I say "the makings" because the enactment must catch the spirit of the writing or else a new tone will prevail. For the past ninety years critics, directors, and actors have debated the nature of Chekhov's longer plays, which may come into the auditorium wistful, heartrending, uproarious, or all three. Did Stanislavsky sadly fail Chekhov's humor? Did the playwright improperly define his work when he subtitled *The Sea Gull* and *The Cherry Orchard* comedies? A farcical performance can arise from tragedy gone wrong (deficiencies in the text), tragedy done wrong (deficiencies in the playing), or tragedy deliberately burlesqued (*Medea*: "Doctor, I wonder if you can help me. I have this insane desire to punish my man by killing my boys"). Once the comic agony has been discerned in a play, a director and actors may feel tempted to tip it to one side or the other, but if they do they oversimplify and undercut its effect.[8]

As a further complication, plays may be received wrong. No audience consists of people who respond en bloc to given situations and characters. In every playhouse there sit Uxorys and Mrs. Friends, not to mention Friends and Mrs. Uxorys. They add up to algebraic imponderables. The medley of laughers, yawners, naïfs, cynics, and troublemakers—of tastes, genes, and humors—sometimes constitutes a refusal of unanimity. Some people scoff at soap opera and western films; others laugh all the way through *A Streetcar Named Desire* and applaud Stanley when he lights into Blanche. Yet others will not laugh at comedy, farce, or anything else.

The unpredictable composition of an audience is one of those daunting facts of life the theatre has to live with, performance after performance. But the mixed reception accorded one or another variety of comic agony ought to satisfy the intentions of the author and interpreters. They apparently wish not so much to divide the audience, to elicit a mixed collective response, as to stir up the feelings of the individual spectators. These stirred-up sets of feelings dismay many American producers and workshop entrepreneurs. For them comic agony "doesn't work"; it doesn't tilt overwhelmingly to one side or the other. In writing and performance they look for undiluted power.

Some years ago the weekly competition in the *New Statesman* invited readers to submit famous *first* words, utterances by a celebrity in fact or fiction at the moment of birth. The winning entry, spoken by Oedipus as he emerges from the womb of Jocasta, consisted of three words: "I'll be back."

Oedipus has been back, many times, most conspicuously as Hamlet and as Lear (the aged Oedipus at Colonus). Other tragic Greek heroes and heroines who have reappeared in new costumes and conflicts and (sometimes) comedies include Ajax (Coriolanus), Prometheus (Alceste), Hecuba and Agave (combined into Mrs. Alving of *Ghosts*), Medea (Lorca's Yerma), and Antigone (Shaw's Joan).[9] In turn, roles from French, English, German, Italian, Scandinavian, and Spanish plays of the past three centuries have joined the Greek antecedents to form a veritable colony of transmigrated souls in the modern theatre. John Tanner has affinities, deliberately bestowed, with Molina's, Molière's, and Da Ponte's Don Juan as well as Prometheus; the Police Chief in *The Balcony* has affinities (probably accidental) with Alceste as well as Philoctetes; Sartre's Götz in *The Devil and the Good Lord* with Hugo's Hernani, Corneille's Horatius, and Euripides' Orestes; the Stranger in Strindberg's three parts of *To Damascus* with Everyman and Heracles; Melchior in *Spring's Awakening* with Goethe's Faust as well as the Neoptolemus of Sophocles; Arthur in Mrozek's *Tango* with Hamlet as well as Pentheus; and Max in *The Homecoming* with Lear, but a Lear who has a trio of sons instead of daughters. Collectively theatre has preserved some continuity in its characterizations while individual dramatists have wrenched them into new forms and moods.

It would make for a trim analysis if we could say that among the original forebears all roles were thoroughbreds, thoroughly tragic or comic, say, and that their descendants acquired opposing characteristics from the crossbreeding that ushers those transformations into comic agony. But the plays known as Greek tragedies are anything but thoroughly tragic. *Comic agony*, words derived from *kômos* and *agón*, refer to two stages in the performance of a Greek drama and, earlier, before the drama had evolved, to steps in an initiation ceremony or an athletic meet. *Kômos* means something like a triumphal return—of a chorus or a band of celebrants—and *agón* is an ordeal, a sacrifice, or a contest of physical or verbal prowess.[10] Comic agony thus brings an experience of sacrifice or suffering into harmony—or, more likely, collision—with an experience of triumph and uplift. The plays dealt with in this book, all written during the past 120 years, have antecedents that reach back to ancient Greece and precede Aristotle by the best part of a century. Comic agony is older than our earliest *definition* of tragedy. The leading roles in some of the theatre of Euripides (*Cyclops, Ion, Helen, The Children of Heracles*, and *Alcestis*) could be convincingly played for serious or for funny payoffs. William Arrowsmith writes: "From the point of view of traditional tragedy nothing is more strikingly novel than the Euripidean fusion and contrast of comic and tragic effects. Thus at any point in a tragedy the comic, or more accurately, the pathetic or ludicrous, can erupt with poignant effect, intensifying the tragic or toughening it with parody. Nor is this a device restricted to Euripides' so-called 'romantic' plays or his tragicomedies; it occurs even in the most powerful and serious tragedies."[11]

When faced with such anomalies, those commentators who like to keep their genres unadulterated—there are not many such persons left—have concluded that Euripides did not quite know what he was doing and must therefore forfeit their seal of approval. But do any plays fit snugly into broadly acceptable definitions of tragedy, comedy, farce, melodrama, and tragicomedy? Less dogmatic scholars, particularly teachers, may well want to qualify their answers when a student questions the old assumptions about, say, the "definitive" tragedies, the ones Aristotle and Hegel took as exemplary. If the gods decreed that Oedipus would commit patricide and incest, why isn't the play a melodrama? We can bicker enjoyably about his choice and free will. Knowing the curse on his future, shouldn't he have taken care not to kill any man (certainly any older man) and not to sleep with any woman (certainly any older woman)? But we are told that the oracle insisted, "He *will* kill his father; he *will* marry his mother." Choice? Is the play *Antigone* the tragedy of the heroine or of her antagonist, Creon? If we leap from the Greeks to Shakespeare, is *Othello* or *Richard III* a genuine tragedy, when Iago or Gloucester keeps making us chuckle? Shylock, at the mercy of fashion and acting whim, had been a variant of Pantalone, a comic butt, a Machiavellian conniver, and a skit on a skinflint of a father and financier before actors in the eighteenth century alerted themselves to his tragic potential. Since the Holocaust in Europe and the transformation of Shylock into the Outcast of All Time, actors and directors do not remind us, except when Launcelot Gobbo is onstage, that in the First Folio edition *The Merchant of Venice* was grouped with Shakespeare's comedies. Laurence Olivier and Frederick Valk, among others, have battered our hearts as they recited Shylock's exculpatory speeches. And soon after Shakespeare, don't some celebrated Restoration comedies overstep the boundaries of farce?

To the reasonable charge that comic agony is large and loose—elusive—I can only reply that it shares these and other characteristics with the five established genres. Like them, it is a concept, not a confinement, not a receptacle with hard (or even spongy) sides. The accepted genres are abstract separations. They define, if anything, some of the outer limits of dramatic possibility. Most plays hardly touch those limits or do not touch them at all, and the ones that do may touch more than one limit at the same time. Meanwhile the intervention of movements, national or international, such as romanticism or realism or surrealism or expressionism, complicates the notion of dramatic possibility by establishing new (often temporary) limits. Somewhere in the vast and formless cosmos of dramaturgical art, parts of which are encircled by those limits, float the bulk of plays, especially the ones from the modern era. Trends in naming come and go, but many of those plays share one characteristic, which I christen comic agony and which is easier to discern in modern than in older plays, because we have a clearer idea from stage directions, interviews, letters, and other critical paraphernalia of how recent authors wanted their theatre realized. I do not suggest that any playwrights, ancient or modern, ever used the two words to denote an intention or accomplishment. The words simply compress the evidence taken from the plays themselves—seeming attempts to approximate such experiences as turning ashen at the news of a long-sought promotion (and disconcerting the boss) or laughing at a funeral.

As an additional or alternative or supplemental genre, comic agony does not do away with the accepted genres but has lifelines to them all. The chapters that follow refer to those genres to avoid the coining of new words. Theatre is an adulterated art. That being so, it deserves, and may eventually have, an inclusive theory, one that identifies different plays to most scholars' satisfaction and yet makes respectful room for novelties. Such a theory need not also supply a gauge of quality. Analyzing a work of art and judging it call for distinctive types of cerebration, the second type warmed by feeling and prejudice. With the aid of loaded language, critics have sometimes tried to force genre theory to carry out both tasks: this would-be tragedy is "not a genuine specimen"; that would-be comedy "smacks of farce." A play that conforms beautifully (or slavishly) to a generic definition is the author's "masterpiece." Pronouncements like these, prompted by hidebound thinking wedded to snap reaction, tell us a little about the pronouncer, nothing about the work. The as-yet-unrealized inclusive theory, to which this book, like many others, is at best a pointer, should enable actors, directors, students, teachers, and other interested parties to approach new and older plays not with presuppositions, not expecting to certify what their mentors may already know, but with genuine curiosity, the fervor of those who merely, but truly, seek. Recognizing that a play shows marked signs of comic agony merely begins the seeking. The recognition does not by itself elucidate a play's themes, its continuities of topic. For an appreciation, those still need to be separately and sedulously explored.

Because comic agony presupposes distinctive examples of conflict in mood and structure, I have assembled the chapters and their plays under three general headings. According to this division, comic agony falls into three principal family lines, but the division is not meant to be final. The chapters do not place the plays in their time or as steps in an author's lifework. Many critical writings have already carried out these tasks commendably. Nor do the chapters cover every imaginable type of comic agony. The effect, now more common in the drama (and in films, fiction, and documentary art) than ever before, has surely not yet run its course. New samples will materialize, as will variations of them. The chapters take each play on its merits as I find them. That a chapter deals with one play does not mean a parity between that play and another in a different chapter: I am not comparing quality or hinting that Ayckbourn is (or is not) a reborn Shaw. All of these plays have had productions and deserve scrutiny in their own right and light.

The first selection comprises obtrusively serious plays that have a less obtrusive component of humor. The second selection brings forward plays that are obtrusively humorous yet address weighty, if not stern, topics. The third selection consists of plays redolent of slapstick in whole or in part that allow the anguish of the roles to show, sometimes gruesomely, through manic stage business and febrile talk. These plays may tumble into that most perilous of ends, a ridiculous anticlimax, or bathos. The three divisions add up to a quantitative breakdown, by degree, of the opposed ingredients, the serious and the laughable. They are three broad types of drama with what I perceive as distinctive overall "tones." Other critics surely would shuffle the plays and arrange them differently.

In most of these plays the comic agony springs from sexual drives. Sexuality, the bliss and curse of mankind, epitomizes comic agony. The sexuality of the rest of the world looks funny from a distance. All those jokes about other men's wives and other women's beds! But some playwrights succeed in making those "others" appear less distant. The cuckold and the imaginary cuckold, traditional butts in European farces and comedies and in a number of tragedies, such as *Othello*, invite modern interpreters and spectators to sympathize with their gnawing introspection. Molière's Dandin and Shakespeare's Ford must pretend to smile and be somebody else as they listen to accounts of their wives' conduct with predatory men. If the actor in either case can reproduce the mix of comedy and agony (the way Ben Kingsley does as Ford in the BBC television version of *The Merry Wives of Windsor*, directed by David Jones) we can almost witness from his face that his stomach is turning somersaults. Comic agony illuminates a play's roles from within and without at the same time. It strives to convey more of the jumbled reality of sexual and other motives than we are accustomed to finding in its predecessors. Conflicts between women and men have always formed a theatrical staple. Often they incorporate a power struggle—in the *Oresteia*, *The Changeling*, and in *Macbeth* when the hero's ambition takes fire from proving his mettle to his wife. But not until the modern period do we notice many plays in which sexual conflict, in consonance with Alfred Adler's discoveries, *becomes* the power struggle. In *Miss Julie* a contest for power and a contest for sexual supremacy conjoin with such tenacity that one cannot say with assurance which of them supplies the drama's main current of energy. Strindberg compels his pair of antagonists to enact the double conflict by bringing them together on Midsummer Eve, a time of sexual vincibility and longing.

If today's spectators feel torn between mirth and compassion, which were "things incompatible" to a classicist and purist like Dryden, their feelings resemble those of today's dramatic roles in being lifelike. A play that yields mixed impressions, like our lives with their tangled happenings, does not restrict itself to one mood at a time but charts its graph of transient, confused emotions as the characters ride the roller coaster of time and a sickening downward lurch curves into an exhilarating upward glide. But in the comic agony, as in life, at what point does the one end and the next begin? Nobody may know for sure, not even the performers.

PART I
Smiling at Trouble

VIRGIN SACRIFICE
The Wild Duck, by Henrik Ibsen

COLUMBUS: *I am haunted by the horizon, tormented by distances. I am full of anguish, as at the onset of love, and my face is no doubt lit up with madness. Do traces of an ancient knowledge still linger in me? I have a recollection of a lost world. I do not know. I know nothing. Tomorrow I shall know, and I shall no longer be in anguish; but I shall be less happy.*
MICHEL DE GHELDERODE, *Christopher Columbus*

Hjalmar Ekdal in *The Wild Duck* (Vildanden, 1884) embodies comic agony. A figure whose speech and behavior are out of key with his circumstances, he feels like a martyr and looks like a clown. He tries to advance from a tragic initiative to tragic stature, but he has no aptitude for tragic modes and makes himself laughable. He has grown from a spoiled boy raised by two maiden aunts into a slothful, complacent family man, a disarming windbag who brags about his cultural attainments and about the fame and wealth that will lap over him after he completes an unstarted and unspecified (but "astounding") invention. Hjalmar is fond of his wife, Gina, and his fourteen-year-old daughter, Hedvig, but mostly insofar as they revive the role his dead aunts played in reflecting him back to himself as a soul worthy of adoration.

When he discovers he may not be Hedvig's parent, he disowns her. To affirm her love for him, to prove herself his true child, she takes her life. Seeing her dead, he demands of God not "Why did You do this to her?" but "Why have You done this to me?"[1]

How do we respond to Hjalmar's misfortune? With horror and compassion, since it was tragic, brought about in part by himself? Or with amusement, since his grief strikes us as being overblown, if not insincere? Our responses are colored not only by our perceptions of Hjalmar's comic agony but also by the effects of Hedvig's death on the other roles present: on Gina, her mother; on Relling, the doctor who pronounces her dead; on Gregers, her father's friend, who had advised her to make a sacrifice to appease Hjalmar, but a sacrifice of her pet wild duck, not of herself; and most bewilderingly on Hjalmar's father, Ekdal. Old Ekdal is a former lieutenant who enters the last act wearing his full-dress uniform and sword for the first time in the action. He looks at the corpse of his granddaughter, laughs at the thought that she must have wanted to be a hunter, and vanishes into the attic, where the wild duck is kept, after twice remarking cryptically, "The woods take revenge."

Because these roles are at least partially comic we could say the play has a mixed ending. But what of the girl herself? Through the previous acts Ibsen has made her unrelievedly poignant. Her sacrifice seems unjust, brutal. Yet it forms the play's climactic event. In several other plays by Ibsen a child dies and the death implies a sacrificial act.[2] A sacrifice, as against an unqualified decease, has purpose; in contrast to a murder or a vengeful suicide, it has a purpose that is lofty. In the drama we associate the self-sacrifice with societies that have a rigorous code of honor or duty, a moral etiquette: Spain during its imperial Golden Age, classical Japan, and, above all, classical Greece. Sophocles dramatizes a willed self-sacrifice by a young woman, Antigone, and Euripides gives us several such sacrifices.[3] In each case the voluntary death ennobles the girl and elicits sentiments of awe from the other characters and from the Chorus. Nothing quite like this happens in *The Wild Duck*. Not one of the characters pays tribute to Hedvig's death *as a gesture*. Yet that death does follow the self-immolations of the Greek heroines in having a positive result. As Hedvig's father and mother carry her body out of the room, Hjalmar exclaims, "Oh, Gina, Gina, how can you bear it!" This is his one unselfish remark in the play. We can observe, in addition, something residually "Greek" in Hedvig's act of sacrificing her life in place of a wild animal's: it is a kind of fertility ritual. But then, there are other intimations of ancient Greece in this play, not only in the roles but even in the resolutely modern settings.

The first act takes place in the home of Gregers's father, the magnate Haakon Werle. The stage, Werle's study, has green shades on its lamps.[4] Behind the study in a large dining room we catch glimpses of a banquet.

In the next four acts Ibsen reverses the scenic effect. Instead of looking out from a "green" room, we look into one, a spacious attic converted to an indoor nature preserve where rabbits, pigeons, doves, poultry, and Hedvig's wild duck live. Sliding doors and a hanging fishnet separate the attic from the foreground scenery, a skylighted photographic studio, the main room of Hjalmar's apartment. At first the glass panes in the studio roof are half-hidden by a blue curtain. They hint at a clear sky. In the last act, during the sacrifice, we will notice snow on them from the blizzard outside. Storms without and within! The studio, on the highest floor of its building, stands for a mountaintop, and the green attic behind it, for a forest.

The forest and the mountain are two images Ibsen sometimes brings into apposition, most explicitly in *When We Dead Awaken*. There the forest revives primeval and erotic instincts in two of the characters, while the mountain challenges the hero to strive for his highest aspirations as an artist. In *The Wild Duck* the indoor "mountain" and "forest" might be compared with a diminished Mount Kithaeron and its wooded foothills near Thebes, where the female worshipers of Dionysos cavort in *The Bacchae*. Hjalmar sits with his loving wife and daughter in his studio during the second act under an imitation of a blue sky; he is a lesser Dionysos who drinks beer instead of wine. He observes that his hair is wavy, not curly (like that of Dionysos). He plays the flute, one of the two instruments associated with Dionysian revelry—the other is the drum.

Just as the green attic is anticipated by the green study, so the Dionysian strain in Hjalmar is anticipated in the first act by the banquet, a tame, modern bacchanalia. Haakon Werle is throwing a lavish, wine-wetted dinner party to celebrate the return of his unprodigal son. Gregers has kept himself away from home for the previous fifteen or sixteen years at a remote place called Hoidal, the site of his father's lumber mill. To this party in his honor Gregers has invited his boyhood friend Hjalmar, but he wants nothing to do with his father or with the remaining guests, prominent men of Haakon Werle's social circle with connections to the Norwegian court. Although this act contains no *visual* symbol of a mountain to complement the "forest" of a study, these people do personify the summit of society in Christiania, now Oslo. They are known by titles instead of names—the Fat Guest, the Bald Guest, the Nearsighted Guest—rather like "masks" from the commedia dell'arte. After bloating up with food and Tokay, they repair to Werle's music room for songs and games, an informal piano recital, and a round of blindman's buff. They add up to a chorus of toned-down, freeloading satyrs, with the Fat Guest as Silenus the leader and Werle himself as a compromise between Dionysos and Zeus.

These mythical analogies may seem farfetched, but although *The Wild Duck* is not, in my opinion, an imitative Greek play, Ibsen does discern the relics of old myths in late nineteenth-century Norway. Because his plays appear to have infinite contents, reading too much into them is a more salutary practice than reading too little. In the past he was reproved for laying down an excess of exposition in this first act, some of which he did not later revert to. Audiences, scholars, and others grew accustomed to thinking of him as the icy realist of the north. Some people still hold him to that outdated reputation. It is true that he unwinds his realistic action scrupulously, but that is not all he does. When he jumps from Werle's mansion to Hjalmar's studio, from riches to penury, he is still intercalating the Greek elements in his modern realism. Werle had a lot to do with the studio. He proposed photography as a vocation to Hjalmar, paid the rent for the loft, took care of the bills for the photographic equipment and materials. He supplied Hedvig with her wild duck, which he had once shot at and failed to kill. He supplied Hjalmar with a wife: Gina admits she was Werle's mistress before her marriage. He "had his way" with her, as she puts it, and evidently did not want either to marry her or to cast her off. He may even have supplied Hedvig, for Gina eventually concedes she doesn't know whether the girl is the daughter of Hjalmar or Werle. Gregers calls his father "a kind of providence." Like Zeus, Werle rains down blessings—among them, seductions. Gregers, however, mistrusts his father's benevolence. Zeus could on occasion behave mercilessly to his own offspring as when he acquiesced in the madness visited on Heracles or the slavery of Apollo. Gregers tells his father that as a child he was always terrified of him; now, as a man, he looks back on Werle's doings and sees "a battlefield with broken human beings on every side," with Gregers himself, as he sees it, being one of the casualties.

Gregers is a strange, tortured man, a lonely dreamer. Much as we can detect something of Nietzsche's Dionysos in Hjalmar, who feels "cozy" with his devoted womenfolk, so in the ungregarious Gregers we spot something of Nietzsche's brooding, oracular Apollo. During his decade and a half at Hoidal he relished, not his closeness to the life of the forest nor his work at the mill, but the solitary nature of his existence, which gave him the chance to "mull over a great many things." Ibsen uses a device in Gregers's dialogue that keeps him at a distance from the spectator: he almost never volunteers information of a personal kind. Most of what we learn about his history comes from other roles, and most of that he neither confirms nor contradicts. Dr. Relling, who also lived in the woods at Hoidal for a time and now rents an apartment downstairs in the same building as Hjalmar's, knew and disliked Gregers. He mentions that Gregers went around "to all the farms and cabins with copies of something he called 'Summons to the Ideal.'" This catchphrase, no less cryptic than Hjalmar's "astounding" invention, did not set the folk at Hoidal on fire. But it tells us that Gregers, for all his Apollonian tendencies and his apparent taste for a cloistral life, had tried without much success to make contact with others.

When he returns to the city he has just about given up hope of converting people to his ideal. Then he meets Hjalmar, who, as a boy, was everybody's idol, Gregers's included, and because of the renewal of the friendship, because of what happens *between* the two of them, rather than because of a spontaneous decision by Gregers, his missionary impulses flare up again. He will inform his old friend that Gina was a soiled acquisition, Werle's former mistress. He doesn't wish to sabotage Hjalmar's marriage, only to put it on a new footing. He will bring the past into the cleansing, cold light of truth. "There's nothing in the world," he says, "that compares with showing mercy to a sinner and lifting her up in the arms of love." He expects that Hjalmar, his wife, and his daughter will cling together despite everything and will "win through to a self-sacrificial, forgiving spirit." The noble plan goes awry not only because it is misguided but also because of adversity that Gregers does not foresee.

He has grown up the product of a strained marriage. His mother, a neurotic invalid, constantly reproached his father for deceiving her with Gina, who worked for them as a maid-cum-housekeeper. When Gregers left home his mother had not yet died. Before or after his departure he developed what he calls a "sick conscience." Nothing quite accounts for this conscience and the lengths to which it drives him. His father says he inherited it from his mother; yet Werle himself has a sick conscience, and if it was hereditary in the first place it might just as convincingly have come down from him. The conscience may also derive from Gregers's acute disquiet over having abandoned his mother when she was dying and feeling betrayed. Or he may be ashamed of his father, whom he considers a rich exploiter, an attitude that would become fairly common some thirty years later among the young heroes of expressionist drama and films. Or he may feel that in relation to others he is not a worthy person—he suggests this, as well as contempt for his father, when he says he hates his name—and that he must therefore neglect himself in order to serve others.

We might trace other possible sources of that conscience. Gregers's and Hjalmar's fathers once worked as business partners. They were prosperous entrepreneurs until the state indicted them for cutting timber that grew on public land. At the trial Gregers's father was exonerated, but Hjalmar's, convicted and desolated, went to prison and lost the right to wear his army uniform. In court Gregers, who admired his friend's father, testified against him—out of fear, he says, of his own parent. Although we never discover whether the testimony Gregers gave decided the verdict, he believes it did. He now feels under a moral obligation to Hjalmar's family for having ruined Old Ekdal, blocked Hjalmar's wished-for career as a poet and scholar, and helped to force him into the menial profession of a portrait photographer.[5]

Whatever the causes of Gregers's sick conscience, he needs it to perform his role. Theatrically speaking, it *is* his role: it shapes his stage conduct. So insistently does the conscience harangue him that when he hears about a spare room going for rent in his friend's apartment, he moves right in on Hjalmar and his family, the better to straighten them out. Gina naturally has no desire to see Gregers, much less take him in as a lodger. She remembers him as an enemy, his mother's ally against his father and against her. Gina's distaste allows a glimpse into one more conceivable reason for Gregers's conscience: an affair between them, which Ibsen allows for but does not endorse and which neither the man nor the woman acknowledges. The implications of such an affair, going on while Gina served in the Werle household, are momentous, both for the story and for the enactment, especially for the encounters between Gina and Gregers and between Gregers and Hedvig, who on this assumption might actually be the daughter of Gregers, not of Hjalmar or Old Werle.[6]

Whether enemy or former lover, Gregers will not be kept out of Gina's home. As soon as he is installed, he lights a fire in his room with the chimney damper closed. He fills the place with smoke, which he tries to dispel by tipping water on the stove and flooding the floor. Gina, who reports the incident (from the story), calls him a pig. Gregers's double blunder in bringing fire and water on the household does not inspire much confidence in him as a savior. He has the heart and fervor of a grand preacher but lacks the incandescent rhetoric and temperament. The episode with the stove—bringing warmth and having to douse it—might stand as a condensed version of his life.

In a number of discussions of *The Wild Duck* Gregers is viewed as though the other roles' unfavorable opinions of him, especially those of Gina and Relling, his enemies, summed him up. Mary McCarthy calls him an "odious, baneful creature."[7] Alan Reynolds Thompson says he "is not merely detestable but ridiculous." Thompson also thinks that Gregers, homosexually attracted to Hjalmar, means to lure him away from his family.[8] Ingjald Nissen surmises that Gregers does not really want Hedvig to sacrifice the duck; unconsciously he wishes her to kill herself but is shocked when she does so.[9] Gregers does do harm. Further, he is priggish and clumsy. But odious, detestable? The dean of twentieth-century Ibsen critics, Hermann Weigand, concludes that Ibsen was actually scathing his own personality: "Gregers is Ibsen's self-projection in caricature."[10]

Ibsen himself dropped a noteworthy warning. Before the first Norwegian production he wrote to the manager of the Christiania Theatre that "Gregers is the most difficult character in the play to portray."[11] Now if Gregers were merely a malevolent creep, his role would be anything but difficult to handle, and not very rewarding for that reason. Condemnations of him do not reckon with the ferocity of his conscience or with the residual innocence that connects the conscience with his deluded idealism. He would have liked to improve his parents' marriage, but how, when he was the offshoot of that marriage? "I've had a chance to see at close range," he says, "what [an untrue] marriage can destroy in two people." The "two people," I would guess, do not include his father: they are his mother and himself. On encountering Hjalmar anew, he discovers a parallel situation: not simply a friend living a lie but also a parent and child who may be hurt if Gina continues to conceal her affair the way Werle did his.[12] For Gregers it is now too late for cures, but Hedvig is young. In saving Hjalmar's marriage Gregers can still save Hedvig from a sick conscience like his. Better yet, he can induce *her* to be the savior. Once again, if readers will pardon me for hammering home a point, it is the encounter with another role that actuates Gregers's behavior, just as it is the encounter with him that prompts Hedvig. Onstage the critical scene between the two characters should dramatize their coming to purposes, without specifying what the purposes are.

Hedvig quickly senses the innocence in Gregers and talks freely to him about the wild duck. It belongs to her, but her grandfather and father "look after it and build things for it." The duck is a mystery, she says. Nobody knows it, or where it came from. Gregers suddenly remarks that it has been "in the depths of the sea." Hedvig, surprised, says that is the very phrase she uses herself when she thinks of the attic. She apologizes because it sounds "stupid." Gregers instantly rebukes her:

GREGERS: Don't you dare say that.

HEDVIG: Oh yes, because it's only an attic.

GREGERS: Are you so sure of that?

HEDVIG: (*astonished*) That it's an attic?

GREGERS: Yes. Do you know that for certain? (*HEDVIG, speechless, stares at him open-mouthed*)

The attic is not an attic. Although divided from the workaday studio only by sliding doors and a fishnet, it might be said to be in conflict with the studio, and it is, as Gregers says and Hedvig knows, "a world of its own." It looks different at different times of the day and in different weather. It's a world not only of re-created nature but also of the past. It contains cupboards with picture books in them, an old cabinet with drawers and compartments (recesses, secret hiding places), and a huge clock that no longer works. In the attic "time doesn't exist."[13] Hedvig cannot read the books, which are "mostly in English," but she looks at the pictures: "There's one just enormous book called *Harryson's History of London*; it must be a hundred years old, and it's got ever so many pictures in it. At the front there's a picture of Death with an hourglass and a girl. I think that's horrible. But then there are all the other pictures of churches and castles and streets and great ships sailing on the ocean." The man and the girl, as they share a vision of a world of which only traces linger, move away from psychological realism and into fantasy. Hedvig has defective eyes, and her parents have been warned by "the doctor" (Relling?) that she will "inevitably" go blind sooner or later. But Hedvig's deficient eyes also suggest that Ibsen is dealing with another sort of sight altogether.[14] She is a dreamer, like Gregers, with a poetic sense of life and of other people. In the picture of Death with the hourglass and the girl she has foreseen her own death, the following day, on her fourteenth birthday.

If the conjunction between Gregers and the girl in whom he plants the "Greek" idea of a sacrifice is poetic, what about the confrontations between Gregers and Relling? Relling, a hard-nosed general practitioner, hates Gregers and hates ideals. He tells Hjalmar, "You've got this clever wife of yours, padding around in her slippers and waggling her hips and keeping you neat and cozy. . . . And what about your Hedvig? . . . And wait till that marvelous invention comes to the world!" Since Weigand's book first appeared and took Gregers to be Ibsen's caricature of his own idealistic self, Relling has been taken with even more monotonous frequency to be Ibsen's spokesman or mouthpiece or raisonneur. We have, then, the spectacle of Henrik Ibsen at fifty-six belaboring his earlier self with a mouthpiece in order to use *The Wild Duck* to repudiate his former "theses" or "philosophy." Through Relling, Ibsen is in effect saying, "Forget about those other plays of mine. I've changed my mind. Ideals are destructive. Don't rock the boat. Don't tip the gravy train. Everybody needs his illusion. Let us all prize the modest happiness we can find." Relling has confidence in his prescription. He has tried it out on the theologian Molvik, with whom he shares the downstairs apartment. He has rescued this futile man of God from "self-contempt and despair" by dubbing him "demonic." Molvik has been "injected" with a "vital lie," for vital lies are necessary when "most of the world is sick."

The question we are obliged to ask is How effective are Relling's vital lies? Molvik is not too happy. He walks around (in Relling's shadow) drunk or hung over most of the time. He often lets the ends of his sentences trail away as if he didn't know what he meant to say. After Hedvig's death, the one occasion when he has a chance to display his authority, he mutters, "Praise be to God. Dust to dust, dust to dust." At that point Relling cuts him off with "Shut up, you fool; you're drunk." Nor does Relling's other experiment, Hjalmar, seem very happy. He has a miserable time at the dinner party. The other guests make him aware of his inferior social rank and expect him to earn his meal by reciting poems and showing photographs. He has promised to bring home something for Hedvig, and he does. A menu. When she looks disappointed, he offers to tell her how each dish tasted. But then he feels ashamed and hides his embarrassment by grumbling about the burdens he has to shoulder as the "family breadwinner." (Most of the bread in the household is actually won by his father.) Hjalmar looks forward to the day when his invention will restore the family name and fortune so that his father can once again wear his uniform in public. That, says Hjalmar, "is the only reward I'm after." The most one can say for Hjalmar's happiness is that he still hopes for it.

What about Relling? He, at least, as the purported sage of the play, should be living a persuasive vital lie. He seems satisfied with his lot until he runs into Berta Sørby, Werle's housekeeper. We have seen Mrs. Sørby intermittently during the first act. While the dinner party goes on, the guests flock around her and take their orders from her, not from Werle, the host. She does not believe in "exceeding the limits." She will not allow smoking in Werle's study; she calls for the coffee, punch, and liqueurs; she dictates which room they shall be served in; she plays the piano; she leads the mock satyrs in the game of blindman's buff. The play even opens with an allusion to her: Werle, we hear, "is proposing a long toast to Fru Sørby." All in all, she's an authoritative lady. But after the opening act she turns up only once more in the play. She has come to Hjalmar's studio for a number of reasons, and Ibsen has plotted Relling into the scene. Mrs. Sørby reveals that Werle has left town. He is going to settle in Hoidal. She will join him there and marry him. When he hears about the marriage, Relling says it cannot be true, and his voice "quavers slightly." She assures him that it is true, answering him with the salutation "my dear Relling." She goes on to hope that she and Werle will be happy.

RELLING: That's a reasonable hope. Mr. Werle never gets drunk—as far as I know; and he's certainly not given to beating up his wives the way the late horse doctor did.

MRS. SØRBY: Oh, now let Sørby rest in peace. He did have some worthy traits, you know.

RELLING: Old Werle's traits are worth rather more, I'll bet.

MRS. SØRBY: At least he hasn't wasted the best that's in him. Any man who does that has to take the consequences.

RELLING: Tonight I'm going out with Molvik.

MRS. SØRBY: You shouldn't, Relling. Don't do it—for my sake.

But Relling, it is clear, intends to get drunk—or whatever else he does when he goes out with Molvik—if not precisely for her sake, then certainly on her account. He leaves, hesitating on her name-to-be: "Good-by, Mrs.—Werle." Gregers then observes that Mrs. Sørby and Relling evidently "know each other quite intimately."

MRS. SØRBY: Yes, we've known each other for many years. At one time something might have developed between us.

GREGERS: It was certainly lucky for you that it didn't.

MRS. SØRBY: Yes, that's true enough. But I've always been wary of following my impulses. After all, a woman can't just throw herself away.

The few teasing glimpses these exchanges give us into the past lives of Mrs. Sørby and Relling do not so much amplify their roles as stress how little we know about them. Were they lovers during the lifetime of the multiple-wife-beating horse doctor? Did Relling go to Hoidal after Mrs. Sørby decided she couldn't "just throw herself away" on him? Have they been in touch recently? He says at one point that he was "never exactly married." Does this mean he ran from her? Why is she so relieved at having escaped from him? Had Relling ever urged a vital lie on her, so that when she says she hopes she will be happy she is not uttering a mere banality but taking a dig at him?

Mrs. Sørby's scene shakes many of the assumptions often made about the play.[15] Among other results it shows Relling to be a more unhappy and disillusioned man than we could have imagined. He has not been able to come up with a vital lie on his own behalf but has "wasted the best in himself." Perhaps this is why he thinks "most of the world is sick." The belief may console him to the extent that he feels a failure among equals. If we quote his lines against Gregers, we should remember to quote Gregers's lines against him. Gregers does not attack Relling as a person, only as a force. For instance, he notes that Mrs. Sørby was lucky not to have become entangled with Relling, and he tells Relling to his face, "I won't rest till I've gotten Hjalmar out of your clutches." Hjalmar, too, makes some bitter remarks about Relling. In the early part of the play he likes Relling enough to invite him to lunch. But he changes his opinion after he spends a night on the town with Relling and Molvik and sleeps over in their apartment. While packing to leave home he mutters to himself that he would like to have Relling strangled. He calls him "barbarous," "dissolute," a "sneak," and a "snake in the grass"; Relling and Molvik together are "vermin wallowing in sin." This is strong language to describe a man who goes out on binges.[16] Hjalmar adds that, sooner than return to Relling's apartment, he will take his old father with him and march out into the blizzard. Did he see anything untoward going on downstairs or while they were "out"? Was Relling "wallowing in sin" with Molvik?

At one point Relling calls himself "a beast" and Molvik "another beast." His tone is jocular, but so is much else in this dour comedy. Relling is also given to a fairly free use in his conversation of the words *devil* and *hell*, up to his (and the play's) last line. If the studio is a mountaintop, the downstairs is an infernal region inhabited by the Tempter and his acolyte demon. Like figures from a morality play, the chthonian pair are Medicine and Theology, two of the diabolical arts.

But we have no call to wax indignant over Relling any more than we do over Gregers. I am arguing that Relling is no more of an author's mouthpiece than Gregers is an odious, baneful creature. Ibsen has set up his balanced struggle between two advocates for a man's soul, the Idealist and the Tempter, dramatic beings who have the defects of their theatrical humanity. Their arguments also have defects. The hope for happiness, the temptation to stay comfortably in one's niche, can lead people astray just as easily as the quest for the ideal can.

But happiness and the ideal need not be opposed aims. Striving for happiness can count as reaching for an ideal of a sort, just as obeying the claims of the ideal can count as a means of seeking happiness or, at least, peace with oneself. Relling and Gregers differ doctrinally in that the former proposes one's own good as a code of conduct; the latter, unselfishness, the good of others. In practice the two men are not so much at odds: in their very unlike ways they both care about people and faultily do what they can for them, Relling as a pragmatist, Gregers as a visionary. Gregers is right: Hjalmar is living a lie. Relling is right: it is a vital lie. Gregers is wrong: by uncovering the truth he inadvertently wrecks Hjalmar's home. Relling is wrong: the foundations of that home and its "happiness" were fragile.

Yet the home doesn't quite topple. After Hedvig's sacrifice, Hjalmar and Gina will pick up and start again. He has said that she is a "good companion for life's journey." Whether for good or ill, Gregers and Relling are also Hjalmar's traveling companions through life, and so are the other figures. They all add up to the composite portrait of modern man that Ibsen has painted with Hjalmar at its center. There is thus unity in *The Wild Duck*'s parts. Gregers and Relling "belong" to Hjalmar as respectively his leanings toward idealism and his inclination to let things ride. Gina the retoucher is his artistic muse since he is a counterfeit poet. Ekdal, his natural father, has pulled Hjalmar down in the world: that, at any rate, is Hjalmar's excuse. Werle is the second father he needs, the provider. Hedvig, his votary, embodies the love sacrifice he wants made on his behalf. And Mrs. Sørby appears as a nurturing spirit and Mercurial messenger from the provider. Even Molvik has his place in this nexus as a religious consolation that proves useless.

At the same time these roles constitute a Greek drama that was never written, incorporating a maid's sacrifice, a Dionysos, an Apollo, a Zeus, a household goddess of inferior status, a Hera (sister-wife of Zeus but also goddess of matrimony), and an Aesculapius the healer.[17] The modern figures are pale reincarnations of these myth-gilded predecessors. Nevertheless, the reminders of Greek literature confer on the play's time and space a penumbra of shaded edges.

Although the reminders do not affect the action, they may well affect the playing. So does the composite structure of the roles. The dominant chords struck come out of late nineteenth-century realism, but the undertones in performance are mythic and metaphorical, in harmony with the theme of sacrifice. To put it another way, despite the realistic fact that most of the action takes place out of the attic, which is a background scene to look into but is not always open, the dramatic fact that the sacrifice, or critical event of the play, occurs in the attic alerts us that the roles as a collective image are all creatures of that artificial chunk of nature, that "world of its own."

Hence the play has a realistic, but more than realistic, title. Just as the principals live in three environments, a mythical world of the past, a collective poetic image of civilized man, and a modern drama, so the wild duck is a creature who lives in three elements: she swims, she walks, she flies. Or rather, she flew before Werle winged her with his shotgun. Her wing has not properly mended, and she still carries some buckshot in her body. But she survives. She has her cushioned basket in the attic forest and a trough of water that is refilled every other day. As a wild creature she lives apart from the others, the domesticated species. According to Ekdal, a wild duck that is wounded dives immediately for the bottom and bites into the weeds and sea moss. This one would never have come up again if Haakon Werle's "remarkably clever dog" had not hauled her back to the surface, leaving the imprints of his teeth on her. A spectator or reader will trace similarities between the duck and the nine principals. All of them have been figuratively wounded, gone down, and been hauled up again, tooth-marked. Some of them have played both the duck and the remarkably clever dog.[18] Werle, for instance, rehabilitated Mrs. Sørby, Hjalmar, and Gina; Mrs. Sørby will rescue him in return when she takes him, blind and "helpless," under her supervision. Of the nine, Hedvig and Gregers most directly personify the wild duck as a lonely, displaced creature. But the one nearest to "being" the wild duck, Old Ekdal, who disappears at the end into the attic and finally closes with its world, is a hunter who "knows" animals. Ibsen hints at an animality in Ekdal from the beginning. He is the first of the main roles to appear. His part is not large measured either by the number of lines he has or the time he spends onstage, yet the author devotes a paragraph of stage directions to him and very little to the others when they are introduced.

Ekdal wears an overcoat with a high collar, woolen gloves, and a reddish brown wig. He carries a cane and a fur cap in his hand and a brown paper parcel under his arm. Ibsen says not one word about his build or mien and mentions only one facial feature—and that not an intrinsic one—a little gray mustache. This is no merely literal picture. Ekdal is almost as wrapped up as the parcel he is carrying. When he has his fur cap on, the only parts of him that show are his mouth, the tip of his nose, and his eyes. He might almost be an animal: a bear, say. In his younger days Ekdal, the "outdoorsman," the "tremendous hunter," shot nine bears.

In the course of the play it is Ekdal who remarks three times, "The woods take revenge."[19] He first makes the remark in response to Gregers, who has told him that in recent years the woods around Hoidal have been heavily logged. When he says it the second and third times, shortly before his last exit, Hedvig has just died. She shot herself in the breast. He, her grandfather, had recommended that wound as the "safest way" to kill a wild duck.[20] Nature has claimed a human sacrifice in exchange for man's sacking of her resources.[21] As a voice that unconsciously speaks for the wild-animal residue in modern man, Ekdal the hunter protests on behalf of the bears and ducks he has himself slaughtered. As a former lumberman, he deplores the plundering of the woods.

Ekdal, though, is not the wild duck. The uniform and sword he puts on to enter the attic remind us that he is human, a soldier and a killer. The wild duck with her "dragging wing" and "limp," her powers of recuperation, and her ability to adapt to a new environment is every one of the roles and not quite any one of them. Rolf Fjelde writes that they have all "gone down, like the wounded wild duck, into the undertow of life. *The Wild Duck* is a drowned world; once we grasp this basic metaphor of the play and enter into it imaginatively, we can freely explore the channels of the deep, where the lost voyagers rest suspended, nearly weightless, beyond salvage, in their timeless dream."[22] Behind its fishnet curtain, the "drowned world" of the attic, which Gregers and Hedvig think of as "the depths of the sea," ruled over by the wild duck, is a garden, a park, an attempt to preserve a natural refuge. In Ibsen's times the sea could not be depleted like the woods or pillaged like the mines in *John Gabriel Borkman*. Today it is at least as vulnerable as any other environment, fouled by leaks from tankers and spills from surface rigs and submarine oil shafts and organized treasure hunts and threatened by the prospects of "scientific harvesting." (Similarly, mountains many times the height of the ones in *Brand* and *When We Dead Awaken* have been scaled—or, as the press likes to say, conquered—by teamwork.)

The drowned world, though, is a metaphor. It need not be restricted in its application to the sea either in Ibsen's lifetime or ours.[23] The wild duck in her attic evokes vestigial memories in these figures of a beckoning green past. That past is wild. The spirit of animal abandon and the Dionysian urges, buried in them, gone to the bottom, have grown domesticated. They no longer understand the ancient signals, the impulses and reflexes. Like Mrs. Sørby, they are "wary of following them." They have descended (in both senses) from an age of heroism, and perhaps an age of matriarchy. They live in what Fjelde calls their "timeless dream" but are unable to appreciate, say, a sacrifice that is heroic. Hedvig's self-less gesture shames them: it shows up their smallness and the comic futility of their disputes over ideals and happiness. Ekdal embodies the "drowned" nature when he enters at the start, a slayer of bears and a bear by proxy, springing up on the fringe of an opulent dinner party. Thereafter, the play steadily releases animal imagery through to Hedvig's sacrifice in place of the wild duck, when Hjalmar mourns, "I drove her from me like an animal!"

In this city setting, with the green world only a room's width away, a broken-down doctor who lacks whatever it takes to be happy dangles the lure of happiness before others. A high-principled young man who has made nothing of his life tries to allay the stabbings of his conscience by foisting an ideal of truth on a buffoon. A drunken theologian thinks he has safeguarded his meager stock of self-respect but cannot perform as a demon any more convincingly than he could as a minister. Such roles, corroded by time's distance from the heroes of myth are satiric butts. Hjalmar, their common reference, is the most obtrusive, with his spasms of extravagant self-pity.[24] Yet this same Hjalmar can say with simple, poetic clarity, "It's useful sometimes to go deep down into the night side of existence," and touch the drama at its core. In him, as in his bibulous old father, comedy and agony have clashed and cannot be pried apart. He feels grief for the loss of Hedvig, but he regards it as his loss, not hers, much as Agamemnon does at Aulis in Euripides' play after he has agreed to the sacrifice of his daughter. Soon Hjalmar will watch himself grieve and will study the part of the stricken father, as Relling observes, in order to play it the more authentically, that is, with more nineteenth-century pathos. Hjalmar is, after all, an actor by temperament, and the figures around him might almost be roles in which he casts himself. He and his daughter set each other off. They are the action's main currents of comedy and agony. Hedvig never asks for pity, but she is pitiful. So is her gesture of love—killing herself, as Hedda Gabler will do, with her father's pistol.

Most of his other encirclers have weaknesses almost as conspicuous as Hjalmar's. Werle and Hedvig are the two exceptions. Mrs. Sørby with her prissy rationality and hectoring manner and her fear of letting go is occasionally funny. So is Gina when she mispronounces words, not so much in mockery of her lower-class background as in a puncturing of Hjalmar's pretentiousness. He has told Gregers that she is "not entirely without culture," and he winces at her boners.

If Gregers and Relling amuse us because they cannot carry out their self-appointed missions, we smile at them rather than laughing outright, as we do at Hjalmar. As the play ends and the stage empties, they stand together still arguing, the broken dialectic of Hjalmar working itself out. Hedvig's sacrifice stunned them both: their experiments with her father did not produce the hoped-for resolution, a wife, husband, and child delighting in being able to give one another strength. Gregers says, "If you're right and I'm wrong then life isn't worth living." He is near his emotional breaking point, but his sick, stubborn conscience tries to justify him. He says he is glad it is his destiny to be the thirteenth at table. He thereby deepens his identification with Hjalmar, who after being invited to Werle's had found himself number thirteen at the party. Gregers may well be contemplating suicide at this moment, not for the first time in the play, but Relling brushes aside his sorrowful defiance—they have never remotely understood each other: "Oh, go to hell."

So we smile at suicidal Gregers, the guardian angel who hoped to take root in Hjalmar but is no longer needed. And we smile at Relling, the imp who murmurs that change is risky and happiness the only worthwhile objective. But as we smile at them and at our recollections of the other strange disputants in *The Wild Duck*'s comic agony, we think back to Hedvig's abandonment of her young life, and we absorb some of her pain.

FROSTY SPRING
Spring's Awakening, by Frank Wedekind

To Dr. Waldemar Zozo: You, Sir, were the Navy psychiatrist who examined me in Norfolk, Va., about 1942, and told me I was unusually immature. I knew that, but professional confirmation caused me deep anguish. In anguish I was not immature.
SAUL BELLOW, *Herzog*

Wedekind's best-known play, *Spring's Awakening* (Frühlings Erwachen, 1891), another choice sample of comic agony, never disappeared from circulation, in German or other languages, but as a drama about the prudishness of German and Swiss-German burghers and their inhibited offspring, it did seem to be dated by the tidal advances of sex education.[1] News reports in the late 1960s and thereafter told of a *Sexwelle*, a sex wave, which, according to an official of the Federal Ministry of Family and Youth in what was then West Germany, made "Germans want to put their bedrooms on the street." It seemed that "some social scientists say the phenomenon represents an overreaction against old German taboos and the stresses of the Nazi period. One suggested that it could be a sublimation of now-outlawed militarism. . . . While it is undoubtedly part of a wider trend sweeping Western civilization, the wave is said to reflect aspects of German history and culture as interpreted by the Western part of the divided nation. There is a preoccupation with technique—with becoming 'an efficient sex machine,' as some have put it."[2] Nazi authoritarianism was supposed to have "deprived a German generation of exposure to the work of the Austrian Jew Sigmund Freud." As a result, instructional films on lovemaking and documentaries on the incidence of prostitution commanded wide audiences. Mail-order houses specialized in "erotic literature and stimulants." A columnist who proffered sex advice in the family weekly *Neue Illustrierte* became known as the Sexual Pope.

As though to bestow posthumous consolation on Wedekind's generation, an experiment in West Berlin collected "schoolchildren ranging in age from eight to fourteen." They "were encouraged by scientists of the city's free university to undress and enact scenes of sexual intercourse" under the auspices of the University's Institute of Psychology.

The participants were apparently found on nearby playgrounds. . . . Five to fifteen children participated each day, with some fifty youngsters believed to have been involved.

Two psychologists took the children swimming and they returned "voluptuously tired." Everyone lay on cushions and mattresses arranged on the floor to imitate a giant bed.

"The psychologists provoked insinuations of sexual activity that were then played out in pantomime by Thomas and Koksie," the reports said, referring to otherwise unidentified children.

"At first we wanted them to enact or intimate coitus, but that did not come to pass because Koksie, giggling shamefully, turned the other way to the floor."

Later . . . the group played at forfeits, in which everyone eventually got undressed.[3]

In America books on sexual responses (responses sometimes said to have been evoked under controlled and hygienic laboratory conditions) have for decades skated to the top of the best-seller lists if the publishers gave them sufficient advertising muscle. But by 1970 West German psychologists were a little ahead of American publishers as they rounded up preteens from neighborhood swings and climbing bars to subject them to a comic agony in real life that would cause them to start "giggling shamefully." Had Berlin turned into an open sex arena for all ages? The news of the experiment with Thomas and Koksie and other youngsters, who may or may not have been strangers to one another, "shocked the public and the city administration." The sex wave, the public shock, and the experiment conducted by lip-smacking "scientists" supplied evidence that the sort of warped mentalities Wedekind wrote about persist: prurience is another face of prudery. Twenty years later in the Western world, costly, furtively purchased blue movies have given way to videotapes openly displayed on "adult shelves" and rentable overnight at two dollars plus tax ("Pay for two, get the third for free!"). Films that feature undressed, grappling, sweating, groaning, pumping pairs (or groups) of bodies have become laughable.[4]

Spring's Awakening does incorporate sensational sexuality: scenes of flagellation, two fourteen-year-olds making love, group masturbation, and an idyllic homosexual affair between two boys. The play did not receive its first professional performance until fifteen years after it was written. But the sexual escapades are part of a wryly poetic, tragic, *and* comic study of some young people. The three principals are children. Wendla Bergmann, who has just reached her fourteenth birthday (about the same age as Ibsen's Hedvig and Shakespeare's Juliet) is smitten with Melchior Gabor, a boy of fourteen. Melchior has read scholarly material on lovemaking and reproduction. He knows what to do and does it. Wendla becomes pregnant and dies at the hands of an abortionist. The third child, Moritz Stiefel, a girlish boy of fifteen, is baffled and tormented by the "awakening" of erotic impulses. Unable to cope with them and with the standards that have been prescribed for him at home and at school, unable to escape from his misery, Moritz commits suicide.

Summarized thus, the action sounds Teutonically morbid, an impression fortified by the subtitle, *A Children's Tragedy*. But Wedekind splashes comedy into every scene, and the dialogue darts about from grisliness to satire, from lyrical sweetness to farce. The author's astringent humor is most overt in his treatment of the adults in the play, the parents and the schoolteachers, most of whom he ridicules unmercifully. He also makes graceful but persevering fun of the youngsters, as he counterpoints their own hot and tragic view of their plight with his comic coolness. His notes on the play, written some twenty years after he had finished it, are worth considering as an antidote to the conventional critical opinions: "Since about 1901, above all since Max Reinhardt put it on the stage [in 1906 and in a denatured version], it has been regarded as an angry, deadly earnest tragedy, as a thesis play, as a polemic in the service of sexual enlightenment—or whatever the current slogans of the fussy, pedantic lower middle class may be. It makes me wonder if I shall live to see the book taken for what, twenty years ago, I wrote it as—a sunny image of life in every scene of which I tried to exploit an unburdened humor for all it was worth."

One of Wedekind's early translators, Francis J. Ziegler, nevertheless believed that Wedekind had a thesis, namely, "that it is a fatal error to bring up children . . . in ignorance of their sexual nature." This was an explosive remark for the American public in 1912, an unsatisfactory bit of exegesis at any time, and an article of faith in 1970 for the virtual abusers of little Thomas and Koksie. H. F. Garten, one of the few critics in English who has dealt with Wedekind's work at any length, suggests that "Wedekind lays the blame on the narrow-mindedness of the schoolmasters and the moral cowardice of the parents who shrink from enlightening their children on the facts of life."[5] This sort of talk about Wedekind's laying blame or setting down a thesis or promoting enlightenment misses the point that the parents and schoolteachers in the play have muddled through the same sort of upbringing as the child's. It is not so much that they are cowards as that they know no way of speaking to the children about sex. If they tried, they would blunder horribly. Sensing this, they turn evasive. Cowardice is one thing; ineptitude is something else. The grown-ups might have made life easier for the youngsters if they had been able to think back to their own adolescent years, but if they did, Wedekind would have been writing a modern German (or American) sex-advice column and, with any luck, have commanded a different sort of attention and a much larger income as the Sexual Pope. The play's parents cannot speak to the children about anything. They offer themselves up for comedy. In stark contrast, self-destructive impulses (related to the erotic ones) obsess the three young principals.[6]

Wendla's entry into womanhood on her birthday marks the beginning of the action. Her mother, Frau Bergmann, has made her a long dress—Wendla calls it a penitential robe—and justifies the length by claiming that Wendla would be cold in a shorter garment, as though growth means merely more square inches of skin exposed to the elements. But we see what is in her mind when she says,

"Other girls are gawky and gangling at your age. You're just the opposite.—Who knows what you'll be like when the others are fully developed?" She worries that her daughter may look more tempting with a short hemline. Wendla replies strangely, "Who knows? Maybe I won't be around." This is the first of her premonitions that she will die young.

The premonitions, casually voiced, soon make it clear that Wendla is a personality of some consequence. Hers is one of the few rewarding girl's roles in the drama—not quite a Juliet or an Iphigenia but comparable to Hedvig or Isabel in *Intermezzo*. She is far more substantial than the run of insipidly naive heroines who have never had a dirty thought or the cutely precocious Shirley Temple mimics who never matured. With the instinct of a blossoming woman she rejects the "penitential robe" and decides to go on wearing her little girl's dress, which will do more for her.

Wendla does not have a bad home life. It contrasts favorably with that of her school friend Martha, whom we meet two scenes later.[7] When Martha threaded a blue ribbon through the yoke of her nightdress, as some of her friends had done, her mother hauled her out of bed by the hair: "I lay on the floor and shrieked and yelled. Enter Papa. Rip! Off comes my nightdress! I head for the door. 'So that's it,' he shouts, 'you'd like to go out like that, wouldn't you?'. . . It was freezing. I went back in. I had to spend the whole night on the floor in a sack." What fixes our attention in this part of the scene is not so much Martha's being treated by her parents as an incipient whore because she wears a blue ribbon in her nightdress, or her father's behavior in ripping the nightdress off her, or even her punishment, sleeping in a sack, but Wendla's seriocomic reply: "I'd be glad to sleep in your sack for you." There speaks the modern, guilt-charged temperament. Wendla wants to suffer, even do penance, for others.

As they talk the girls walk through an outdoor scene. The spring wind along the street feels blustery; it makes their hearts beat faster. Melchior goes by. Martha and a third girl admire his "marvelous head" and compare him to "the young Alexander when he was a pupil of Aristotle's." Wendla speaks less committally about Melchior. She mentions that at a recent party he told her he "didn't believe in anything: God, an afterlife, or anything at all." His remarks seem to have provoked her at the same time as they appealed to her.

In her next scene, the climax of act I, she meets Melchior on a sunny afternoon in a forest. She has been out to gather woodruff for making May wine. She has lain for a while in the moss, dreaming. Melchior, after roaming through the forest, says he almost took her for "a dryad fallen from the branches." It seems that Wendla periodically visits the poor to take them food, clothes, and money. She enjoys these excursions. Perhaps they lighten her middle-class conscience: she is *doing* something. Melchior attributes her pleasure to the local pastor's preachings about the joy of self-sacrifice. The assumption sounds unlikely.

Wendla does not really sacrifice anything she takes to the poor, only a little time. The charity looks like a substitute for a more drastic kind of giving. We are reminded of how she thought earlier of taking Martha's place in the coal sack as she tells Melchior that she lay in the moss a few minutes before and dreamed that "I was a poor, poor beggar girl. I was sent into the streets at five in the morning. I had to beg all day, in rain and storm, among rough, hard-hearted people, and if I came home in the evening, shivering with hunger and cold, and didn't bring as much as my father expected, I'd get beaten." The mention of being beaten returns her thoughts to Martha, who is "beaten night after night. Next day you can see the welts. What she must have to suffer! . . . I pity her so, I often cry into my pillow in the middle of the night. . . I'd gladly take her place for a week or so. . . . I've tried beating myself to find out how it feels inside." But beating oneself is not the same as being beaten. She suddenly picks up a switch from the ground and asks Melchior, "Wouldn't you like to hit me with it once?" He would not. What, and draw blood? Is she mad?

The climax of the scene (and of the act) disqualifies all criticism that tells us: Oh, if only parents and children had sat down together and bartered grievances and information—had, in the jargon of our time, thrown down barriers and eliminated a communications gap—this particular spring would have come in tranquilly to the chirping of birds and the unfolding of petals. Not a hope. Wendla pleads with Melchior to flay her. He assays a few tentative strokes with the switch. She cannot feel a thing, she says, and urges him to hit her on the legs. He still cannot strike hard enough to hurt her. He throws away the stick and begins to punch her with his fists. Then she feels the pain and cries out. But he cannot stop his arms from working or his eyes from pouring tears. By now Wendla is screaming. Melchior lets up and runs away, still sobbing. He is ashamed of his lack of self-control. Or the misdirection of his lack of self-control?

In the next act Wendla's older sister, Ina, has just given birth for the third time in two-and-a-half years. Frau Bergmann announces, "Just think, Wendla, the stork paid Ina a visit last night. Brought her a little boy." Wendla retorts, "That explains the never-ending influenza" that Ina has evidently been said to suffer from, to account for her pregnancy. She inquires whether her mother was there when the stork dropped in. Frau Bergmann says it "had just flown away," after leaving Wendla a brooch as a consolation gift. The girl responds to more of this fencing with some choice syncretism. Outside the house she can see "a man three times the size of an ox. With feet like steamboats. He's holding a bedstead under his chin and fiddling 'The Watch on the Rhine' on it." But sarcasm doesn't work. She still has to ask her mother straight out, "How does it happen?—You can't seriously expect me to believe in the stork—at fourteen." Frau Bergmann prevaricates. She cannot say. She would prefer to be—and breaks off the sentence. She will tell Wendla "everything. . . . But not today . . . tomorrow

. . . next week." Finally, under more pressure from Wendla and after saying she deserves to go to prison and to have Wendla taken away from her, she sinks into euphemism: "To have a child—one must love the man—to whom one is married—love him as only a husband can be loved. One must love him so much, one must love him, Wendla, as you at your age are incapable of loving. . . . Now you know." She rushes her daughter away to Ina's for chocolate and cakes, as if the girl were four, not fourteen. Wendla's dress, she notices, looks shorter than ever.

A couple of scenes later Wendla is up in a hayloft with Melchior, about to part with her girlhood once and for all. He tells her to get away from him or he will throw her down, which is exactly the way to tempt Wendla Bergmann to stay. Then she is asking him not to kiss her, and saying, "Don't, don't!" The scene here has broken lines in place of text.[8] Explicit stage instructions are unnecessary in this ancestor of bucolic movie seductions. But what above all else distinguishes this scene from its thousands of bastard descendants is a brief speech by Melchior: "There's no such thing as love! That's a fact.—It's all just selfishness and self-seeking.—I love you as little as you love me." Wedekind avoids romantic slosh. He shows us two children attracted to each other, making use of each other.

Wendla is now in love with love, but Wedekind shuns the option of letting us into her emotional state. She walks in the garden to keep away from her mother's watchful eye, saying she will look for violets. She feels ecstatic, and yet sufficiently outside herself to be awed by her feelings.

When she reappears, a long stretch later in the action, she is in bed with palpitations, headaches, giddiness, shivering. The family doctor prescribes exercises and a weird intake of pills: "Begin with three or four a day and increase the dose as rapidly as you can stand it." Ina, a mother of three, has no advice for her sister but does speak one beautiful line that is an unconscious metaphor for Wendla at fourteen-and-a-half: "Your plane tree is changing color again already.—Can you see it from your bed? A short-lived splendor, hardly worth the joy we feel to see it come and go."

Frau Bergmann tells Wendla she has anemia. Wendla can force the truth out of her only by saying she is sure she has dropsy and will soon die. If this is not a life-and-death disease, why does her mother keep crying? Frau Bergmann at last tells what she knows but cannot resist adding an accusation: "You're going to have a baby, Wendla! A baby! Why did you do this to me?" (The pompous humor of her question sounds very like Hjalmar's reaction to the news of Hedvig's death.) Wendla answers that it is impossible for her to be pregnant: she is not married. Besides—her sentiment corresponds to Melchior's earlier one—"I never loved anyone but you, Mother." The words have a comic innocence and yet are pathetic. Wendla has not loved and is not loved. She surrendered to a hunger.

She then wants to know why her mother did not tell her "everything." Frau Bergmann replies with a question: "How could I have told such things to a fourteen-year-old girl? It would have been the end of the world. I've treated you no different than my mother treated me." Her counsel now is: Trust in God; hope for the best; be brave. The arrival of a neighbor called Mother Schmidt interrupts the dialogue and concludes the scene. Mother Schmidt, who does not enter the room or the action, is, we are later informed, an amateur abortionist. As a result of her ministrations, Wendla dies.

We could say that Wendla's death derives from her mother's refusal to tell her "everything" and to provide her with contraception, the sort of double denial promulgated by the Rehnquist Supreme Court in its *Rust* v. *Sullivan* ruling (May 1991), which banned federal abortion advice. But Wendla's fate also derives from the absence of a domestic or overseas Peace Corps or some other communal program likely to be touted by today's social workers, a "project" on which this counterpart of a contemporary suburban teenager could expend some of her missionary energies. Wendla has the soul of a martyr, but her goodness gets squandered on daydreams of suffering. Yet it seems to me that Wedekind is writing to a broader theme: the bittersweet agonies of puberty and adolescence. In retrospect one looks back on these years fondly and talks about calf love. But they are a testing time, and today, as always, not every youngster surmounts them.

Wendla's opposite, Moritz, is as much of a glutton for punishment as she is. And his life is almost as closely linked with Melchior as hers is. Moritz, a year older than his friend but far less independent and less informed, encourages Melchior to serve as his protector and mentor. On a warm Sunday evening out of doors they talk about the mysterious "stirrings of manhood." But Moritz cannot stop fretting about his homework (Central America, Louis XV, sixty verses of Homer, seven equations, a Latin exercise), due the following morning. Next year's classroom has space for only sixty boys. Unless his grades improve he is one of seven who will flunk. Then what will his parents do? He feels terrified, especially when he thinks that they "could have had a hundred better children than me."[9] In his quaintly formal schoolboy lingo, he asks: "Don't you agree, Melchior, that the sense of shame is simply a product of a person's upbringing?" He can speak of this sense of shame, just about, but he cannot overcome it or reconcile himself to it. "I can remember even as a child of five feeling embarrassed if anyone turned up the queen of hearts; she wore a décolleté." He thinks of the queen of hearts because "I hear Mama carried me under her heart." That, and the fact that hens lay eggs, constitute his knowledge of reproduction. Melchior promises to undertake "quite an interesting assignment"—to write up a clear, brief explanation of sex. Moritz asks him to add illustrations in the margin. Melchior suddenly says,

"You're like a girl," and then lets the matter drop. Moritz doesn't take up or challenge the statement. To him, with his tacit (and later explicit) acceptance of feminine yearnings, the queen of hearts may invoke bosom envy.

His sexual desires not only flutter between masculine and feminine; they are
also tainted by his fear of school. He hesitantly mentions his first sexual dream,
of legs in blue tights climbing over a lectern. Wedekind again feeds humor into
nearly every speech in this scene without playing down Moritz's misery. Probably because of this misery, to most of the older children Moritz is a comic butt.
One of the girls says, "He embarrasses you when you meet him. At the children's
party . . . he offered me some chocolates. . . . They were soft and warm! . . . He
said he'd had them too long in his trouser pocket!" Moritz as the source of warm,
flowing chocolate from a pants pocket: it is a devastating comment, especially
from a girl. The boys jeer at his anxiety over grades. One day, as we learn from
the story, he stole into the classroom to look at the register and find out whether
he had been promoted. He had—provisionally. Still, he is all "happiness—
bliss—jubilation" for the time being. He adds, "If I didn't get my promotion, I
was going to shoot myself." The boys take this remark as crude bravado, all of
them except Melchior. The comfortable verbal interplay between the two friends
contrasts with Moritz's uneasiness with his other contemporaries and with his
elders.

Moritz continues to drive himself. He sits up until three in the morning
contending with verb conjugations and the like. The next day he falls asleep in
class. But he says to Melchior, "You feel so good when you've won a victory over
yourself. . . . I mean to work and work till my eyes pop out of my head. . . . If I
don't get through, Papa will have a stroke and Mama will go to the madhouse."
The irony in Moritz's fate is that the best he can hope for is to stay in the class.
He is competing with another boy for the lowest position. The other boy has had
six failures during the term, Moritz five. Catastrophe looms. He lives on the
edge of the abyss.

Melchior invites him home to drink tea, unwind, and chat about the essay
on reproduction, now written. The house has an agreeable ambience; Melchior's
mother, Frau Gabor, is the most approachable adult in the play. Moritz, warmed
by tea and friendliness and the temporary relief from school and parental pressures, turns garrulous. He tells Melchior a story related by his grandmother
about a queen who was "fabulously beautiful" but could not see, hear, eat, drink,
laugh, or kiss because she lacked a head. But along came a king with two heads.
A magician moved one of them onto her shoulders—really advanced transplant
surgery—and they lived happily ever after. Moritz says, "I can't get the headless
queen out of my mind. If I see a beautiful girl, I see her without a head, then suddenly I myself seem to be a headless queen." His fellow-feeling for the headless
queen, the most potent signal in the play for his feminine desires, has a variation

rung on it by the author when the two boys come around to talking about Melchior's sex essay. Moritz says, "I was most strongly affected by what you wrote about girls. . . . To have to suffer wrong is sweeter than to do wrong . . . [it] seems to me the essence of all earthly bliss. . . . A girl keeps herself free of everything bitter till the last moment, and then has the pleasure of seeing all heaven break over her. . . . By comparison, a man's satisfaction seems to me shallow, stagnant."[10]

Moritz does flunk at school. He turns to the only adult he knows who might assist him, Melchior's mother, and asks her to lend him the fare to America. If she cannot, he may have to put an end to himself. Wedekind encapsulates this part of the story in Frau Gabor's letter of reply. She wants to soothe Moritz, but "frankly, your veiled threats to take your own life . . . have slightly alienated my sympathies." Like Wendla's mother, she consoles with useless exhortation: "Chin up! . . . Such crises of one kind or another confront each of us and must be overcome. If everyone had recourse to poison or the dagger there would soon be no human beings left in the world."[11] With this avenue closed to him, Moritz sees no escape. He wanders out of town and toward some marshes. Like many an O'Neill protagonist to come, he does not "belong." "I've signed no contract with the Almighty. . . . I don't hold my parents responsible." Even into the dusk of this scene, a presentiment of many German films of the 1920s with their underlit, tormented faces and acres of bosky shadow, Wedekind keeps injecting comedy. The plight of Moritz is to be laughed and wept at—simultaneously. "I was an infant when I came into the world, or no doubt I'd have been smart enough to become someone else." He is going to die, but the thought that he has never had sex with a woman holds him back. He is still talking to himself: "There's something to be ashamed of [*shame* again] in having been human without getting to know the most human thing of all.—You were in Egypt, dear sir, and did not see the Pyramids?"[12] The memory of a certain voluptuous Fräulein Snandulia, with whom he danced at a party, tempts him to stay alive. Another décolleté: "Her silk dress was cut low back and front. . . . In front, so low you could almost pass out. She couldn't have been wearing a slip." A broken line interrupts the dialogue again, presumably to show that, as a pitiful gesture to life, Moritz is masturbating.

From the low-cut Snandulia his thoughts edge away to the "many happy evenings" he has spent with Melchior—to a female role from a male role—and then to the grave and beyond the grave to faces that beckon, "the headless queen, the headless queen—sympathy awaiting me with soft arms."

A young woman comes up behind him and seizes him by the shoulder. Her name is Ilse; she models for artists and sleeps with them. A young woman, an available, slightly older woman—it is a reprieve! She talks of having been mistreated by an artist, hit and then kissed, brutal love of the sort the masochistic Moritz is bound to envy. Then she exacerbates his masculine longings: she invites him home with her to drink warm goat's milk. She will curl his hair, give him a rocking horse, baby him.

Ilse has been away from home for four nights. She has just come from the "priapia," a fraternal organization that sounds like a phallic, avant-garde collection of young Rotarians or Jaycees. When she asks Moritz to go with her, he remembers that he has left some homework undone: the Sassanids, the Sermon on the Mount, and the parallelepipedon. Ilse is cold. She takes off, saying, "By the time any of you [schoolboys] are ready, I'll be on the rubbish heap."

Moritz has missed his chance, thinking about his homework when "a single word would have done it." Like the General in *The Balcony* he pictures the young woman for an instant as "an unruly filly" wearing black silk stockings, on his bed with "great crystal mirrors" over it, and there he would love to . . . strangle her. But he longs, no matter how, to be a man before he dies.

Or a woman. "To be you, Ilse." Brutalized, manhandled, but kissed. He masturbates again (two broken lines this time) among the willows of the marshes and the reeds, the *Königskerzen*, which Eric Bentley has translated literally and suggestively as "king's tapers." Moritz burns the discouraging letter from Frau Gabor. In its sparks he sees "shooting stars." Darkness has settled over the marshes. The expiring flame of the letter marks the transition from twilight to night and the end of Moritz's life.

We do not see him die, nor do we know how he died when his funeral begins in a later scene. The local pastor (the one said to believe in self-sacrifice) has come to bury Moritz, not to praise him. Assailed by a Christian impulse, he consigns the dead boy to hell everlasting for having taken his own life. Moritz's father, in his only appearance in the play, says, "The boy was no son of mine. I never liked him—from the beginning." The school principal remarks that a suicide "saves the moral order the necessity of passing judgment." But judgment has been passed. Not one of the grown-ups has a generous word to speak in memory of Moritz. Two citizens commiserate with his father, not for having lost a son, but for having had a bad son.

Only the children, some of them, pay tribute to Moritz. Ilse and Martha throw flowers on his grave, ivy and anemones. Ilse, the last person to see Moritz, reveals that he shot himself. She heard the report of the gun as she was leaving. Next morning she returned to take the pistol out of his hand. He had blown his head off, ending his life as a mockery of the headless queen. The last word he spoke that Ilse remembers is *parallelepipedon*, a reference to some unfinished math. A parallelepipedon is a solid figure bounded by six parallelograms. An example is a coffin.

Moritz's life ends, like Wendla's, as a trope. She evokes a vision of the plane tree and its burst of temporary color. She has premonitions before dying of a "monster," the fetus, flying into her and of the old man outside the window playing that once-popular song by Max Schneckenburger, "The Watch on the Rhine"—an Old Man Death. Moritz dies, a "headless queen" among the "king's tapers," an unmourned flame. Both children are claimed by the late frosts and rigors of spring that sometimes precede flowering.

The epic structure of *Spring's Awakening* allows Wedekind to devote some of the play's nineteen scenes to secondary characters and subplots without losing the impetus of the double main plot. We see into the lives of some of Wendla's girl-friends, Martha and Thea, and also Ilse. Among the boys are two who, like Moritz, are fearful of these girls. The relationship between them develops into a more definite homosexual love than that between Moritz and Melchior. Hän-schen Rilow and Ernst Röbel have a scene together in a vineyard that corresponds to the lovemaking between Melchior and Wendla in the hayloft. Ernst is the boy who competed with Moritz for the lowest grade in the class; now that Moritz is dead he will get it. Hänschen's earlier appearances have included a solo scene in which he studied a reproduction of Palma Vecchio's Venus and sent himself into masturbatory frenzies and terrors: "You suck the marrow from my bones, you crook my back, you steal the light from my young eyes. . . . My heart! I'm hav-ing convulsions!" After this he dropped the picture into a toilet bowl. Hänschen is the only boy who speaks about Moritz at the funeral with affectionate rever-ence. He throws a spadeful of earth into the grave and remembers Moritz's "angelic simplicity."

In their love scene Ernst and Hänschen lie down together in the vineyard during the grape harvest, sated with the fruit. They talk about themselves and the autumn evening. Near the end, Hänschen leans over and kisses Ernst on the mouth. For many years the scene went unperformed, and it has been omitted from some translations. Yet it is charming and fragile throughout, as candid as any of Gide's and less apologetic, and it has none of the affectation of commer-cial homosexual theatre. Ernst pleads, "I love you, Hänschen, as I have never loved a living soul," and the passion rings true. Hänschen seems convinced that passion of this intensity belongs only to the interregnum between boyhood and manhood: "When we think back in thirty years, maybe we'll just make a joke of it."

The linchpin of the main plot, Melchior, may well be the author's self-portrait, although it hardly matters whether he corresponds to the Frank Wedekind his school contemporaries knew. Melchior claims that behavior—his, at any rate—springs from selfishness. He may say this as a reaction to the self-sacrifice preached by the pastor, the schoolmasters, and his parents. He is capable of a neurotic blowup, as when he flays Wendla on the legs and then punches her, an attack predicted in the "worst dream" he ever had, in which he found himself "flogging our dog Lolo so long he couldn't move his legs." The children, boys and girls, like him. He is a favorite among the teachers. Seeing him with Moritz, one teacher says, "That my best student should feel himself attracted to my worst is quite incomprehensible to me." For all his talk of the inevitability of selfishness, Melchior is troubled when he comes across examples of it, such as Faust's abandoning Gretchen. He and Moritz have read the play at school. He says of Faust's faithlessness: "Suppose Faust just promised to marry the girl and then left her; as I see it, he wouldn't be a bit less to blame. . . . Gretchen would die of a broken heart." Later he will see himself as a junior Faust and Wendla as his Gretchen after he learns that she died. He will feel despicable, not so much for not having kept faith with her as for not having been able to love her.

After Moritz's death the sex essay, the "explanation" Melchior wrote, is discovered. The teachers, graphologists all, trace it back to Melchior. These teachers are a bunch of caricatures. Wedekind gives them names like Zungenschlag (Tongue-thump) and Sonnenstick (Sunstroke). They summon Melchior to a faculty meeting. After preliminary talk about whether the windows should be kept open or shut and about the possibilities of Moritz's death setting off "a suicide epidemic such as has already broken out in various other schools" (the if-everybody deduction again), they accuse Melchior of being the author of "a treatise twenty pages long in dialogue form, entitled 'Copulation,' equipped with life-size illustrations and teeming with shameless indecencies, a document that would meet the most extravagant demands of an abandoned libertine, a connoisseur in pornographic literature." Melchior doesn't deny the charge. He doesn't have much chance to say anything. But he manages to affirm that what he wrote "is fact, no more, no less. . . . Please show me one offense against morals in the document." He might almost be Wedekind speaking about his play to people who later called him a pornographer. Like the play, the "treatise" is composed "in dialogue form." We can assume it was modeled on Socratic argumentation and may even have had a certain dignity in its presentation, likely to anger the teachers all the more if they took it as either clever imitation or a mockery of classical, metaphysical catechizing. In any case, they have no respect for their pupils, as they have none for one another. Buffoons or no, they are cruel disciplinarians. Melchior is expelled.

His father then determines to send him to reform school. Frau Gabor opposes this move bitterly and eloquently, even threatening to leave her husband if he goes through with it. She is to blame, she says, if anybody is (*blame* yet again), but she cannot believe her son to be anything worse than artless, childlike, and innocent. Her speeches in this scene show the adult world during some of its few admirable moments in the action. But Herr Gabor argues: "Anyone who could write what Melchior wrote must be rotten to the core; the very marrow is infected. . . . This was no unintentional lapse, but the documentation, with horrifying clarity, of . . . a natural drive toward immorality for its own sake. This piece of writing is evidence of that extreme degree of spiritual corruption which we lawyers describe as 'moral depravity.'" His forensics do not impress Frau Gabor. A reform school will destroy Melchior with its "crudity" and "filth."

At this point Wedekind twists the situation inside out with stinging suddenness. Herr Gabor reveals that Wendla's mother came to see him that morning (not long before Wendla's death), bringing a letter from Melchior, in which the boy admits "he has sinned against her, et cetera, et cetera, but that naturally he'll answer for everything." Herr Gabor asks his wife what he should do with Melchior now. With the hurt pride and perhaps the jealousy of a more than usually understanding parent of the opposite sex, she does not hesitate. Her toleration and sympathy crumble, as they did before, when she wrote to Moritz. Melchior must go to the reform school.

In reform school a brief scene—another one omitted from some earlier translations—shows us the conditions Frau Gabor had feared her son would be exposed to, although that sheltered lady would hardly have imagined the game the young inmates have devised. They stand in a circle, placing a coin on the floor, and the boy who first ejaculates (not merely urinates) on the coin wins it. Melchior, invited to join in, politely declines. He worries about becoming corrupted, but if he stays, can he keep his distance from the others without arousing resentment? Won't he make himself different? At the same time, he is more afraid of taking part in the contest, because "they're killing themselves, that's what prison's done for them." Wise though he seems for his age, Melchior swallows whole those old wives' tales about "self-abuse"—or are they old husbands' tales? And some of the other youngsters in the play are as terrified as he is of the consequences of masturbating.[13] But he does not give the reform school time to dirty him. He climbs through a skylight, wraps a handkerchief around the lightning conductor, and slides down sixty feet to the ground. The last boy who tried this trick had to be picked up in pieces. Melchior is more agile or luckier.

In the final scene he has taken refuge in a graveyard. His coat is in rags, his pockets are empty, and his conscience plays with him. He is being pursued by the rest of the play. He thinks of Wendla's pregnancy and worries because the girl always takes the brunt of careless lovemaking. Perhaps he should follow Moritz's example, suicide: "No mortal ever wandered among graves so full of envy." Yet he does not have the nerve to die voluntarily, and he cannot believe he has sinned. He longs for release: "If only madness would overtake me."

This will happen. The "madness," though, is more akin to a dream than to a demented condition. Melchior comes in turn upon the grave of Wendla, the ghost of Moritz, and an apparition called the Man in the Mask. In this unrestful resting place, where leaves ominously rustle and "ragged clouds race across the moon," the action dissolves into nightmarish coincidences, a dramatic heightening of the afflictions of his conscience. He knocks over the cross on Moritz's grave without noticing. Then, among the hundreds of tombstones, he chances on Wendla's and is stunned to find she is dead. The inscription coyly says she "died of anemia" and adds, "Blessed are the pure in heart." He concludes that she died from the pregnancy and that "I am her murderer."

The ghost of Moritz "comes stomping over the graves," his shattered head under his arm, like Anne Boleyn's in the old music hall number. As a headless queen, he can perhaps be saved by Melchior, who would somehow have to perform as the two-headed king. He repeatedly asks Melchior to give him a hand, though, not a head, and professes to be pleased with his present existence, if it can be called an existence. He is "above it all." He keeps mentioning how much he laughs these days; he never did when he was alive. He even smiled when he attended his own funeral and watched the proceedings. He is trying to lure Melchior into death, offering him "peace, contentment." Melchior replies: "If I agree, it will be from self-contempt. I see myself as a pariah. . . . I can't conceive of anything that could stand between me and doom. To myself I am the most execrable creature on earth." Moritz is asking why he still hesitates, when the "thing" that could stand between Melchior and doom appears.

The Man in the Mask refuses to identify himself. He is a function, not a person. To save Melchior from his conscience and Moritz's dead handclasp, he first reassures Melchior about the cause of Wendla's death: "That little girl would have given birth splendidly. She was superbly built. It was Mother Schmidt's abortion pills that did for her." He will take Melchior away, "among people," and acquaint him with "everything of interest the world has to offer." He would, he says in a flowery locution, "give your survival my best attention." He chastises Moritz for having surrendered to mortality—and morality, "the real product of two imaginary factors . . . 'I ought to' and 'I want to.' . . . Your parents would no more have died of [the disgrace] than you need have done." Thus the Man in the Mask persuades Melchior to shed guilt, live, grow up, and become the author of *Spring's Awakening*.

Critics usually assume that the Man in the Mask is also a limited self-portrait, Melchior grown up, partly because Wedekind himself played the role more than once, partly because the work is "dedicated by the author to the Man in the Mask." If these critics are right, the dedication is a joke, and a feeble one, a pointless stab at some self-aggrandizement. I would not assign an unmistakable meaning or identity to this role, but its dramatic function during Melchior's ordeal in the graveyard *is* unmistakable. He brings Melchior out of his melancholia and then steers him away from a tragic ending, suicide. He is a life force debating with a death force, for a claim on Melchior's soul. He confirms this role by saying to Moritz that he appeared to him, too: "You don't remember me? Even at the last moment you were hesitating between death and . . . life."

During the debate Melchior listens and tells himself that "they can't both be the Devil." But one of them is. Since Moritz's translation from life to death, the Devil has taken over that poor youngster's decapitated likeness and turned him into Mephistopheles the Tempter, who promises the Faustian Melchior amusement and detachment, the cool pleasures of remaining "above it all." As his opponent, Life, the Man in the Mask happens to be the only wholly sympathetic adult in the play, the only one who can say, "I would give your survival my best attention." He saves Melchior from the fate of Moritz and Wendla, pulls him past the "spring" and into the later seasons of maturity. He will take him "among people."

Wedekind's irony does not mean that such an adult existed. The Man in the Mask is an unfulfilled wish, a smudged hope in the author's imagination, and in Melchior's. For if the scene is a dream—as Moritz's headless ghost reminds us it must be—then both the ghost of Moritz and the Man in the Mask are Melchior. He has reached the crisis in his young life, the combat within his private "morality" between those "two imaginary factors," the I-ought-to (I ought to punish myself fatally for what I have done) and the I-want-to (I want to go on living).

The Man in the Mask wins the debate. Melchior goes off with him. The ghost of Moritz remains alone—poor dead Moritz, only now emptied of the diabolical presence, to deliver the last lines, which are comic and agonized: "So here I sit with my head on my arm. . . . I shall go back to my little plot, to set up my cross that that madcap trampled down, and when everything is in order, I shall lie on my back again, warm myself with the putrefaction, and smile." Wedekind, we recall, said he wrote the play as "a sunny image of life." The sunny image may be stretching matters, especially in the sepulchral last scene. But of life? Undoubtedly. Life as a stirred-up amalgam of Schiller's joyous ode and the misgivings of a rejuvenated Faustling. Wedekind scorns to end the comic agony with a sentimental reconciliation between opponents. Instead, the Man in the Mask reconciles Melchior with adulthood. That is the meaning of the dedication to the Man in the Mask. The play becomes a paean to life.

SIRELESS IN RUSSIA
Uncle Vanya, by Anton Chekhov

O you heavenly charmers,
What things you make of us! For what we lack
We laugh, for what we have are sorry, still
Are children in some kind.

SHAKESPEARE (OR FLETCHER?), *The Two Noble Kinsmen*

Three-quarters of the way through the action of *Uncle Vanya* (Dyadya Vanya, 1898) a pistol fired offstage startles the audience. Ivan Petrovitch Voinitsky, known in the family as Vanya, rushes onstage in pursuit of his brother-in-law, Serebryakov, a retired professor. Enraged beyond control and fighting off Serebryakov's wife, Vanya fires again point-blank. As he does so, he utters the word "Bang!" But the exclamation doesn't help: like the first bullet, this second one misses.

The incident, which displays Vanya near the end of his rope, cannot sum up one of Chekhov's more richly adumbrated roles, but it does suddenly dramatize the futility Vanya feels at this moment. He has an incapacitated hatred, a resentment so strong that his very will to kill robs him of the physical means to succeed. He has just become aware that having been exploited and—worse—taken for granted for a quarter of a century has worked on him like a spiritual castration. We become aware of it, too, but the surge of pity we experience for Vanya gives way, precisely as it collects, to our desire to laugh. For with that one despairing word the pathetic figure becomes clownish, scarcely able to take aim, so impatient for the bullet to fly that he must hope to speed it on its way, to force it to do more damage, by exploding himself into the word "Bang!" And so we are tempted to laugh, without meaning spite, much as we laugh at any unavailing act. But our laughter does not succeed in breaking through cleanly. Like the pity, it is checked in its turn by our alertness to Vanya's unappeased hatred, which, as act III closes, modulates into despair, shame, and self-disgust.[1]

Vanya's hatred for Serebryakov serves as only one of the active ingredients in this drama. It flourishes in partnership with his helpless love for Serebryakov's wife, Elena, whom he deludes himself into thinking he could have won ten years before. Vanya's simultaneous hatred and love become apparent with his first speech in act I. He has just woken up from a nap, and the objects of his hatred and love are already on his mind: "Ever since the professor and his wife came here to live, life has been out of joint."[2] Both the hatred and the love are also affected

44

by the interplay among these three and Vanya's niece, Sonya, and Doctor Astrov, who visits them not simply for medical reasons. If we look past the several fringe roles for a moment, the triangle in the main plot resolves itself into a pentagon or quintet in four movements. As in all of Chekhov's last four plays, the hatred and other stinging emotions arise from unrequited love. This drama offers five studies of incompatibility. But behind or below an apparently loose structure lies the drama's causation, and this, also common to Chekhov's last four plays, consists of the absence of a father and the unavailing search for a replacement.

Ivan Petrovitch Voinitsky. Formal patronymics in Russian literature (and life) remind us of the significance of the father in this patriarchal, prerevolutionary society. A holding like the Voinitsky estate, which includes a twenty-six-room mansion and a farm, amounted to a community of peasants (who, before 1861, would have been serfs) and their families, besides the household servants and *their* families, with the owning-governing family at its center and the father at its head, playing multiple roles as entrepreneur, business manager, local squire, magistrate, counselor, mediator, and friend (or overseer) to the permanent and hired help.

Vanya's father, a man with some political affiliation or other and referred to posthumously in the play as the Senator, did not take on the customary paternalistic duties. A quarter of a century before, he purchased the estate as a dowry for his daughter, Vera (who was Vanya's sister, Sonya's mother, and Serebryakov's first wife). Vanya not only relinquished any claim to the estate but also labored to pay off a lump of the mortgage out of brotherly love for the dead sister and the living brother-in-law, and out of avuncular love for Sonya. He made a quixotic gesture that went on and on, eventually costing him, apart from the mortgage dues, a secure (even easy) retirement and a wide slice of his life. People who are perennially put upon by parents, siblings, employers, or others often live to regret their selflessness and its attendant sacrifices. They squirm from the flow of untold gallons of stomach acid or worse, sometimes without realizing why. Vanya knows why: his altruism has turned bitter and exacerbated his hatred. He can no longer bring himself to continue to draw up the accounts and supervise the farm, work he has been doing for twenty-five years. In act I he comes out of his sleep—wakes up to his plight—to enter the play, aged forty-seven but feeling eighty-seven. When he later accuses Elena repeatedly of being indolent, he may be fending off the same accusation from others. As summer vanishes into fall Sonya will tell him that the hay, which they should have had bundled and used for fodder or sold, lies rotting in the fields. Chekhov has set Vanya up as the person most eligible for the father role. He is the only son of the Senator. He had a strong attachment to Vera and will do everything he can to preserve the estate for her daughter. A bond exists between Sonya and him more like that of daughter and father than of niece and uncle.

In addition, the shape of the play, particularly its succession of locations, seems to point to Vanya as the operative figure. In the earlier version of the drama, *The Wood Demon*, Voinitsky deliberately shot himself, not Serebryakov. He did it offstage, also at the end of act III, and did not miss. As a suicide he ended up a dramaturgical construct; as the incompetent murderer he becomes a personification of comic agony.[3] His subsidiary but significant role becomes enlarged in *Uncle Vanya*, as the new title implies.[4] The four acts move from a garden (I) indoors to the dining room (II), thence to the living room (III), and finally into Vanya's study-cum-bedroom (IV), almost as though the settings are closing in on him. A man of culture, intelligence, and sensitivity—perhaps too much sensitivity for his own peace of mind ("I might have been a Schopenhauer, a Dostoevsky")—Vanya ought to have handled the tasks of paterfamilias with a talent buffed by long practice.[5] Elena recognizes his qualities, even while she does her utmost to evade his advances. A continual bickering among the members of the family troubles her. She pleads that Vanya ought to bring them all together.

First, though, he wants to bring her together with himself. He believes that ten years earlier, when he was thirty-seven and she seventeen, he stood a chance with her. He let the chance escape. Was he too shy to propose? Too attached to his sister or her memory? Did he feel too old even then? Or suspect even then that she would turn him down? Elena gives no sign that she would have accepted Vanya at any age, or even that she may do so if Serebryakov dies shortly. (If we care to project the story forward, however, that moaning invalid will probably outlive the rest of them.) Vanya remains a bachelor, childless, honest, eaten up by his twin passion over the husband and wife whose images drive each other into and out of his emotional flux.

Perhaps Vera ran the estate effectively while she lived. The play offers no hints about that or about when or how she died. As one outcome of her death, the property did not pass on to Sonya, who may then have been a minor. Instead, the widower Serebryakov acquired it, at least nominally: the play's first stage direction tells us that the action takes place on "the Serebryakov [not the Voinitsky] estate." But for most of the year this retired, dried-out scholar remains away, an absentee owner, while he concentrates on his specialty, art history, allowing Vanya and Sonya to manage the house and farm. From them he receives reports he hardly bothers to scan. During the brief summer he visits the estate with this second wife and disrupts its routine, not by interfering in the stewardship but by sitting in his room writing all day—worthless criticism, according to Vanya. He takes his meals and tea at irregular hours. Because of his ailments, predominantly gout, he keeps most of the household awake at night. He admits to being impractical. Even if he wished to, he could never fill in for the missing father.

Since the estate annually earns a narrow margin of profit, Serebryakov would now like to sell, investing the proceeds, some of which will go toward a new house for his wife and himself. "Of course" he will not dispose of Sonya's property without Sonya's consent, and "of course" he will make some provision for the future of Sonya and Vanya and the Senator's aged widow, Vanya's mother. But he considers these matters secondary, if he takes them into consideration at all, until Vanya, in a paroxysm of wrath and sarcasm, yells about them and then goes out of control with the pistol.

Serebryakov will cope with the "fathering" of the estate by disposing of it. Understandably. He feels near the ebb of his life. At one time he enjoyed repute in the art world. That he has now forfeited, if we can believe Vanya, because his writings proved to be pedestrian, based on worn and wan ideas. At one time women adored him, and he persuaded Elena, a beauty some forty years his junior, to marry him; but now, griping about his old age, cranky over his sickness and exhaustion, living in fear of being struck down by angina or some other instrument of fate, he craves the respect he believes owing to his rank as a professor at the same time as he begrudges recognition for the new generations of scholars. He informs Elena that she despises him. If she does, she is too well-bred to say so, perhaps too well-bred even to let herself think so. The loyal, misplaced admiration of the Senator's widow does not console him for the certainty that he has become a nuisance, an encumbrance, an irritant to everybody else.

The third possible "father" substitute, not a member of the family but its doctor, is Mikhail Lvovitch Astrov, reconceptualized from the "wood demon" of the earlier play and a forebear of today's sometimes isolated, sometimes incorporated environmentalists or conservationists and vegetarians, who compete to save the human race and its habitats from polluters. Thanks to his artistic and historical imagination, Astrov cuts a glamorous figure in the household, except with Serebryakov, who distrusts doctors for fear of how they may diagnose him. Sonya loves Astrov and loves what he stands for: in act I she bursts into a speech in which she echoes phrases obviously lifted from his mouth about the tempering, beautifying, ennobling values of forests in the life of human beings. If he loved her in return, they could marry, team up to maintain the estate, and bring it into harmony with its surroundings. Sonya would also take him in hand: she would see that when he was hungry he ate, instead of resorting to vodka, and that he slept when he felt tired instead of letting himself be drawn into impossibly long work days and indulging in self-reproaches for malpractice, neglecting patients, and failing to save the ones who died. Sonya was cut out to conduct both him and the estate. But alas for this ideal partnership as a fill-in for a father: after Sonya has persuaded Elena to sound him out, Astrov denies that he loves her. He apparently hasn't toyed with even the possibility of marriage. Like Thoreau, he cherishes his privacy, although not so rigorously.

It is Elena he finds seductive. He keeps coming back to the house during the summer months to meet her, not Sonya. In certain respects she is his counterpart, the attractive, artistic outsider. He suspects that she asks him about Sonya in order to clear the emotional underbrush and ease her own approach to him. She leaves him bewildered, impatient, when she then refuses a tryst with him in the forest. But Astrov also visits the house in other seasons, when Elena is not there and nobody is sick, making the twenty-mile trip by troika from his home. He specifies why: he finds it restful to sit in Vanya's study, where a drawing board has been set up for him, and to devise maps that chart the decline of the landscape: deforestation, overpasturing of the grasses, ponds and wetlands allowed to degenerate into swamp. There is not even, he says, the excuse of some purported advantage to reap from commercial growth—of the sort Chekhov will write about two plays later in *The Cherry Orchard*, when Lopakhin buys up Ranevskaya's estate to exchange the beloved, once-famous orchard for tourist cabins—or from nominal profits bled out of the slow deterioration caused by this century's scablike spread of the suburb, with its excrescent office buildings, malls, and car crushes. No, this rural blight has come about because of carelessness, ignorance, sloth, neglect. Astrov's equivalent today would be filming documentaries that urged legislators and public television viewers to conserve the depleted rain forest and our own north by northwest; he is less the diabolical figure suggested by the earlier sobriquet *demon* than a sporadic fanatic who is literally "good-natured." In one of Chekhov's most prophetic touches, as Astrov quits the comfort and peacefulness of Vanya's study for his long ride home, he stops and looks at a map of Africa, remarking, "Out there . . . the heat must be terrific." He is staring at the continent whose native peoples, wild animals, and vegetation would, in the century to come, sink most graphically, most abysmally, into famine, extinction, and desert. Thus Astrov walks out of the play, overworked and underappreciated (except by Sonya), a doctor with no cure for his own malaise but too wedded to his vocation and his avocation to dream for an instant about an alliance with Sonya or more than a fleeting encounter with Elena.

The two men Vanya envies, one for his past appeal to women, the other for his present appeal, reveal themselves for their differing reasons as less desperate than he is but hardly more contented.

If the men fail to qualify for the father's role, what about the women? Vanya's mother, the widow Maria Vasilyevna Voinitskaya, might have taken over on the death of her husband, the Senator, if she had had the requisite regent-cum-queen mother personality. She has not even a glimmer of it, and we can speedily dismiss her. She emerges only rarely from her political pamphlets and books. When, as an adamantine radical of yesteryear, she lifts her gaze from her publications, she frowns on persons who have ever modified their political or artistic views, if these were views she once shared. She takes no part or interest in household matters and invites comparison with one of Molière's rigidified roles. Her faith in Serebryakov, for example, remains as unshaken as Madame Pernelle's in *Tartuffe*. When her son cries out to her, "I'm raving. . . . Mother, I am in despair! Mother!" she tells him "sternly" to do as her son-in-law says. If Serebryakov were an antique Dionysos, she would be his most loyal maenad, his doddering Agave, willing to butcher her son verbally if she thought him a traitor to the cause.

We can make a comparable detour around the old nurse Marina, one of those unflappable Chekhovian retainers. But either of the two other women in the play could, with the right allotments of brain and bravado, have seized command, have gone so far as to become a female tyrant on the lines of Kabanova in Ostrovsky's *The Storm* and bullied the estate into something like self-sufficiency or—why not?—prosperity. Sonya and her stepmother, Elena, make a fascinating study in contrasts, not unlike the pairs of opposed women, almost always a blond and a brunette, in Shakespeare's comedies.[6] Chekhov plots these two into apposition in a number of scenes where we observe their sympathy for each other springing almost unaccountably from their differences. *The Wood Demon* contains a reference to Paris and Helen of Troy, and although Chekhov omits the line in *Uncle Vanya*, we can assume that Elena, who keeps her name, is one of those sirens for whom men once cheerfully, proudly died. But not in this age and place. Here they gawk at her languid deportment, the lazy walk and the yawning presence, but nobody will perish for her. Vanya may want to kill (rather than die) for her and then botch the attempt; but in the end we can only conjecture whether he does mean to kill her husband.[7] Nor does anybody ask anything of her (except the hardest thing of all for her to give, herself) or show any inclination to accept her as any sort of an authority, wife though she may be of the sterile head of the house. This Helen is fatigued by—unable to cope with—being the cynosure of a male universe.[8] Her beauty, no source of pride, is at best a burden to bear through time until it will dissolve. She has few opportunities to become oblivious to it, and in the action of the play most of those occur when she fulfills her only function, ministering to the morose and demanding Serebryakov, who, as an invalid, is anything but imaginary.

Elena's role will be more rewarding for an actor and her spectators, I would venture, if she is not a flirt or a schemer but an innocent whose beauty confuses her and is her undoing, who does not set out to snare men but cannot help charming them. Sonya tells her she must be a witch for having cast a spell on Astrov that continually lures him back to the house; and so she is a witch, if we understand Sonya to mean an involuntary bewitcher. But she is also stifled, a pianist who in one scene yearns to express herself in music, not words, but is forbidden to by her husband. Elena evidently married Serebryakov precisely (if mistakenly) to share a spiritual life with him and avoid the dominantly physical partnership she might have committed herself to with someone of her own age.

Astrov is her true opposite number in that he has an effect on her and Sonya comparable to the effect she has on him and Vanya—in both cases without trying. They each shun love; together, they each yield to a spasm of desire; they each feel abashed at their wary pretexts for meeting.

Yet for all her apparent fecklessness, Elena realizes and articulates more keenly than anyone else the need for somebody to take charge of the estate. She is the one who pleads that "there is something very wrong in this house" and elevates that "wrong" to a global plane as she urges Vanya to deal with it: "You are an educated, intelligent man, and I should think you would understand that the world is being destroyed not by crime and fire, but by hatred, enmity, all these petty squabbles." What I am getting at here is that one cannot defend a staging that gives birth to an evil Elena without willfully distorting the play. Chekhov's mature writing eschews motiveless—or, come to that, justified—malignity. Even as unsympathetic a part as Yasha's in *The Cherry Orchard* becomes strained, limited in its acting opportunities, if mulcted for villainy; in his most repelling moments, Yasha, like the others in that play, is to an extent a victim of circumstances.[9]

If Elena is not "bad," can Sonya be "good"? Playing her as flawless, saintly, will risk overlaying the role with priggishness. To pursue the busy life she maps out for herself, Sonya has to overcome doubts that almost amount to self-hatred. While Serebryakov and Vanya feel old and wasted, she thinks of herself as young and wasted. Nothing is going to happen to her: a long future stretches ahead until the time when she will find the "rest" and the peace she speaks of transfixingly in her last speech. She has learned to tolerate her father, to accept his intolerance of others, if grudgingly. (Vanya is more fatherly toward her than her father is.) She has a sad disposition. So, according to Marina, had her mother: Vera, heavyhearted at having married Serebryakov, may have "killed herself with pity" for him. Marina's evocative words could easily apply to Sonya if she were unlucky enough to get her way, to marry Astrov and have to live with his pessimism and drinking. If he married her, he would probably drink all the more. But so long as he keeps his distance—hurrying out of the room, after an apology, to put on a tie and look formal as soon as she appears—everything about him captivates her. Her uncle and grandmother palter over abstract questions of art, literature, and politics, but he, a cultured scientist, speaks with vitality and convincing evidence of reality—of the earth and growth. He can be passionately positive. She has come to look on him as hero-rescuer-dryad. He fulfills that image of the ideal in the opposite sex that is sometimes thought to ignite the spark of desire. He stirs her wonder.

Elena has a comparable effect upon her. When Sonya doesn't speak to Elena for a couple of weeks, she doesn't feel jealousy or resentment, as Elena fears, so much as awe at Elena's beauty, which is garnished, very likely, with city fashion and sophistication. Chekhov has supplied Vanya's age, Astrov's, and Elena's, but not Sonya's. One can easily visualize her as shorter and younger than Elena, who, even without meaning to, must look down on her. In act III, Elena, who has offered to elicit Astrov's true feelings, says to her at one point, "Trust me, little dove." (Some published translations distort the Russian word *golubka* to "dear" or "my dear"; others flatten it to "little one" but at least retain the diminutive sense.) In a 1973 "all-star" production, Mike Nichols cast as the Sonya Elizabeth Wilson who was, or was made up to look, not as young as Julie Christie, the Elena. There were gains and losses in this casting, the obvious gains coming from Wilson's sensitively tuned performance. I have no idea whether this was the first time a director had suggested that Sonya is no juvenile lead. One could make a convincing factual case for Nichols's choice.[10] It puts a new complexion on the scenes between this stepmother and this stepdaughter. It also colors certain other relationships among the characters, for Sonya's father, grandmother, and uncle treat her as a child, almost as a domestic. Nevertheless, whatever the age of a Sonya in production, that treatment, disparaging at times, prevents her as the only "doer" in the family from being taken seriously as a dispenser of order, even if she wished to play that part by going it alone without Astrov. Neither Elena nor Sonya is prepared to assume a paternal or even a maternal role.

The main quintet of players—a sextet if one includes Vanya's mother—allows for a few "bars" contributed by four peripheral characters. An unnamed peasant enters infrequently to summon Astrov. Another peasant, a watchman (for want of a more precise job title) named Yefim, remains out of the house and perhaps not even visible as he intermittently makes a tapping noise during the night and evening hours in act II and at the end of act IV. Is he testing shingles, clapping clapboards, listening to beams for structural stresses, but in the darkness? Is he blind—a blind watchman—a conjecture that seems borne out by the presence of his dog? A number of critics have concluded that his taps mark relentless time, like ticking or a heartbeat. The sound effect then prefigures the snapping celestial string that seems to denote the end of an era in *The Cherry Orchard* (and is heard there, like the tapping here, in acts II and IV).

The next fringe figure, old nurse Marina, adds a comic, grandmotherly warmth to the action, as if to compensate for the coldness of Maria Vasilyevna. She tries to act as a calming influence on Sonya by calling the others in the house geese and ganders, especially when they squabble; she robs their assertions and questions of significance as she reduces them to animal noises. As a counterpart of Anfisa and Ferapont in *Three Sisters* and Firs in *The Cherry Orchard*, Marina does not talk about herself.[11] The play's first scene lets her serve as Astrov's interlocutor and host: she assists him in defining himself, in helping him convey his feeling of impotence about the past and the lack of appetite over the future that he shares with the others. In the following act, when he says meaningfully to Sonya, "I look forward to nothing. I don't like people. . . . It's been a long time since I've loved anyone," she cannot refrain from asking him, "No one?" He replies, "I have a certain tenderness for your nurse—in memory of old times." Lovable, comforting Marina is also more successful than Elena is in calming Serebryakov when he goes into one of his snits. Like Yefim with his tapping, she has a characteristic activity: she knits a stocking. In these times of symbol-freighted criticism, our deduction mechanisms whisk us toward Clotho, the Fate who weaves. Marina's part, however, is fatalistic, not fateful. It may well be that Chekhov, the unwitting co-father of Stanislavsky's acting System, simply provided the performer with an apt stage shtick, the sort of busy work—knitting is private, absorbing, but allows for taking part in a conversation—that untold hordes of Method directors would copy a half-century and more afterward, when an actor in a secondary part needed "some activities to concentrate on." In her opening scene the old nurse describes the disorder that has fallen on the house as a result of the irregular hours at which meals are now taken. It will be left to Elena and others to trace reasons for the disorder, but Marina announces it. In the last act she similarly announces the reversion to domestic order. Shortly before the departure of Elena and Serebryakov, and then of Astrov, the separations begin, the dissolution of the dramatis personae. Vanya and Sonya remain, both heartbroken, looking forward after a lazy, maddening summer to a long bleak winter of nothing more enterprising than keeping accounts. Marina then consoles herself by announcing: "Now we'll go back to our old ways. Breakfast by eight, dinner at one, and in the evening we'll sit down to supper; everything in its proper order, the way other people live. . . like Christians. [With a sigh] It's been a long time since this old sinner has tasted noodles."

If Marina personifies the brisk, this-too-shall-pass attitude of the servants, who form a core of stability in Chekhovian society, Ilya Ilyitch ("Waffles") Telegin personifies the dispossession of the landed class in an earlier phase. Telegin's uncle owned this estate and sold it to the Senator, and Telegin himself either owns or once owned property. In his evolution as a role, Telegin has even lost the estate that was his in *The Wood Demon* when, under the name of Dyadin (a word possibly cognate with *uncle* in Russian), he gave refuge to Elena's previous incarnation after she fled from her husband. In *Uncle Vanya* he haunts the house, a lachrymose, laughable, guitar-playing apologist for himself, defending his very being to Serebryakov and Elena, inserting voluble irrelevancies into conversations, and breaking into tears whenever Vanya, whom he idolizes, expresses rage or unhappiness. But does he belong there? And if not there, where? Telegin signals the arrival in Chekhov's drama of the disjunct individual, who is not a member of the principal family but clings to somebody who is. Such a figure will often also cling to some thing (such as an outworn or inappropriate ideal) with a combination of doggedness and incoherence that undermines the effort.[12] Telegin's guitar wafts out background music that lulls the characters at the start of act IV but turns plaintive as the act comes to an end and they recede from us and from the sultry weather of act I into their wintry future. He slightly compromises this artistic function by lending a note of pathos to the traditional greedy parasite from the New Comedy of Plautus: he embodies the modern parasite, the pitiful hanger-on.[13] Telegin, more than anyone else in the action, is not merely fatherless. He is rudderless.

Still, no performer is an island. Even a soloist who recites monologues might be said to enlist the spectators as direct receivers of the lines, as substitutes for fellow artists; and to invoke from them a trust not unlike what actors count on from one another. Disjunct roles, far from being theatrically isolated, are equal members of a family of stage relationships. To Anton Chekhov, more than to any other playwright, we owe our twentieth-century conviction that good acting is good sibling revelry. The main reason is that, with few exceptions, he does not create bravura, much less heroic, nineteenth-century solo parts, but ensembles, twentieth-century ensembles, their coherence reinforced by the dramatic structure. *Uncle Vanya*, the last play in which he used soliloquies as extended asides, and after which he caught up in this respect with Ibsen, Strindberg, Hauptmann, Shaw, and the other turn-of-the-century giants, gives us a Sonya, an Elena, and a Vanya who commune privately with themselves and the audience in what-to-do-next meditations. Once again, the absence of a father leaves these figures fumbling for guidance. Their indecisiveness, taken amiss by many early audiences, is what brings them close to us today. Chekhov's older contemporaries, among them Tolstoy, possibly felt comfortable with brazen characters who knew what they were about, cherished clear-cut ambitions, and made them come true—who looked upon the world as will and idea. That particular taste, along with many others, went out of style with the encroachments of realism.

The spell thrown on audiences by Chekhov's plays owes much to his gradual blueprinting of the dramatically familial relationships, to his deftness in touching on his principal and perennial themes, such as dispossession and love unrequited, and to the peculiar Chekhovian "mood."[14] The playwright induces this mood by mixing what we often take to be immiscible contents, comedy or farce with sorrow or rage. Vanya's "Bang!" illustrates this mixed moment of comic agony.

But other moments of comic agony befall, especially during the chain of encounters leading up to the "Bang!" In each case they depend on the plotting, the sequential disposition of the characters, on exactly who is present onstage and who absent—and when—so that, denied the fatherly presence, the others feel they need to dispense advice or even take charge. And the mixed moments swim in mixed motives. Early in the third act Vanya tells Elena to "be a mermaid. Let yourself go for once in your life, fall head over heels in love with some water sprite, and plunge headlong into the deep." Because she finds this unasked-for advice offensive, he tries to mollify her by promising a peace offering of autumn roses he gathered that morning. When he leaves, Elena tries to alleviate the uncertainty about whether Astrov loves Sonya. She summons Astrov on the pretext of letting him show her his environmental charts. He in turn grows offended when she appears indifferent to his heartfelt pleas about the decay of "his" forests. The audience, however, appreciates that Elena is flustered by the responsibility she took on, distracted by trying to figure out how to broach the matter of Astrov's feelings for Sonya without seeming like a tactless and interfering stepmama—at the same time as she feels drawn to him herself. He assumes she has too frivolous a mind to care about what political commentators in our day call a "serious issue." Then he accuses her of questioning him on her own behalf, of wanting to find out whether he loves *her*. Astrov is wrong, but he is right. She may have thought she would interrogate him for Sonya's sake while, without realizing it, she wanted an excuse for a private meeting with him. Astrov never took her for a parent or guardian, and he does not want to play her—or anybody else's—real or imagined father. He would simply like to have sex with her.

As they kiss and she endeavors (not strenuously enough) to break out of his embrace, Vanya enters bearing the promised roses. Embarrassment all around. Stunned to see how hastily she took his advice to let herself go for once in her life, Vanya "puts the bouquet on a chair" and "agitatedly wipes his face and neck with a handkerchief" as he mutters, "Never mind . . . No . . . Never mind." Elena can say only, "This is awful." Astrov, however, waxes suddenly irrelevant: "The weather today, my dear Ivan Petrovitch, is not too bad. It was overcast in the morning, as if it were going to rain, but now the sun is shining. As a matter of fact, it's turned out to be a beautiful autumn . . . and the winter crops are quite promising. [*Rolls up the map.*] The only thing is . . . the days are getting shorter. [*Goes out.*]"[15] Is this a weather report or a weather forecast? Here we have one of those many instances in Chekhov that require the characters (and the audience) to hear one thing and understand another. We can take the speech not exactly literally but as a blunt and funny try at escaping from the three-cornered awkwardness. Or it may connote that, with that first kiss, Astrov feels cheered, believes he has broken through Elena's defenses, and must make an announcement, but in cryptic language. (As a consequence, in the next act he will renew his request for an assignation with her in the open air.)

A few minutes afterward, at the family gathering called by Serebryakov so that he may tell them what he thinks ought to be done with the estate, only Maria Vasilyevna harkens devotedly to her son-in-law's speech. The others in the onstage audience seethe. Sonya's ominous suspicion that there is no future for her with Astrov has been confirmed by Elena and is driving her distraught. The genteel Elena herself now longs to make and keep an appointment with Astrov but is terrified that she may earn Sonya's hatred and may also commit herself to an affair beyond her control. She will quell both the longing and the fears by fleeing the estate the following day. Vanya listens, distracted, to an address given by the man he detests after having blunderingly witnessed what he takes to be the definitive loss of the woman he loves. As the import of the speech sinks in, he sees he is liable to be evicted shortly from the estate that remains in the family only because he supplied the capital and sweat. If he does not assert himself now, he will forfeit everything to this pelican of a deputy father.

The combustible situation would smack of melodrama if Serebryakov were laying down rules. But his speech is considerate, self-deprecatory, and tentatively phrased, opening with a humorous reference to the last line of *The Inspector General* and going on to invite the help and guidance of the family.

Vanya's interruptions, when they come, may at first sound rude and unjustified and yes, funny. They may. One cannot parse this speech or any of the preceding sequences with finality. Sonya, Elena, Vanya, Astrov, and the others are no more than roles, manipulable creatures—not people, not even characters until actors temporarily inhabit those roles after conferring with a director and conferring later, if they don't trust the director, with their acting coaches. Astrov's odd remarks about the weather or Serebryakov's courteous, inflammatory speech or Elena's attempts to keep Astrov at a distance can be read with ironic inflections or with embellishments (curled lips, quizzical brows, head turnings, half-smiles) that run counter to the obvious denotations of the lines, or rather to how they are conventionally scored. In truth, no sooner had plays out of the great eruption of late nineteenth-century realism won acknowledgment as modern classics than ironic and other revisions and decorating of them began in earnest.[16] Since it is possible to graft a generous spectrum of motives and behavior patterns onto these roles, there is no question in my mind that the ironic colorings have often opened the plays out in instructively unforeseen ways.

Tadashi Suzuki and his Company of Toga deconstructed (or reconstructed) *Uncle Vanya*, together with *Three Sisters*, in a performance entitled *The Chekhov*. Suzuki's actors occupied something like an abstract version of a Kabuki set. They took many lines from Chekhov and translated them intact into Japanese, but they revamped the action. Six of the actors encircled a mostly passive Sonya (known here as the Young Girl, so Suzuki evidently wanted her to convey a portrait of innocence). These six, playing most of the other roles from *Uncle Vanya*, each wore a Groucho nose, spectacles, and mustache, black swallow-tailed jacket, lavender gloves, no shirt, and no pants. They crept, leapt, and hobbled around the playing space in coordination and inside shopping baskets, oversized wicker panniers cut open at the bottom. They borrowed a barked, highly emphatic form of vocalizing from the Noh theatre. Like the six, the Sonya wore glasses and held a parasol, as did all the actors in the *Three Sisters* portion of the program.[17] At one startling moment amplified claps of sound seemed to devastate all the figures onstage; they recovered with tortured, spastic slowness, as though reacting to the dropping and aftereffects of a nuclear bomb or of a Chernobyl-like disaster.

The strongest of the eight staged versions of *Uncle Vanya* I have seen, Laurence Olivier's from Chichester, played straight into the dialogue without irony. The casting, which gave Sonya to Joan Plowright, Elena to Rosemary Harris, Vanya to Michael Redgrave, Astrov to Olivier, and Serebryakov to Max Adrian, entrusted the roles that are subsidiary but almost omnipresent to Fay Compton, Lewis Casson, and Sybil Thorndike. Olivier shaped a succession of exquisitely interdependent acting sequences that illuminated the principal movement of the action: the awakening of Vanya from his servitude, his brief rebellion against an indolent invalid who had no right to assume the father's title to the home, his unresisting slide back into the pit of monotony, and the end of the swift summer and the onset of winter. The production, on film and possibly by now on videotape, has excised some speeches and consequently trimmed the roles of Maria Vasilyevna and Telegin, but it is marred hardly at all by lapses into that Victorian tone from which British Chekhov sometimes seems unable to break free. Stuart Burge, who directed the filmed version, repeatedly positioned the camera judiciously for the interplaying by means of "two shots" and deep-focus takes of a figure speaking in the background past a foreground of the head or bust of a figure listening (and reacting). Even an anamorphic lens could hardly have captured more fluently the simultaneous connections and distances between the characters.

In the closing scene the summer visitors leave, and the repeated words "They've gone," uttered in succession by Astrov, Marina, Sonya, and Maria Vasilyevna, and soon, "He's gone," referring to Astrov and spoken by Marina and then Sonya, clang with a sad finality, reminiscent of the cadence in Old Capulet's memory of his youth: "'Tis gone! 'tis gone! 'tis gone." The drama has given up its search for a father by alighting on Vanya and the woman who shares his plight and gives him the title Uncle.

I wonder whether Chekhov was prescient, even unknowingly, in making a hidden play or subplot out of the search for a father, which, to repeat, had occurred in *The Seagull* and would recur in his later full-length plays.[18] This is not the place (nor have I the inclination, much less the qualifications) to look into such questions as how effectively Czar Nicholas II (r. 1894-1917) functioned as a "caesar" or leader or national father; whether Russia's sheer extent made (and still makes) central and humane government unfeasible; why the Soviet experiment in communism—a form of political organization originally conceived of as a family on a national, political scale—swiftly grew perverted and turned into its opposite, a monolithic and imperial despotism that outdid in the scope of its brutality such antecedents as the Inquisition; how for well over half of this century Mother Russia's neighbors (foreigners all or, in today's jargon, ethnic minorities), co-opted into her heterogeneous union, were restrained; how the countries on her western borders could be held in submission; and whether the collapse of monopolistic power in Eastern Europe came about only when Gorbachev became the first Soviet leader since Lenin to be perceived, rightly or wrongly, as, at first, someone with the benevolent, genuine intentions of a father and, later, as a family tyrant, a parent against whom to rebel.

In *Uncle Vanya* the fumbling admissions of love, the taking refuge in nostalgia and regrets, the inept judgments, evasions of leadership, and feelings of victimization come comically and agonizingly to a head in that "Bang!" Vanya impulsively blows the household apart—for a moment only. It will never again quite settle into what it was.

INWARD JOURNEY
The Ghost Sonata, by August Strindberg

One of the most enigmatic plays ever, *The Ghost Sonata* (Spöksonaten, 1907) could justifiably borrow an alternative title from a composition by Edward Elgar.[1] His *Enigma Variations,* composed eight years earlier, has a hidden main theme. Critics started to track down the enigma—as much of it as they could find—by relating the titles of the fourteen variations to the initials of some of the composer's fourteen friends to whom the variations are dedicated. As an example, the best-known variation, "Nimrod" (the mythical hunter) is dedicated to A.J.J., whose surname is Jaeger, the German for "hunter." The "larger theme," says the composer, comes through in the music only by suggestion. I have heard a claim that the musical notation corresponds to the profile of the Mendip Hills, which Elgar loved, but whatever the source or truth of this comparison, and from whatever topographic vantage point that profile must be viewed for it to resemble the pattern of the notes (transposed, surely, for a single instrument), the enigma has so far remained raveled. Each critic at best clears up not *the* enigma but *an* enigma of his or her own confecting. Here beginneth the first lesson in modern and postmodern interpretation: criticism, rather than feeding off works of art, may come around to devouring them.

Following Elgar, Strindberg may have meant his main theme to escape elucidation. He often said he liked to write and paint directly out of his unconscious, provided that it kept sending him material. We might assume that he created arbitrarily by merely letting the results happen through his arm. But his scientific ambitions and logical thinking become evident in his many prose writings, among them his essays on the history of the theatre, his celebrated preface to *Miss Julie,* and his "Notes to the Members of the Intimate Theatre." There is method in his randomness. Although his work predates surrealism and may even have inspired that movement, Strindberg himself was too much the conscious artist to warrant the designation of presurrealist.[2] But I believe he would have welcomed audiences of surrealists, pre- or post-.

The three "movements" of this sonata for stage and actors, this enigma in three scenes, are like recollections of three distinct dreams, linked by the reappearance of certain characters and ideas. What Method-trained artists call the through line proves tricky to recognize (let alone reconnoiter), enwrapped as the play is in symbols, a plenitude of physical detail (architecture, surroundings, furniture, unusual objects), motifs, coincidences, and contrarieties. Harry Carlson has detected a succession of mythical hints and correspondences.[3] Evert Sprinchorn discerns "parallels" that include three figures from history and art with whom Arkenholz, the hero, shares characteristics.[4] In the end the play guards its secrets, and the best a critic can do with it is attempt to contribute to the range of intimations, which are released almost unwillingly by its comically agonized elements.

Most of the seventeen roles are referred to by title, such as the Colonel, the Mummy, the Superintendent, the Fiancée, the Milkmaid, the Dead Man, and the Woman in Black, in the manner used occasionally in Strindberg's earlier plays (the Captain, the Stranger) and picked up by expressionists in Germany a decade or less later. Some of them also have names: the Student Arkenholz, the Old Man Hummel, the Young Lady Adele.[5] Several lesser figures receive names only (Baron Skanskorg) or names and functions: Johansson, Hummel's servant, or Bengtsson, the Colonel's valet. One role, the Cook, who enacts a critical part in the third scene, did not appear in Strindberg's original listing of the dramatis personae. To unravel the logic, if any, underlying the mixed identification, one would need to follow the play, if it could be managed, into the playwright's own interior.

Because of the complexities crammed into this third of four "chamber plays," as the author called them, the very sequence of events in the thirty-plus pages of action defies a thoroughgoing summary. That's all the more reason for not undertaking one. But the settings deserve a paragraph.

Ghosts need a home to haunt. The first set shows a street corner and, built on it, two floors of a residence that also faces a side street, as if at a crossroads. In the square in front stand such public amenities as a bench, a fountain, a phone booth, and one of those stubby European pillars with advertisements plastered on it, including one for a performance of Wagner's *The Valkyrie*. The house can be regarded as the main role (as distinct from the hero) or by extension as the featured instrument of the sonata. It serves as a repository of scandals and crimes from the past and, despite the modernity of its exterior, is a source of infection within, like the Augean stables or the house of Atreus or some other dwelling that forms the backdrop for a Greek tragedy. The action of the three movements consists of a journey that goes within—from the street to a "Round Room" visible from the square and overlooking the corner (in two directions), finally penetrating to the "Hyacinth Room," which is not visible from outside. In the second scene, in the Round Room, the author prominently displays the wallpapered door to a closet, a white marble statue—enclosed by potted palms and a curtain—of a young woman, a tiled white porcelain stove with a mirror or mirrors either above it or on each side of it or incorporated in the tiling (depending on which translation you prefer), and views of a green room and of the Hyacinth Room. In the green room the Colonel, the presumed owner of the house, sits and writes. In the Hyacinth Room, which will form the setting of the third scene, the Young Lady sits and reads. She will move to a harp for the third scene when Arkenholz visits her in this "bizarre" and "oriental" room decorated with hyacinths "in all colors." A large statue of the Buddha has in its lap a shallot bulb with a sphere of white flowers sprouting on the end of its stalk. Strindberg seems to want this room to create a stifling feeling, perhaps of wet heat like that of a greenhouse, because of the suffocating array of hyacinths. A death screen used in scene ii remains available in scene iii, an anticipation of the final stage image when the scene will melt away and give place to Böcklin's painting, *The Isle of the Dead,* "in the background." For this inward journey the audience might almost be seated on a trolley and transported from the exterior through a wall or window into the Round Room and then glide into the adjoining Hyacinth Room, which subsequently goes dark and gives way to the Böcklin painting.

More resolutely than in many other examples of comic agony, dialogue in *The Ghost Sonata* declines to traffic in the usual patter of psychological realism. The roles—some amusing, some anguished—have hardly any consistency of motive or consistency of impact upon one another. I propose, therefore, to study the play as a piece of music by looking at its thematic development, which has much in common with the development of *The Wild Duck* and *Ghosts. The Ghost Sonata* also has an affinity with the author's *Miss Julie,* written almost twenty years earlier and so frequently performed and discussed internationally during his life that it must have remained omnipresent in his mind. (As Evert Sprinchorn reminds us, however, the playwright "had seen parts of [*Miss Julie*] in rehearsal," but a year after writing *The Ghost Sonata,* when he put on a special performance to honor Charlotte and Bernard Shaw, who were visiting, "this was, astonishingly, the first time in his life that Strindberg had ever seen his naturalistic masterpiece on stage" in its entirety [*Shaw Annual,* vol. 13, 1993, 11]).

I find eight principal, interlocked themes worth the attention of directors, actors, and designers, although it would be foolhardy to say either that these make up the only content of the fugal arrangement or that my definitions of them are, well, definitive. Readers familiar with the play may well wish to jiggle them about or customize the list. A further caution: as a rule, we weigh the significance of any figure's remarks against how we assess that figure. Is he a liar? Does she have peculiar but pertinent likes and dislikes? Is a particular question designed to elicit a particular answer from the listener(s)? In the case of *The Ghost Sonata,* though, I suggest that this normally healthy habit does not apply: every opinion and piece of information may have to be taken at face value. Even then it will be cryptic. And so we proceed to the generalized themes.

Ghosts, funerals, and death. A Japanese screen is put up around the dying personages. The action opens with news of a fire and a death, in which Arkenholz played a heroic part. Earlier in the play we hear of a consul but not about his consular activities; he is known as the Dead Man and once lived in the house. Arkenholz, blessed with "Sunday sight," is the only living person who can see him. Hummel dies in scene ii. In scene iii the Young Lady expires or, more accurately, begins her trip toward death, not long after Arkenholz describes Hummel's funeral and some revelations brought forth on and by that occasion. The final tableau gives us the Böcklin painting *The Isle of the Dead*, whose title implies segregation of some or all of the dead and may also comment retroactively on that mock-up of an island, the Round Room of scene ii, with inhabitants whose existences have scarcely altered for twenty years or more, as though they had become marooned in time.

Heredity and true and false parentage. This theme ties the play most closely to Ibsen's drama. Hummel mentions his son, whom we do not see; the son is spoken of later as the lover of the man who bore the mace at Hummel's funeral. But Hummel says at one point that he wants Arkenholz to be his heir, as though he has disinherited that son. The Young Lady, treated by the Colonel as his daughter, proves to be the daughter of Hummel, who thus might be said to foster a remote incest between her and Arkenholz, his son by quasi adoption. The Young Lady's mother is the Colonel's wife. She squawks from time to time like a parrot and has a mummified appearance. The white marble statue of a young woman represents the "mummy" in her youth and flowerhood. A Woman in Black is the illegitimate daughter of the Dead Man (or Consul) and the Wife of the Superintendent. We are led directly to the next theme.

Adultery. The gist of some of the adulteries mentioned in the story, never dramatized in the action, looks to be treachery or revenge. Others come about for no explained reason—if adultery needs a reason beyond its occurrence. Together with the dubious parentage discussed above, the adulteries have implications that are almost impossible to sort out. We come to know little about the individual adulterers, except to notice that the author describes in a general way some turn-of-the-century wife-swapping or marital musical chairs being practiced under the guise of middle-class respectability. This restlessness must have been shocking to audiences of the time, and perhaps still is to audiences now. Or maybe the adulterers appeared funny—as they would have been if handled by Feydeau, one of Strindberg's younger contemporaries who was at the peak of his popularity when *The Ghost Sonata* was written. It is as though the author, toward the end of his life, has come to disbelieve in fidelity. The Young Lady is the result of an affair Hummel once had with the "mummy," whom he took to avenge himself on the Colonel for stealing his, Hummel's, fiancée, now a white-haired old lady who has the German-Swedish name of Fräulein von Holsteinkrona. The Fräulein stares into a mirror that looks out of the Round Room window all day, as though she amounts to no more than the transparent image of her that passers-by could notice from outside. Baron Skanskorg has also been the lover of the "mummy." Skanskorg is now getting a divorce from his wife, who is not in the action and who seems to be the sister or stepsister of the Woman in Black.

Parasites, including vampires. Hummel, we learn, has bled his victims dry. One of them was Arkenholz's father. He also blackmailed his son's male lover, the one who, out of respect or relief or gloating, bore the mace at Hummel's funeral. When Hummel clasps Arkenholz's hand, he seems to drain the strength out of him. Once, when Hummel was a servant, he behaved "like a vampire, sucking the marrow out of the house." The same is true now of the present Cook, who is said by Adele to belong to "the Hummel family of vampires." She has drained away the strength of the house's inhabitants by boiling all the good-ness out of the food and watering the wine and drinking the gravy from the meat. The priest at Hummel's funeral embezzled his church's funds. Strindberg will take up this theme of parasitism again in the fourth chamber play, *The Pelican*, and in other writings. The person in the household who prepares meals, whether a cook or a mother, may act like a vampire, denying sustenance to helpless chil-dren, or by analogy sucking vital fluids out of them.

Servants and masters. Hummel, the servant, some time ago displaced his master, Bengtsson, who left him and went to work for the Colonel.[6] The Colonel, originally a commoner, freed himself earlier from his rank as a nonentity by giv-ing himself a military title to which he had no right. Johansson, who pushes Hummel around in a wheelchair, has been reduced to a life of servitude, from which he is freed only with Hummel's death. Hummel even wants to turn Arkenholz into his factotum.

Transformations. This is the principal theme of an earlier work, *A Dream Play*, in which Strindberg emphasized in a prefatory note the need for fluidity of the roles and settings, for instant—almost magic—alterations of sights and sounds.[7] In scene i of *The Ghost Sonata* the house looks innocent and reputable enough from the street; viewed from within, it has been transformed into a pit of corruption. The "mummy" frequently talks like a parrot. So does Hummel when the inhabitants of the house, which he hoped to take over, challenge and defeat him in a sort of trial. Although no stage direction specifies that Bengtsson and Johansson recover their independence and former status while the Colonel and Hummel lose theirs, we should see both sides of the transformations of rank. One way of arriving at the transformations, equally theatrical, is by putting on and/or taking off masks, by which I mean not only literal face coverings—although they might be used—but also new clothing or other outward appear-ances, personalities, accents or pitch of voices, which create unexpected identities.

The supernatural. Hummel, we are told, is a "black magician." He manages to enter houses through the windows.[8] Arkenholz, a Sunday child, has second sight. This enables him to perceive an apparition called the Milkmaid, a non-speaking figure who is something of an enigma in her own right. She enters the first scene to drink and wash at the fountain. When Arkenholz arrives and asks to borrow her cup, she seems terrified, possibly of him or possibly because she thought herself invisible to mortals but has come under the scrutiny of this Sunday child. Hummel thinks Arkenholz is talking to himself. When he learns that the Milkmaid was present, Hummel in turn feels terrified. She is very likely a ghost of a young woman whose death he once caused, for when she returns to the square and raises her arms above her head like somebody drowning, staring at Hummel, he sees her and "shrivels up" in panic. In the following scene she returns momentarily, like a token of his conscience, to signal Hummel's approaching downfall.

Secrets. Scene i posits a mystifying situation, in which, among other happenings, Hummel invites Arkenholz to work for him (after seeing a performance of *The Valkyries*) and promises to introduce him to the house and the Young Lady. Scene ii, however, dispenses with Arkenholz until the very end and spends itself on the unveiling of secrets, initiated by Hummel. Before the transformations have taken place, the secrets in each figure's past may not be revealed. Then truth enters to act like one of those double-strength cleansers. It works by destroying secrets as though they were no more than stubborn stains, and so the class and power structure is restored. Secrets are the engines of narrative and what writers keep up their professional sleeves: secrets are their final flourishes when they want to hold an ending at bay.[9] But often they are more. In nineteenth-century melodrama and its most legitimate offspring, twentieth-century crime fiction, secrets percolate through the entire story as this or that one's illegitimate parentage or illicit sexual encounters come to light. Secrets unwind differently amid *The Ghost Sonata*'s comic agonies. The play mocks conventional melodrama and its hokey secret-mania. In the second scene a glut of secret material pours forth. But in scene iii a big, new secret looms—and remains intact, open to informed and other species of guesswork, but not resoluble. At the end of the scene before, in which the accusations and counteraccusations have turned up varied sorts of corruption, Arkenholz recites some verses, apparently addressed to Adele, about the triumph of goodness and innocence (the last line runs: "The guileless are good"), accompanied by her playing of the harp. The two young people are seen at a distance in the Hyacinth Room, to which the setting then changes, as though mounted on a turntable.

If scene ii consisted largely of accusations, as family and other secrets were torn open, scene iii contains several family confessions by Arkenholz. He and Adele both speak feverishly of their love for the hyacinth. He asks: "Don't you know the story behind that flower?" She answers, "No. Tell me." He says, "First you have to interpret it," and proceeds to give a cosmic explanation of the hyacinth's form. As the scene proceeds, he speaks of the shallot and the narcissus. He wonders why the most beautiful flowers are poisonous, asks why Adele would not marry him, and answers himself: she is "infected at the very core" of her life.[10] Whereupon Adele weakens like a fading flower, and at her request Arkenholz closes her off behind the death screen, repeating his poem about innocent goodness and expressing his pity for her. He never does get around to telling her the "story behind that flower," the hyacinth, which remains within the play's withheld secret, its enigma.

At this point I have to break into a digression about *Miss Julie*. What has made that short, early drama particularly fascinating to audiences is that it consists of a multiple, compressed conflict. The principals, Julie and Jean, are opposites in almost every respect, and the action therefore becomes a study in contrasts: A woman versus a man. A female against a male role. A virgin against a practiced sexual partner. An aristocrat by blood, bored with life and voicing a low opinion of herself, against an ambitious member of the working class, a laborer's son. A representative of past power, of the decadent nobility, against a representative of the future, a self-made proletarian. A person obsessed with maintaining (or later, salvaging) her family's honor against a person obsessed with attaining money and a respectable standing in the community. A woman haunted by a fear dream (falling from a pillar of inert stone) against a man driven by a wish dream (climbing a tree, a living substance). A lonely figure seeking guidance without humiliation ("I mean to have a partner who can lead and doesn't make me feel ridiculous") against an accepted member of his class who knows what is and is not done (though "now and then," brags Jean, "you meet somebody with guts enough to work his way up in the world"). And finally, a tragic character, lost in time and space, a woman who seems to have plotted her own disgrace, against a comic figure, an upstart or arriviste, with his acquired French name, warming a glass of wine in his hand, talking glibly about the European train system and about buying property in Switzerland and a count's title in Romania.[11]

In spite of the nonrealistic narrating by Julie and Jean of their dreams, the bacchanalian dance by a party of peasants, and the resounding mythical overtones throughout the play, *Miss Julie* has remained one of the striking examples of "naturalism in the theatre," admired by Zola, the coiner of that phrase, and by generations ever since. Some of Strindberg's late plays are also approximately naturalistic in form, such as the fourth chamber play, *The Pelican*. He never altogether forswore naturalism but shifted to whatever style felt appropriate as he wrote.

The Ghost Sonata would seem to be at the far end of the dramatic scale from *Miss Julie* as it leaps restlessly from topic to topic and theme to theme. Yet there are resemblances between the two plays. The couples in both yearn for what cannot be. Jean has worshipfully looked "up" at Julie from below the class barriers that separated them since he was a child, and she has become infatuated with the notion of a strong love partner, possibly even a brutal one, for she turns masochistic in her moments of melancholy and displays a sadistic streak when angered. Adele, the Young Lady of *The Ghost Sonata*, has nothing of Julie's frenzy as a role. She makes no advances to Arkenholz. She only entertains him with cool hospitality and appreciates that he is a hero, a public benefactor celebrated in newsprint after his courage in the collapsing house. He, however, is immediately, fiercely attracted to her on first sight in scene i, when she wears a riding habit, and later, when she waters her hyacinths at her window. That's a Freudian symbol if there ever was one, and there's another when she accompanies him on the harp. But much as we suspect from the opening of *Miss Julie* that the liaison between the Count's daughter and his valet has a forbidden flavor to it, so the meeting between Arkenholz and Adele, arranged by Hummel, could almost be a Faustian pact and therefore cursed from the start. A quotation in the dialogue from Goethe's *Faust* reinforces this impression. Adele is the unattainable, and so is Julie, even after Jean has taken her sexually.

The void that separates Adele from Arkenholz becomes apparent early in scene iii, when he avers that there is nothing he would not do to win her hand. She replies that he can never have her, and when he asks why, she says he mustn't ask. In a similar exchange a few moments later, he asks whether she knows what he thinks of her. She replies that he mustn't tell her, or she'll die, and he answers that he must, or *he* will die. He goes on to proclaim himself a truth-teller, like his father, and when he talks about her being infected, she collapses, says she is dying, as she predicted, and begs him to put the screen in front of her. In some way that is not explicit to the audience he has told her that he knows her secret and that it is fatal, and she insists that giving words to it will kill her. But these sentiments are communicated—virtually concealed—between conversational gambits about the unreliability of the house, Arkenholz's memories of the funeral, Adele's unhappiness with the Cook, and other seemingly stray matters. Adele's death, then, is prepared for in the dialogue that precedes it, but inconspicuously.

What exactly—or even inexactly—does she die *of?* Does she catch the moral disease in the house? Has the corruption spread even to her flower-decked outdoor room indoors? If not, we may well puzzle over the continuity between the third scene and the two that lead to it. At the onset of that scene she requests that Arkenholz sing to her flowers. Instead of responding, he asks whether the hyacinth is the flower of her soul and goes on to describe, in language that recalls the bursting of the giant chrysanthemum at the end of *A Dream Play*, how he loves the hyacinth "above all other flowers," even though the hyacinths in this room do not return his love, even hate him. It is shortly after this choice specimen of pathetic fallacy that he wants to know whether she has heard the story of the hyacinth—and then does not get around to telling it.

Ovid has a truncated version of the myth in book 10 of *Metamorphoses*, in which he describes Phoebus Apollo's love for the graceful youth Hyacinthus, with whom he "went ranging after boyish pleasures," among them throwing the discus.[12] Ovid says that when Hyacinthus "ran out to meet it where it seemed to fall," the discus turned like a boomerang, "glanced [off?] a rock and struck the boy full face." In other versions of the legend the discus did not reverse itself spontaneously because of some spin imparted to it by accident: the wind god, Zephyrus, who had also taken a fancy to the boy and was jealous of Apollo's attentions, diverted the discus, causing Hyacinthus's death. Grieving Apollo then caused "the blood that filled the grasses at his feet" to turn

to a brighter hue than Tyrian purple,
And from its lips there came a lily flower,
And yet, unlike the silver-white of lilies,
Its color was a tinted, pinkish blue.
Nor was this miracle enough for Phoebus:
He wrote the words "Ai, Ai" across its petals,
The sign of his own grief, his signature.[13]

Now if Arkenholz can stand in for Apollo, thanks to his being a Sunday child with special sight reminiscent of the oracular god's, can Adele, surrounded by her hyacinthine clusters, which Arkenholz loves and at the same time finds deadly, while he loves her and finds *her* deadly—can she be the play's Hyacinthus? Sundry hints seem to affirm it, and with Strindberg hints are about as much as we can hope for. His imagery reaches us glancingly, like the discus off the rock. In order to gain entry into the house, Arkenholz, we recall, must first attend a performance of *The Valkyries*. Many drawn-out episodes take place in that opera's four hours of playing time, one of the most striking being the gathering of the titular women, Brünnhilde and her sisters, the daughters of Erda and Wotan, the team of battlefield soul-scavengers trained by their father. Like those "masculine" women, Adele first appears in a riding outfit, which would give a woman a masculine look, even a woman as beautiful as she is. The first sight of her, in scene i, throws Arkenholz into despair. He weeps, after quoting the line from *Faust* to the effect that any man would be happy if he had the good fortune to win such a woman. There are further allusions to the absence in her of a femininity that would be conventional for the time. She hates housework and the thought of bearing a child. He must not have her and may not ask why. But our clairvoyant latter-day Apollo has gathered why. Like his father before him, he must speak the truth, however much it hurts. The most beautiful flowers are poisonous. The sources of life are infected. These pronouncements could mean that the suffering young woman is the unhealthy, even diseased, product of the corruption in the house, out of bounds to Arkenholz and a rough equivalent of Osvald in *Ghosts*, paying for his father's sins.

Conversely, we could make an only partly defensible leap and say that the Young Lady is male, or partly male, an hermaphrodite. She is a partial "he," who might even be Hummel's son, the one whose lover bore the mace at Hummel's funeral but did not venture out of the story into the action, the son to whom Arkenholz relates selected details of her/his father's funeral. This hypothesis may not be susceptible to hard proof but has much to recommend it.[14] Something beautiful has grown out of the evil in the house, a flower blooms in the dung, a figure too fragile for love or marriage, an angelic presence that is beyond owning, an ideal that is too piercingly beautiful to be allowed to survive. In his letters to Harriet Bosse, Strindberg talks about the Séraphita-Séraphitus paragon, the *époux-épouse* taken from a story by Balzac, one of his favorite authors.[15] A hermaphrodite with male and female sex features has a role in the *Satyricon* of Petronius, and in the film *Fellini Satyricon*. A creature too delicate to endure the rigors of ordinary life, the "demigod" is abducted and subjected to a harsh journey across mountains and hot wastelands.

If we hark back to Miss Julie, from whom the role of Adele is transposed, we remember that she too had something like a son's upbringing from both parents and is confused about her sexual appetites. Her sequence with Jean in her bedroom apparently represents her first lovemaking with a man. Although until recently engaged to be married, she treated her fiancé with contempt and cruelty. She too favors riding outfits (without forgetting whip and crop). She is, says Strindberg in his preface to that play, "a relic of the old warrior nobility," an earthly Brünnhilde.[16] Arkenholz, though, is no agent of corruption like Jean. He comes on as a savior at first but is unable to rescue Adele or to hold on to her. Thanks to his mantic vision, he predicts his plight in scene i, when he describes how, the day before, he witnessed the collapse of the building, noticed a child, snatched it up in his arms, and escaped, only to find his arms empty. Adele, that unfortunate soul, is lost, like the world in *The Dream Play* that Indra's Daughter could not save, and Arkenholz must leave this haunted house empty-handed. The final image of *The Ghost Sonata*, that *Isle of the Dead*, pictures a boat with dead souls in it traveling across black water, like souls transported by the Valkyries. The sight of the painting is the closest point to which the playwright could bring himself in implying a rescue or peaceful redemption.[17]

The Ghost Sonata has plentiful provisions of agony. But where is its comic quotient? I would say suffused throughout, but especially in the first two scenes. Just as in *Miss Julie* Jean plays the comic side of the battle of the sexes, so most of the figures who populate the two first "movements" of *The Ghost Sonata* earn their comic leitmotivs. As exceptions, Arkenholz, Adele, and the Milkmaid remain mostly serious, though the first two do lapse now and then into comic overplaying of melodramatic attitudes. The other roles are gargoyles, from the spiderlike Hummel and the pretentious Colonel to the parroty Mummy, the vacant von Holsteinkrona, and the Cook out of Lewis Carroll.[18] In the several productions I have seen, none on a high professional level, the actors and presumably the directors wanted to get the poetry across and indulged in what they felt were suitably highbrow exercises in elocution, which did little more than make the continual ripple of new topics seem disjointed and impossible to concentrate on. During her colloquy with Arkenholz, Adele remarks that only in asylums do people say everything they think. Agreeing, he says his father ended up in a madhouse.

ADELE: Was he ill?
ARKENHOLZ: No, he was well, but he was crazy.

Not only are these lines Groucho Marxian or Jimmy Durantean, but they make us wonder whether Arkenholz himself is "altogether there." Besides, he is about to break into outspokenness, and even if he is sane (doubtful, because traditionally people with oracular powers like his were at the very least possessed), Adele implies that the house itself is an asylum. Can the fugal development of this play accommodate comic roles? I believe that without them, the play itself, not merely Adele, quietly dies.

PLAYING THE ROLE FOR REAL

Enrico IV, by Luigi Pirandello

All stories are haunted by the ghosts of the stories they might have been.
SALMAN RUSHDIE, *Shame*

Certain of Pirandello's plays serve as models of comic agony. *Right You Are (If You Think You Are)* and what he called his theatre-in-the-theatre trilogy (*Six Characters in Search of an Author, Each in His Own Way,* and *Tonight We Improvise*) have a dramatic form in which a play nests within another play, the comic "outer" play being in generic conflict with the agonized "inner" one. Obtuse figures in the outer play remain amusedly and amusingly indifferent to the agonies that arise in the inner triangles and may go so far as to mock them. About those triangles in his inner plays Pirandello withholds certain information. As a result, we cannot choose sides among the tortured souls entangled in them, except by whim, because we do not quite know who, if anybody, was in the right, who, if anybody, in the wrong. Thus, what we take to be structural deficiencies in what happens offstage—factual gaps or missing clumps of story—seem to be deliberate omissions. Two examples: there are no independent witnesses of the earthquake in the story of *Right You Are,* and in *Six Characters* the Father's secretary, who is also the Wife's lover, does not appear.

As in *Six Characters* and *Tonight We Improvise,* the inner drama of *Enrico IV* (1921) consists of a performance that is in some respects studied and yet needs to create an impression of spontaneity, of happening for the first time while telling us of recurrences.[1] But so fractured is it in time and space that I believe analyzing the play as inner and outer dramas makes less sense than trying to delimit its story and action.

The story takes place in three stages or at three different ages—three historical periods, the first two widely separated in time and place. In the original historical triangle from which the story derives, stage one, the fourth German emperor named Heinrich (Enrico, Henry) and the seventh pope named Gregorio embarked on a power struggle (IV v. VII) that depended on recognition or role attribution. In order to assure allegiance from the German nobles, Heinrich needed to have *il Papa* acknowledge him as emperor. Once recognized in that role, he intended by treacherous manipulation of power (that is, by statecraft) to call on the nobles, plus twenty-seven bishops in Germany and Italy, to support him in displacing Gregorio. But first, to secure recognition from Gregorio,

Heinrich used as an intermediary Matilde of Tuscany, who was technically his foe although the two of them may also have been lovers. She begged Gregorio to come to her castle at Canossa for an interview, while Heinrich developed numb shins as he knelt for hours in the snow outside the castle awaiting Gregorio's verdict. This version of Heinrich's humiliation may or may not be accurate, but it serves as the first stage of the story only of *Enrico IV*.

For the story's second stage we leap forward from A.D. 1077 across eight hundred years. Like fretful archaeologists, we sort out and rearrange matter dropped at various points of all three acts. Around 1900 some young people, club members in Umbria, planned a pageant or cavalcade. Matilde elected to play her namesake, Matilde of Tuscany. One of her admirers, a stiff and remote young man with an absorbing gaze, promptly took on Enrico (Heinrich) IV and, to do justice to the part, boned up on German and Italian medieval history. We do not learn who performed the role of Pope Gregorio. During the pageant, conducted on horseback, the royal horse reared up and unseated the rider, who cracked his head on the ground. When he recovered consciousness, he seems to have misplaced his identity, as he continued to play out the pageant, not to mention the rest of the life and times of the German emperor.

Over the course of the next twenty or so years, the story built to its third stage. From different figures in the action we find that the devoted sister of Enrico (as we will call the young man, whom the playwright gives no other name) turned the rooms of her villa in Umbria into approximations of Heinrich's throne room at Goslar and sundry settings in Saxony, Lombardy, and along the Rhine. She hired valets, "privy councillors," and a steward who would bring in occasional women for sexual duties and otherwise play up to Enrico's psychosis so that he could inhabit it fairly congenially. This benefactress, another of those critical people in a Pirandello story who does not break into the action, believed her brother was close to recovering his sanity. During her last illness she instructed her son, Di Nolli, to see that his uncle was well cared for and to visit him. She died about one month before the action opens in the year 1921.

Di Nolli, by one of those flukes that make for provocative drama, has become engaged to Matilde's daughter, Frida. He has also, as the action gets under way, come to the villa to see his demented uncle and brought Frida with him. Matilde, whom Enrico once loved, insists on accompanying Di Nolli, possibly to keep watch over Frida, but more plausibly because she once found Enrico's eyes haunting. She is accompanied by Belcredi, the man Enrico once rightly took for his rival, for he is now Matilde's lover. The arrival of the two pairs of lovers, youthful and middle-aged, will not amount to a pure social occasion. It incorporates a doctor's house visit (common in 1921), since Di Nolli also has on hand a psychiatrist with the delectable name of Dionisio Genino. By carrying out an experiment that only a dramatist could dream up, the latter-day Dionysos hopes to shock Enrico into his prepageant past, out of what is perceived as a delusion of grandeur and back into himself, only a "himself" aged by some score of years. Alas, instead of being cured by the experiment—seeing life-sized portraits of his young self and a young Matilde step out of their frames—Enrico goes berserk and, among other rash acts, puts a sword into his rival's gut.

What the psychiatrist had not bargained for is that before the experiment took place Enrico told his retainers that he recovered his sanity twelve years earlier. If this is true, the experiment does the opposite of what Dr. Genoni intended: it drives the patient back into his psychosis. But is he sane beforehand? Or is he lying or mistaken when he speaks to his retainers? Has he in truth not recovered, then or ever? Has he acquired the madman's manner of feigning sanity, of behaving with such sincerity, such conviction, that people can't help saying, "He can't be mad"? Or, come to that, was he ever technically, certifiably insane, whatever insane meant in 1921 and means today? And whether he was or not, did the purported shock treatment offer him a longed-for excuse to slay the skilled swordsman he looked on as his rival—and with a sword, no less?

Whatever the hard reality of the action, and of the story that both supports and undermines it, Enrico, who has dreaded playing the role of a twenty-six-year-old emperor for the rest of his life, a role for which his age increasingly disqualifies him, is at last doomed to that age cell. Motioning his retainers to gather around him, he declares that henceforward they are together forever in their mock-up of the late eleventh century, for if he admits to the sanity he claimed earlier, he brands himself a murderer in those days of capital punishment in 1921.

But what is "hard reality"? What does such a term of evasive convenience bandied about by the likes of prosecutors and politicians have to do with Pirandello's drama and characters? As many students of what was once called the author's "relativism" have observed, this play confuses any preconceived notions we might have formed about the reliability of information and the witnesses who supply it.

Yet as we follow the unrolling episodes of the action, we may notice that it observes the unities of time and place. Although the story makes trips to the eleventh century and roams through ancient German and Italian lands, the action satisfies the requirements of neoclassical critics by taking place in less than twenty-four hours and in one setting, the villa. What we make of those episodes, however, is another matter—or more than one. A lesser playwright would tantalize us less. We would find closer correspondences, say, between the triangle in the story (Heinrich, Matilde of Tuscany, Pope Gregorio) and one of the triangles in the action (Enrico, Matilde Spina, Belcredi). Belcredi might understandably stand for the pope, but so might the psychiatrist, Dionisio. The play, though, informs us that metaphorically, educibly, Dionisio does represent a papal figure, while Belcredi becomes his henchman or functionary, for in Enrico's reenactment of the medieval tier of the story, Enrico keeps referring erroneously to Belcredi, even after being corrected, as one of Gregorio's voices, an envoy named Pietro Damiani. In alluding to the second tier of the story, set twenty-odd years before, he cries that his horse shied because somebody (he does not specify the person but unmistakably implies that it was Belcredi) goaded the animal with a spur, thereby causing his head injury and lasting affliction. In other words, Enrico believes that Belcredi literally unseated him as "emperor," whereas Gregorio confirmed the original Heinrich in his throne or seat.

As one who loved and respected the early Italian comedy of both the "erudite" (scholarly) and "artistic" (professional) kinds, Pirandello mimicked its varied entanglings of masks, identities (which include bloodlines), and representations. Matilde enters wearing "a violent if expert makeup which gives her the haughty head of a Valkyrie."[2] She has dyed her hair. Her face is masklike and (for the purposes of this play) aptly Germanic.[3] Enrico also has dyed hair. On his cheeks are red blotches, a pitiful attempt at visual rejuvenation—pickling the emperor's twenty-six years—and at the same time a reminder of the makeup or mask of a clown. The playwright says nothing about Belcredi's face or features but does mention his "curious, bird-shaped head" and so gives us an impression of beaky prominence and of the alert snatches of movement that characterize land birds: another mask of sorts. The psychiatrist's "mask" is a "fine satyr's face." The four "privy councillors" and the two valets are, so to speak, body-masked in their eleventh-century uniforms. The play makes little attempt to individualize two of the councillors, but it does give some limited acting chances to the other two, the principal councillor of the quartet, Lolo, whom Enrico knows as Landolfo, and Fino, known as Bertoldo, a jittery new appointment. Frida and Di Nolli, as befits equivalents of the *innamorati* (youthful lovers) from the commedia dell'arte, go unmasked. But when they impersonate the portraits, those youthful versions of her mother and his uncle respectively (which the mother and uncle hope to rebecome with the aid of cosmetics), the frames are conceptually their masks.

In his stage directions for Matilde's entrance Pirandello calls her a "widow for many years." But he does not name her husband or say anything about him. She may have acquired her title of marchesa from the marriage, but she may equally well have inherited it from or through her parents. The triangle, then, has been a four-sided figure now missing one side (or angle). She has held on to Belcredi. She keeps him by her more as an escort and limited confidant than as an object of desire or even a comforting presence. She doesn't love him, maybe never did. She cavils at his words, quarrels openly, laughs at him. The stage directions make him her "friend," not her husband. Enrico in his twenty-year isolation may not realize that. But the lines she speaks about *him* suggest that before the pageant and his accident, she might have married Enrico (or had an affair with him) if he had asked her.

We assume Frida's father was the husband of Matilde, but nobody says so in the play. Frida is nineteen. Enrico dates his accident to about twenty years earlier, and Matilde roughly confirms that gap in time, although her arithmetic could add up to twenty-two years. If twenty is the correct figure, either Matilde married very soon after the accident and Frida was conceived shortly after that (or before) or else Frida might be the daughter of Belcredi—an improbability. Or she might be the daughter of Enrico.

Matilde calls herself "impulsive" and admits she was fascinated by whoever Enrico was before the pageant. I have already suggested that the persistence of that fascination, aggravated to some extent by curiosity, could account for her taking part in this visit. If Enrico really is the father, his clasping Frida to him shortly before he stabs Belcredi is meaningful, and his line "You are mine, mine, mine! And by right!" is literally true: it refers to the daughter who is, not to the mother who once was. It is worth noting that a stage direction about Matilde remarks that she "provokes facile gossip against her daughter as well as herself."

The absence of the other deceased figure, Enrico's sister, together with what we learn about her, has the effect of further deepening the play's ambiguities. She came away from the "tender" meeting with her brother, not long before her death, suspecting that his mental health was about to improve. She might have noticed that his lucidity, for so long concealed, had now started to leak out. Or he may have told her he was no longer mad. Or that he had never been mad. Certainly she made exceptional sacrifices for him. The twenty-year upkeep of the villa and the trouble she incurred to maintain its false character, as well as her instructions to her son, might be taken as evidence of an ultrasisterly devotion. Where did she live in those twenty years? Another villa? A castle? A hovel? How rich was she? No wonder Enrico confuses her with his mother after he has been rattled by the portraits scene—and conceivably before that, too. She it was who asked to have the portraits of young Matilde and young Enrico in full regalia transferred to the villa for her brother's sake. Painted before the cavalcade, they would, she might have hoped, stir him to a remembrance of flings past: himself and Matilde before he donned the part of the emperor and could not tear it off. The remembrance would help him get over the delusion and the accident. It may not have occurred to her that the sight of the portrait might confirm him in his imperial role, might reify that role. The sister must have been a titled lady by birth, in which case Enrico is also of an aristocratic line, or she took over the property and perhaps a title when he was declared legally insane, or else she inherited her wealth and her son inherited his rank of marchese from her husband.[4]

It is not unusual for a young man to look like his uncle. We may therefore ask how close the resemblance is between Di Nolli and the youthful Enrico. Without forgetting the dim lighting, we permissibly wonder whether Enrico would not notice immediately a difference in the painting he has had in his confined quarters for eighteen years. Alternatively, we may wonder if the resemblance would not be even closer and the difference negligible if Di Nolli were Enrico's son. The issue (in two senses of the word) of incest repeatedly crops up in Pirandello criticism; and here we have the implication of repeat incest—in successive generations—if Di Nolli is to marry Frida, who could be Enrico's daughter.

The impatient reader may well ask at this point: Does it matter what we don't discover in the play? What do we discover? The impatient critic would like to brush aside such questions by saying that it is worth following up every clue in sight, since we can never be sure how far speculation about the once-forbidden will take us, and by adding that we get some idea of how resourceful Pirandello is only if we investigate the bonds between his characters as aggressively as we do those in *Hamlet* or *Ajax*, *Hippolytus* or *Don Juan*. But there is a more compelling reason: the fact is that we are not confronting facts in this play. We have the impression that we know who is who and what has happened. This playwright has the knack of leading us by the nose across unstable terrain. Not until we look back over it do we see that we feel not quite confident about what we thought we experienced en route. I am not speaking here of coincidences or misunderstandings among the roles, which are the very stuff of drama, but of the dubieties in the story, in its essence. Why did we look back in the first place? I believe Pirandello has built into his story quantities of subliminal but serious teasing. Certain passions haunt him. They haunt his roles. We may, in some measure, share them.

As a prelude to Dr. Genoni's shock treatment of Enrico, he and two of the other visitors, Matilde and Belcredi, adopt guises meant to soothe away any suspicions entertained by Enrico in his supposed state of madness and historical displacement. This time, in 1921, during the third stage of the story, Matilde plays not her namesake but Heinrich's mother-in-law, Adelaide. The psychiatrist plays Ugo of Cluny, an abbot who goes between Enrico and Pope Gregorio. Belcredi, for whose presence Landolfo can find no watertight pretext, plays a monk, also from Cluny. All three are ill at ease in their roles and unfamiliar with the period, Belcredi especially so after Enrico rejects Belcredi's nominal role and insists on taking him for Pietro Damiani. They bumble and get by only because of the sleight of tongue of the experienced "privy councillors" and Enrico's unwillingness to listen: the scene turns into his interrupted tirade. We do not learn until after the encounter between him and the trio that he was not (so he says) insane and that he recognized Matilde and Belcredi. The scene as he played it almost surely means something other than what it appeared to mean: his speeches were a form of disguise to match or counter their costume disguises. But this scene also constitutes our first meeting with Enrico. We take him as the lunatic the exposition has prepared us to watch. Perhaps we hardly notice a double significance in lines like the one in which he swears to Matilde (playing his mother-in-law) that he loves her daughter (historically Berta of Susa but, in the present tense, Frida) and does not want to be divorced (parted) from her. In that same discontinuous speech he talks of the death of his mother (not his sister) one month before, tells Matilde that she wears makeup to recollect an image of herself young, but tells Belcredi that he, like Enrico himself, has different recollections of "the realities of the past, which have lived on inside . . . like a dream." Given a liberal, vaguely philosophical interpretation, the "realities of the past" could mean almost anything, but here, as specifics, they surely allude to their mutual hatred and to Enrico's feeling that Belcredi has come to see him in order to gloat over his plight.

Enrico-as-Heinrich later panics, as though he fears that Belcredi-as-Damiani wishes to seize his crown. Matilde reacts to this distrust by collapsing into a chair and almost swooning. Their behavior makes a capital, melodramatically supercharged curtain for act I; but in Pirandellian truth Matilde has perceived in that gaze of Enrico's (and perhaps has found the impression fortified by his equivocal words) that he understands what is going on, that he sees through her. She says as much in the following act, and Belcredi derides her perception. But she may also have seen something more damaging to her vanity: that Enrico no longer loves her. The jealousy that originally heated his hatred for Belcredi still simmers but no longer needs to be brought to a boil by the old, frustrated love for her, which has been replaced by those "realities of the past . . . inside." He shouts at the disguised trio that he has "changed, changed, changed." He is no more the portrait of him holding the pose of the imperial twenty-six year old. He has become a different sort of poseur.

Another dramatic double entendre in his harangue harks back to when he (and/or Heinrich) was a child: "Even an emperor has a childhood—he doesn't know he's an emperor in fact—he's just a kid at play, letting time go by." Far from having been an emperor, the modern Enrico may not even have had a title. His nephew, the "young marchese" Di Nolli, has one, so does Matilde Spina the marchesa, and so does Belcredi the baron. By playing the role of emperor, Enrico outranked the last two—at least during the rehearsals, if any, and during the performance of the pageant and, it would seem, in his own mind. Now if he was originally a commoner, his nephew's title does come from Enrico's unidentified (and very likely wealthy) brother-in-law, with whom his sister made an advantageous match. While it may be true that counts, marquesses, barons, baronets, and similar species, some of them inevitably self-appointed, floated around Europe at any time of aristocratic dispossession (that is, at any time) and while boulevard comedies in France, Italy, Britain, and elsewhere have often featured titled characters (created by untitled authors who steep their work in bogus class claims), Pirandello evidently had some motive for bestowing nobility with such a open hand in this play and then conferring the false title where it was so wanted. Whatever the degree of, and fluctuations in, his insanity, Enrico has played the role with flourishes that recall the familiar Napoleonic syndrome of countless madhouse tales.

Our initial compassion for this commoner who tries to live his royal but constrictive role (we have trouble sifting him out from the role itself) grows strained as we watch him take pleasure in his emperor's perquisites. He tastes his revenge ahead of time. He lords it over his "privy councillors," who are little more than vassals, and he practices his own form of shock treatment, anticipating the doctor's, when he astounds them by saying that he has been sane for years. As a grand finale he stabs the foe who keeps saying he is not mad. In premeditating his revenge, however, Enrico almost certainly does not expect to kill Belcredi, but rather to humiliate him and Matilde and perhaps merely to frighten, or at most to nick, him with the sword. Seeing what he has done leaves him aghast, not triumphant, as the closing stage directions make explicit. The weapon and his revenge proved sharper than he intended.

Belcredi is the one who says, even before the accident, that Enrico appeared slightly or more than slightly exalted, had a self-consciously stagy manner, but was an excellent actor. Belcredi also mentions that after the accident, when Enrico continued to play the emperor, some of the others in the cavalcade provoked him. He rounded on them with his sword, and says Matilde, "at a certain point he was hit." She does not specify by whom or how or whether there was a serious wound, but Belcredi, the expert swordsman, mentions that Enrico "bore down on a couple of us" after drawing "his imperial sword." As with the goading of Enrico's horse, Belcredi may have been the party responsible for the "hit" (in Enrico's mind he definitely is), but the play text does not pin that responsibility down.

In the course of the action Belcredi himself assumes several personae. He starts out as the skeptical commentator, helping Matilde to revive memories of Enrico, sparring lightly from time to time with the psychiatrist, and portraying Enrico as a personality more sharply sensitive than most of their other acquaintances. At the same time he is the butt of Matilde's mockery, against which he complaisantly defends himself. From Enrico's attitude toward him, both when Enrico discusses the visit with his councillors and when he seems willfully to take the baron for Pietro Damiani, we also think of Belcredi as a villain, a scarcely tolerated and at times unwanted hanger-on of Matilde's, who helped spur Enrico into madness out of crude envy of his qualities as a superior being. Finally, after the stabbing, when Belcredi is carried offstage, Matilde lets out a "piercing shout" that can only denote that the baron is dead. For those last few minutes Belcredi seems more than Enrico to be the victim, not the villain, and to deserve compassion. We might say that if he did not cause the accident or harm Enrico after it, his melodramatic end is all the more affecting. On his entrance in act I the stage direction observes that neither Matilde "nor other people have ever taken him seriously. . . . He would be very vivacious if his agility . . . were not encased in a sleepy, Arab laziness that comes out in his strange voice, which is rather nasal and drawling." Pirandello has given him enough "vivacity" to make him a significant figure but has burdened him with a recognizably aristocratic offhandedness: he lacks the compelling, histrionic, brash presence of his lower-status rival.

Belcredi and the other principals in the play, in one scene or another, or in more than one, make fun of Dr. Dionisio Genoni and his profession. The shock treatment Genoni envisions, even if it were to work flawlessly, without the attack of nervousness from Frida, strikes us as being itself mad in the circumstances, so that the play falls, at least in part, into the "Physician, heal thyself" premise adopted by Molière and taken up by Shaw, among others. Belcredi says: "All they do is talk. The best talker, the best psychiatrist. . . . They tell you right off the bat that they can't work miracles—when a miracle is precisely what we need. . . . They don't work miracles—but they always land on their feet." The sentiments seem so familiar, since psychiatry and especially psychoanalysis and, even more, its half-hourly fees and defensive-aggressive questioning have become everybody's second favorite topic ("Aren't you a psychoanalyst?" "What makes you ask?") that we might forget that the lines were written in 1921. Jokes about psychiatry notwithstanding, shock treatment of one sort or another has since become commonplace, with what overall results I can't say. And Dr. Genoni is not written as a clown, though the role is often played as one, but as a scientist who could, if required to, produce ample evidence about the efficacy of his plan. Nor is it the psychiatrist's shock that sends Enrico into his murderous rage. He has announced the pleasures of revenge well ahead of time, in the second act, and that revenge includes punishment of Matilde. Thus, if Enrico believes Belcredi is either her husband or her lover, then demeaning him will inflict a double wound. Belcredi may wind up a melodramatic victim, who, despite his mild razzing, does not conspire in his own death. Enrico, by contrast, is a tragic victim who does bring about his own fall—into the condition from which he had hoped to escape. To blame Genoni for this is to put Enrico on a generic par with Belcredi. But perhaps it is already too late to save Genoni from a bad press and more farcical interpretations. In case anybody thinks Pirandello is making facile fun of the shrink, however, he has not only "a fine, satyr's face, insolent and rubicund, with protruding eyes," but also "a short, pointed beard that shines like silver" and "refined manners." He "is almost bald." The description fits the playwright: this role wears the mask of Luigi Pirandello. As an ironic flourish, the latter-day namesake of the god of wine, drama, release, and other intoxicants is trying to win Enrico back to sanity, to sobriety.

I have little to say about the young couple. Again like the *innamorati* of the commedia, they are not richly imagined and will hardly be noticed unless played by offbeat actors. Frida is little more than an appendage to her mother and a contrary image to emphasize Matilde's maturity. Di Nolli treats her more protectively than he does his uncle, whom he seems to know only slightly and wants cured as swiftly as possible to shake off the promise made to his mother, even if honoring that promise means some ill treatment: the four councillors are told by the steward in act I to keep Enrico out of the way of the visitors until they are ready for him and to "use force if need be! Those are the Marchese's orders."

When we consider the role of the marchesa Matilde, we can trace resemblances between it and one of the stock parts of nineteenth-century farce and boulevard comedy, namely, that of the older woman who believes she still enchants men as she once did. The portrait often tends toward caricature, the sex-mad dowager or the unfulfilled wife yearning for a lover, any lover, or, failing that, an object for romantic dreams. The type recurs in Labiche, among other playwrights, and gets an American airing in Sturges's film *Sullivan's Travels* in the form of the middle-class widow who locks the Joel McCrea character in her bedroom and from whom he escapes (through a window and hanging on to ripping bedsheets) into a rain butt. In *Enrico IV* she has her loyal lover whom she treats with contempt that verges on cruelty as she pines over the other man, the one she lost, the exciting mystery. The part is not without its pathos, even its agony.

The sharpest agony in this drama, though, belongs to Enrico. He blundered into a trap of his own making. Even without committing the murder of Belcredi, he will, he fears, always be branded a madman. As an unusual instance of comic agony we have the agonized character who laughs at the "sane" people he thinks of as his persecutors and at the same time may suffer from the (unprovable) loss of two children. In this portrait, is Pirandello saying that it is futile to look for a convincing definition of madness, that the borderline between it and sanity that people used to go by no longer holds up? That there are "layers" of "sanity"? Does the irregular behavior and speech, sometimes curiously, monotonously insistent, connote an attempt to tell us something about the burdens of madness, as R. D. Laing argued in *The Divided Self* and *Self and Others?* Did Pirandello anticipate by some forty years this understanding of insistent communication when he dramatized Enrico's attachment for twenty years to the trappings of Heinrich IV? I cannot believe we are meant to accept the claim that the would-be emperor became unmad after twelve years, when he started to live again in the twentieth century. Sane? There is a feverish quality in the way he talks in the twentieth-century role that makes us wonder about his mental state even before the accident. Are we reckoning with a madman who plays a sane king, a sane man playing a mad king, or a modern Italian commoner and a medieval

German king both sane or both insane?

I have seen Enrico played by Jean Vilar, Herbert Berghof, and Rex Harrison. For Harrison the role was, I would say, artistically out of reach, although he had the courage or rashness to assay it twice in commercial productions, on Broadway and later in the West End. It is true that in places Enrico might yield as a part to the sort of insolent charm Harrison displayed in films like *Major Barbara* and *The Rake's Progress* and *My Fair Lady*. But his performance, which I saw in both theatres, was a bit too knowing, as though he was winking at spectators to show himself in control, when the opposite impression might have yielded more theatrical advantage. Vilar maintained a mask that was saturnine and inexplicable. In combination with his sonorous but almost uninflected bass voice, his somber presence radiated majestic, monolithic authority, and simultaneously withheld shows of emotion, so that one might almost imagine that this was the character of an emperor striving (not too hard) to abase himself by imitating a commoner. At the time I felt and wrote that Enrico was one of the roles we would never see better performed than by Vilar.[5] But subsequently I saw a production at Washington's Arena Stage with Herbert Berghof, very different in the title role: he was by turns a wheedler (reliving days and nights on his knees in the snow at Canossa?), a ruler entertained by his own pretensions, and a snarling fury as he jumped, skipped, darted along the tightrope of that hypothetical dividing line between whatever it is we call sanity and whatever we choose to call insanity, never in control as a character but under impeccable control as an actor, tipping first one way and then the other, making even the acts of recovery smell of danger, so that freezing the performance at any moment would make it look out of kilter, in a state of perpetual imbalance.

SUMMARY
Comedy in Hiding

The five plays examined in this first segment of the book used to receive polite, even guarded, stage treatments. By now the professional and academic theatre communities and other fascinated parties assume that all plays invite interpretations more broadly amusing than before. Denied an infusion of comedy, and even in spots a touch or two of farce, plays such as these will only partially reveal themselves. Adherence to the traditional genres will suppress some of their essentials.

In teaching, the genres have come under suspicion except for the purposes of raw or elementary differentiating between types of plays. Most of us do still adhere to them, more as baggage tags to show approximately the plays' destinations than for detailed identification. Film critics, however, who could have availed themselves of the dramatic genres, chose instead to develop their own array of specialized subdivisions, such as film noir, science fiction, the romance, disaster, gumshoe, and killer-chiller, which they nevertheless refer to as "genres."[1]

"Divisions of genre serve a purpose somewhat like a scaffolding: useful as preliminaries but in the end to be discarded," notes Irving Howe.[2] Much as genre distinctions can be "useful as preliminaries" in differentiating between broad types of work, the same general technique applies with comic agony. The three subdivisions used here roughly place a play by noting whether it is dominated by serious drama, wit, or farce. We can go on to explore the structure and workings of each play, as in these chapters, and to divide up the divisions, if we insist—and I don't—into smaller, more consistent units, which are more like the film categories. For each of us some plays will obstinately remain borderline cases and are not a jot inferior as artistry for clinging to the edges of more than one definition, as comic agony itself does.

If Ibsen and Shaw subverted the genres, so did Wedekind, Chekhov, and Pirandello, each in his own way. Among actors and directors in this country, however, the one who usually gets the credit for the Ibsen-Shaw discovery, the concealment of opposites, is Chekhov, thanks to his popularity at that fount of theatrical training, the Actors Studio. As attributed to Chekhov, the discovery unyokes pity from Aristotle's (and Lessing's) insistence on the unit of pity-and-terror-linked and turns it into a special brand of Broadway compassion, so that Chekhov becomes less tragedy that conceals comedy than comedy overridden by schmaltz.

In the quintet of plays discussed so far, comic agony illustrates serious-minded drama variously concealing and distorting wit and the occasional out-break of broader, farcical humor. It mocks the principal male roles by curtailing our sympathy for them. *Spring's Awakening* may have become an exception today, although German audiences at Max Reinhardt's introductory showing of the play are unlikely to have expended much sympathy on poor effeminate Moritz or Melchior the seducer. In four of the five plays, pain that proves comic eases the transitions between realism and fantasy and between one fantasy and another. As its final effect, comic agony closes each play on a note that, for its time, appeared unresolved.

To these five plays I append more instances of this outwardly serious vein of comic agony: Anouilh's *Poor Bitos*, Babel's *Sunset*, Brecht's *Galileo*, Cocteau's *The Infernal Machine*, Frisch's *The Firebugs*, Giraudoux's *Ondine*, Hampton's *Total Eclipse*, Ibsen's *An Enemy of the People* and *Little Eyolf*, Miller's *The Price*, Pinter's *No Man's Land* and *Old Times*, Pirandello's *Right You Are* and *Six Characters in Search of an Author*, Ribman's *Harry, Noon, and Night* and *Journey of the Fifth Horse*, Sartre's *The Devil and the Good Lord* and *The Respectful Prostitute*, Strindberg's *To Damascus* and *Crimes and Crimes*.

PART II
Taking the Joke Seriously

JEST AND SUPERJEST
Man and Superman, by Bernard Shaw

The majority of revolutionists are the enemies of discipline and fatigue mostly. There are natures, too, to whose sense of justice the price exacted looms up monstrously enormous, odious, oppressive, worrying, humiliating, extortionate, intolerable. These are the fanatics. The remaining portion of social rebels is accounted for by vanity, the mother of all noble and vile illusions, the companion of poets, reformers, charlatans, prophets, and incendiaries.

JOSEPH CONRAD, *The Secret Agent*

Shaw calls *Man and Superman* (1903) "a Comedy and a Philosophy."[1] The comedy and the philosophy interact all through the text, but the comedy comes first in the playwright's designation. It should likewise come first in our appreciation of the play. G. Wilson Knight writes, "Shaw's real message is *in the humor itself.*"[2] The ideas enunciated, above all the intricate variations on the man-and-superman theme, acquire a special urgency as ideas entertained by the particular roles, who are, almost all of them, comic figures, from the antihero to the antivillains. These roles thrive, like those of Molière or Racine, on weaknesses and imbalances. Yet, since Shaw no more plays favorites with them than Ibsen does with his, two of the least agreeable of them, Violet, a money-grubber, and Ramsden, a reputation-grubber, speak lines that reverse a situation, make it suddenly more truthful, and permit us to glimpse the desperate feelings concealed by Shaw's glittering dialogue and stage directions.

The four segments of *Man and Superman* form an interlocking unity, much as the comedy and the philosophy do. The two unperformed segments, the preface in the form of an epistle and "The Revolutionist's Handbook and Pocket Companion," a sixty-page pamphlet, throw light on the segments to be performed. These are the play in four acts, apparently based on a simple novelty—boy scorns girl, girl nevertheless gets boy—and the long dream interlude during the third act, often called the Don Juan in hell scene and occasionally performed as a severed play. A spectator may never see the preface and handbook or know they exist, but they provide useful pointers in interpreting the play and an interlude for directors, actors, designers, critics, teachers, students, and others who engage in anatomical dissection of the drama.

"The Revolutionist's Handbook," for instance, written by the protagonist, John Tanner, tells us about Tanner, what manner of man he is, not merely what kind of a revolutionist. Only by indirection does it tell us anything about Shaw and his views. Most of what it does say about Shaw is that he looks on his protagonist with a cold eye. The handbook is something of a spoof. So, intermittently, is the epistle. Shaw addresses it to A. B. Walkley, the dramatic critic of the London *Times*, one of the playwright's friendly rivals during his years as a practicing critic. He thanks (and blames) Walkley for having got him going on this Don Juan play in the first place and dedicates the work to him. Here, Shaw reminds Walkley that, as in all his drama, he insists on making spectators think "in order to bring them to conviction of sin. If you don't like my preaching you must lump it. I really cannot help it." But the constant raillery in the epistle challenges Walkley and other readers to watch out for sleight of hand by the author in the manipulation of the roles and the manipulation of our responses to them. Shaw's dedicatory message to Walkley, who, it might be said, misunderstood him least of his critical contemporaries, shows that the prefatory material was aimed squarely at critics and intended to provoke them. So is the final, straightfaced postscript, added in 1933.[3] Naturally, the critics Shaw was provoking took as literal statement everything in the epistle but the few literal statements. The most heartfelt one is the one most often ignored: "Worst of all, I have been accused of preaching a Final Ethical Superman: no other, in fact, than our old friend the Just Man made Perfect! This misunderstanding is so galling that I lay down my pen without another word." That is to say, John Tanner and his counterpart, Don Juan, can hardly be looked upon as candidates for a Shavian utopia, much less as silhouettes of the author.

The four-act play has a main plot that overturns the traditional love pursuit. Tanner does not go after Ann Whitefield; she goes after him. The apparent love rival, a poet named Octavius and nicknamed (by Ann) Ricky-Ticky-Tavy, or simply Tavy, obviously does not stand a chance with her from the start, or later. Like the rest of the male roles in the play, Tavy has a part that the action does not altogether define. His real "meaning" lies in the comedy and the philosophy.

Tanner, as a self-styled M.I.R.C., "member of the idle rich class," is a reformer who does not believe in the conventional political system or in marriage. But according to the will of Ann's father, just dead, he is appointed her legal guardian, jointly with her father's friend, a die-hard liberal, Roebuck Ramsden, who detests everything Tanner professes to stand for. Tanner irritatingly professes all the more in front of Ramsden. He delights in shocking the aging bachelor and his sister-cum-housekeeper, as well as Ann, her mother, and Tavy.

Does anyone still believe that Shavian roles are undersexed? Almost every encounter between a man and a woman in *Man and Superman* turns on sex or has sexual undertones. The play posits Ramsden as not Ann's father: we cannot mistake his "jolly uncle" affection for her, which she trades on. Given the inescapable competition between Ramsden and Tanner in their joint guardianship of Ann, Ramsden repeatedly badmouths Tanner, overtly because of the younger man's book and opinions, actually because of his virility. Hector Malone, Sr., a self-made billionaire who enters the play in the last act to prevent his son from marrying Tavy's sister, Violet, becomes susceptible to Violet almost as soon as he meets her, while Ann's middle-aged mother, Mrs. Whitefield, is fonder, she says, of Octavius and Tanner than she is of her own daughter. The only male in the play not enamored of any woman, Henry Straker the chauffeur, worships the car he drives and is unnaturally possessive about his sister, Louisa.

Shaw seems more, not less, aware than other writers of the potency of sexual urges. He cannot get away from them. When the figures in his plays—Tanner, for instance—preach continence or highbrow pastimes as an alternative to sexual fulfillment, it is because they are oversexed, not undersexed. Like monks, they resist the urges because they are so vulnerable to them. Jack Tanner is a modern Don Juan. He fences, too, but with his tongue, not a sword. Even the up-to-date weapon is more fittingly sexual.

The Don Juan legend never retreats far below the surface of this play. A fantasy recalling that of Mozart and Da Ponte plays tag with a hard, satiric realism quite like Molière's. The first act is dominated not so much by Tanner's Don, although he makes flashy first impressions, as by Ann, who keeps her three swains in their appointed places by drawing freely on a Doña Ana-like dutifulness to her parents. The second act belongs to the Leporello, Straker, who, rather than following his master helplessly through one thousand and three love affairs, leads or literally steers him. In the third act the play forsakes the fashionable inner- and outer-London settings of Portland Place (Ramsden's home) and a country house near Richmond, as it travels by early automobile into the Spanish Sierras. Here Shaw retrieves the mood of the *capa y espada* dramas of Spain's Golden Age and their conflicts between love and honor or between love and duty, as well as the lung-clearing atmosphere of the Spanish-derived plays of Corneille, Hugo, and Molière.[4] Martin Meisel has pointed out that the opening tableau of this act is a quotation from Verdi's opera *Ernani*, based on Hugo's play.

In the lengthy Don Juan in hell scene, which butts into this third act, Shaw's love comedy and the legend of the Don at last merge. This sequence in hell brings the philosophical themes to a climax. Even after it, in the fourth act, which is the emotional or dramatic climax, Shaw is reluctant to move out of Spain, having settled there. The scene is Granada, a resort, the 1903 equivalent of Cancun or the Virgin Islands, where tourists' luxury escapism almost rubs shoulders with local poverty.

Shaw's delving into the Don Juan legend and old Spain seems to be the consequence of reasoning that goes roughly as follows: What is wrong with the world is humanity. Evolution has not improved human beings morally, as the neo-Darwinians in the nineteenth century presumed. The most logical step, and therefore the most illogical, is a new human breed, the Superman. Nietzsche gave intellectual substance to the notion of an *Übermensch* in the 1880s, and it became all the rage for thirty years or more in Europe before undergoing onslaughts of ridicule at the hands of Sternheim and others. But where would one look for this new breed's progenitor? The person must be capable of moral improvement. A rebel is required.

Don Juan is one of the three prototypical rebels in literature. He can be (and has been) forced to absorb the other two: Faust, who sought knowledge and understanding beyond human ken, and Prometheus, who defied Zeus by bringing fire and the arts to mankind. If he is to incorporate Prometheus, though, the new Juan must be more than a rebel. He must be a reformer. Hence we have John Tanner, who is not a Communist out of partisan necessity, a man born poor who magnifies his personal grievances into a political creed, but a Communist by intellectual and moral choice, rather as William Morris was.[5] By placing Tanner in modern Britain and calling him a new Don Juan, Shaw presents a parallel between the societies that the two men rebel against: Spain in the grip of the inquisitions and a code of honor and duty, and turn-of-the-century England with its own code of honor and duty—two smug, imperialistic, and expansionist powers.

But each of the other men in the play is a rebel of a kind too: they add up at first to a gallery of potential Supermen. As the play advances they lose that potential.

Octavius seems a strange candidate for Superhumanhood. The Ricky and Ticky in his nickname, affectedly adapted by Ann from Kipling's plucky mongoose, apply more descriptively to him than does that little rodent's carnivorous appetite. Handsome to a fault—or beyond—he taps his way blindly through a fog of illusions and mawkish upwellings. He does not have a hope of capturing Ann. He even relishes his defeat, as she tells him once she has shaken him off: "You know you are really getting a sort of satisfaction already in being out of danger yourself." And, "You are like the bird that presses its breast against the sharp thorn to make itself sing." A bird? Tavy is a songster, a poet, the play's one artist. Traditionally rebels are artists in the drama, or else, like Tanner, they have an artistic flair. A contemporary playwright, most of all a Broadway or television artisan, would mechanically make Tavy a bohemian. Shaw had little use for bohemian behavior and dress, regarding them as a pose. Tavy doesn't pose. Utterly, deadeningly honest, a gentleman ridden with romantic ideas—if they can be called ideas—borrowed from the fifteenth century, he diffidently takes over the part of rival of honor from Spanish drama and Mozart, only now he is the lover with a jawful of clichés, reduced to a "sentimental bachelor" or "an old maid," and a target for Tanner's tongue.

That other Tanner target and rival, Roebuck Ramsden, does not cut much of a figure as a Superman, either. His hearty name (the "buck" and the "ram" compromised more than a little by the "roe") is tailored to his humbugging personality. As a self-proclaimed liberal, surrounded by his mementos of Bright, Spencer, and Cobden, those heroes of an earlier, laissez-faire age, Ramsden is one of the forward-looking visionaries of yesteryear.[6] In his sixties, he has an immaculate body, if a less than immaculate soul. In his study, "not a speck of dust is visible. . . . Even the top of [his] head is polished: on a sunshiny day he could heliograph his orders to distant camps by merely nodding." If he lived today Ramsden would be a customer for mouthwashes, deodorants, skin bracers, perfumes with a "masculine" odor, and scented bathroom sprays. He submits to the prim government of his housekeeping sister.[7] But by a Shavian grace the younger Ramsden shows through the crustiness of the old one and sturdily refuses to turn Violet out of his home when she is supposed to be pregnant and unmarried. Shaw gives us a glimpse of the young radical that Ramsden was once—a sincere radical, too, in his time. But his time has passed.

Violet's husband, the young Hector Malone, is another rebel in his mild fashion. He says he will renounce his father's wealth sooner than the woman he loves. But the woman he loves dominates him, and that is probably why he loves her. Thanks to Violet, he does not even have to surrender the Malone treasure house at the end. Hector is easily gobbled up by the system. So much for rebels who say they care nothing for wealth.

His father is a man of tougher fiber. A self-made billionaire (like Kaiser's hero in *The Coral*, no mere millionaire) up from poverty, the older Malone has come a long way socially, but he proves to be an upstart. He is greedy for his son to buy a titled wife or to marry an impoverished young woman and so honor him, as the father, by following his example. For Malone, as for Molière's Harpagon, there must be a profit in every transaction, even a wedding. This is at least an unbending point of view, and in a financial sense, Malone has done more than any of the other men to change his fate. He brags: "English rule drove me and mine out of Ireland. Well, you can keep Ireland. Me and me like are coming back to buy England; and we'll buy the best of it. I want no middle class properties and no middle class women for Hector." Yet the first middle-class woman he meets, Violet, halts him. He is led, as Tanner puts it, "in a string like a pug dog by the first girl who takes the trouble to despise him."

As the fifth in this sextet of false Supermen, Henry Straker plays himself by plucking a pizzicato variation on Malone. If Malone pulls himself up by his bootstraps when he manipulates property, as though his name were a condensation of *man alone*, Straker makes a place for himself in the sun by manipulating technical competence. This "New Man," this H. G. Wellsian technocrat, has got himself An Education, widely regarded in 1903, and today, as the keys of the kingdom. He went to school for learning (he can correct Tanner when it comes to literary references) and to realize the rising expectations of the lower classes, not for manners.[8] In theory he could free himself from his background, but by temperament he is no radical. He preaches "moderation," and Tanner finds him "swollen with the pride of class." More gravely, he is so hamstrung by British respectability that he will not allow Mendoza to refer to his sister, Louisa, by her first name.

Mendoza himself, the most percussive and the most lyrical instrument in Shaw's ensemble, bursts into the action late but can outplay the protagonist Tanner if the actor doing that part slackens breath. More signally than the other five "rebels," Mendoza has hacked out his path through life according to no rules or precedents, and he has taken it to the very edges of society. He is a philosopher-outlaw with patches of Robin Hood, Hernani, Raskolnikov, and Goethe's Götz in his makeup. As the Devil in the hell scene, he makes a fit antagonist for Juan. Mendoza is described as having "imagination," the litmus test in Shaw for an admirable (not necessarily likable) personality. Shaw's creation of Mendoza was a dramatic milestone: a Jew who is a powerful fighter, a poor man who lives on (nonkosher) rabbit and prickly pears, a man who rules his little tribe of disaffected Old Leftists by strength and strength of character.[9] These are all qualities virtually unthinkable in the stereotyped Jew of English dramatic literature before *Man and Superman* and well beyond Lessing's Nathan the wise.

Nevertheless, Mendoza does not qualify for a Superman rating. He wants to become acceptable to that lower-middle-class cook, Louisa Straker. We hear an echo of this ambition in the hell scene when the Devil (played by Mendoza), embroidering a quotation from Poor Tom (played by Edgar) in *King Lear*, says, "It is universally admitted that the Prince of Darkness is a gentleman." Mendoza has compromised himself so far as to make a corporation out of highway robbery, and when Malone the billionaire acquires a chunk of Mendoza Limited, we can assume that the operation has been blessed, or cursed, with the Midas touch.

Near the end of the play Mendoza sets Tanner and himself apart from the other roles when he says, "Sir: there are two tragedies in life. One is to lose your heart's desire. The other is to gain it. Mine and yours, sir." Tanner immediately contradicts him: "Mr. Mendoza: I have no heart's desires." But Mendoza knows better, and so do we if we examine what Tanner says, how he behaves, what he writes in his handbook.

Shaw tells us repeatedly that Woman, as delegate-at-large to the Life Force, pursues Man in order to get children and security from him. Man, the hope for realizing Creative Evolution—at least, in his creative aspects, as the artist—would like to hold fast to his freedom. The fourth act does show Tanner, as pre-Bergsonian Creative Evolution, captured by Ann, the Life Force, and apparently made her prisoner. But is this what truly happens? Does Jack Tanner indeed represent Creative Evolution? Here we ought not to forget the comedy in the philosophy. Certain of Shaw's nudges in the epistle should put us on our guard, such as his acknowledgments to other artists: "The theft of the brigand-poetaster from Sir Arthur Conan Doyle is deliberate" (untrue: Mendoza is not much like the Conan Doyle figure) or "Octavius I take over unaltered from Mozart" (an out-and-out joke).

Why does Ann pursue Tanner? Why not Tavy? If all that Woman wants is to propagate the species, Tavy can serve Ann well enough, and he, unlike Tanner, is a self-proclaimed artist, if a trashy one. He says he adores her and swears he would do everything in his power to make her happy. He is also less likely than Tanner to take up with (or be taken up by) other women after marriage: this ought to appear as a positive virtue to a woman like Ann, who seeks a man she can hold on to. With Tanner, however, she admits that life "will not be all happiness for me. Perhaps death." To win Tanner lets her in for a struggle that drains her and brings to the fore some of the play's allotment of comic agony. In the last act, after "concentrating all her magic," she finds herself "coaxing—imploring—almost exhausted," then "suddenly losing her courage, with an anguish that she does not conceal," and "panting, failing more and more under the strain."

Ann has formidable quantities of charm, as we learn from the stage direction that introduces her: "Turn up her nose, give a cast to her eye, replace her black and violet confection by the apron and feathers of a flower girl, strike all the aitches out of her speech, and Ann would still make men dream. Vitality is as common as humanity; but, like humanity, it sometimes rises to genius; and Ann is one of the vital geniuses." Shaw insisted that the part be undertaken by a siren-like actress. He chose Lillah McCarthy as Ann's first incarnation. Why does this "vital genius" put her charm to so stern an endurance test? The reason is she knows that Tavy does not love her and that Tanner does. Tanner, she says at one point, "does not know his own mind," and she is right.

Tanner repulses her over and over. He calls her at different times a hypocrite, lioness, snake, and elephant and calls himself "the quarry instead of the huntsman." He proclaims his amazement when Straker tells him he is being pursued. But Tanner the reluctant dragon is in truth the coy wooer. He is sure of himself and sure of Ann's affection. Whitefield's will appoints him a joint guardian of Ann (at her instigation), but the trust is voluntary. Nobody forces him to accept. He says only, "I let myself in for it; so I suppose I must face it." With much the same double impulse, he rushes out of England in his car but leaves clues at every stop, clues that Ann (if nobody else) can pick up. He even does his best to scare Tavy away from her:

Thats the devilish side of a woman's fascination: she makes you will your own destruction. . . .

Of all human struggles there is none so treacherous and remorseless as the struggle between the artist man and the mother woman. Which shall use up the other? that is the issue between them. And it is all the deadlier because, in your romanticist cant, they love one another. . . .

Fool: it is you who are the pursued, the marked down quarry, the destined prey. . . .

Tanner is working up a fury of self-protection, but at the same time he is kicking a rival in the shins. Tavy, not he, is the artist and therefore the "prey" in this "treacherous and remorseless" struggle. Tavy, not he, bedevils himself by propounding "romanticist cant" about love. Therefore, let Tavy beware. Consciously Tanner will not admit he wants Ann. Unconsciously he keeps her on tap and the competition at arm's length.

Sometimes his desire comes almost into the open, but he describes it as a feeling from his past, dead and done with. When they were children, he tells Ann, "I wanted to brag to you, to make myself interesting. And I found myself doing all sorts of mischievous things simply to have something to tell you about." At another time he will concede that he still loves her—among other women—and then tie a disclaimer to the concessions: "Why, I am in love even with Ann. [That masterly *even*.] But I am neither the slave of love nor its dupe." Or he will instruct her to marry Tavy, confident she could not do so. Or he will claim that his childhood love for her has waned because of "the birth in me of moral passion." (He would like to think that the umbilical "moral passion" joins up with a Superman embryo.)

Yet it suddenly occurs to him that "the old childish compact between us was an unconscious love compact." She asks, "The love compact is over, then, is it?" He answers, "No: but the moral passion made our childish relations impossible. A jealous sense of my new individuality arose in me." All well and good—the embryonic Superman within beckoned him forward to a new destiny. But why does he keep her on a string by saying that the love compact is not over? He could snub her. Or be silent. Or surly. But he won't let her go.

While he is refusing to give her up—a double-negative lure—he keeps exerting a positive appeal. His witty talk and his heroic certainties about everything spellbind her. She cannot help saying, "What a shocking flirt you are, Jack!" The exclamation astounds him. He does not realize what he has been doing, speaking in a manner that impresses her while it shocks her (or because it shocks her), just as he did when he was a child. How can she believe him when he says the compact is not still in force? "Why are you trying to fascinate me, Jack, if you don't want to marry me?"

Tanner, not Ann, initiates the pursuit, keeps it alive, clinches it. After she has tried out every wile in her repertory, she is in "anguish" and "failing more and more under the strain." Her despair might seem to be a ploy, a last gamble. It is not, but it works. He instantly renews the flirtation.

ANN: Well, I made a mistake: you do not love me.

TANNER: (*seizing her in his arms*) It is false. I love you. The Life Force enchants me. I have the whole world in my arms when I clasp you.

Ann's line could have provided him with an out, but Tanner doesn't want one. He wants the Life Force to enchant him. He has willed the childhood love to continue, even to ripen. He leads *her* on. The Life Force is in him as much as it is in her. The struggle between the Life Force and Tanner's moral passion is internal, not a head-on clash between the sexes. For all his assured pronouncements against love in marriage ("the essential function of marriage is the continuance of the race, as stated in the Book of Common Prayer," and so on), for all his emphatic personal declarations ("I am heartwhole . . . . I havnt the slightest intention of marrying her"), for all his cold-blooded reformism, Tanner can no more qualify as the first agent of unsullied Creative Evolution than the other rebels in the play can. Since childhood he has been sullied by a heavy infusion of the Life Force. When the play ends he is about to be inducted once and for all into the social system he says he despises. He is, in fact, already a captive of it, thanks to his private fortune. A genuine Superman would have to be genuinely chaste—superhuman—and would have to remain or somehow work his way outside the system.

But Shaw does not let it go at that. Tanner has a mean streak in him. We tend to overlook his meanness because he fascinates people, us as well as Ann. Tanner's arrogation to himself of the social critic's function does not mean he is a paragon. Not a bit of it. This "megalomaniac who would be lost without his sense of humor" gets his hands on what he always wanted, Ann, but he affects to have been humiliated and lets out a tirade against marriage, domestic happiness, and weddings. It is funny, satiric, spiteful. Violet cuts in on him, but we tend to overlook her line, as we overlook his cruelty. She speaks "with intense conviction," and she says, "You are a brute, Jack."

Then there is the state Ann is in during this last scene. Her line, "It will not be all happiness for me. Perhaps death," is taken up again, with a slight variation, after Tanner "hauls her summarily to her feet." She says, "Yes, I feel strong enough now. But you very nearly killed me, Jack, for all that."[10] He has little thought for others. After one particularly nasty insult to her, he collects himself and says "remorsefully": "Forgive my brutalities, Ann." Then he offers as an excuse, "They are levelled at this wicked world, not at you." Maybe so, but Tanner is one of those self-righteous persons who say, "I can't help it; I have to speak my mind," and think they have given themselves license to say anything to anybody, however wounding. Tanner feels himself providentially superior to the rest of the world. Shaw puts this would-be Superman in his place, a married home, and dedicates the play to a critic.

Can this be called a happy ending? Tanner and Ann have each other, and she has told Tavy she means to "enrapture Jack." But what sort of a life will she have with him if he blames her for denying him the exercise of his moral passion? Mrs. Whitefield thinks Ann will be good for the bullying Tanner. But will Tanner be good for the charming Ann? Which has brought the other down?[11]

It is easy to laugh at Ann's stratagems, just as it is easy to feel for Tanner, if we picture him as a beleaguered quarry. But her coquetry hides the depth of her lasting, irrational, and altogether natural passion for him. Tanner is not a "bad" man; rather, his defects are petty. We distinguish him from the other quasi rebels by his ungenerous frankness, not by any grand flaw or bold virtue. His real reason for trying to dodge marriage is vanity: "I shall see in the greasy eyes of all the other husbands their relief at the arrival of a new prisoner to share their ignominy. The young men will scorn me as one who has sold out: to the women I, who have always been an enigma and a possibility, shall be merely somebody else's property—and damaged goods at that: a secondhand man at best." He has been "an enigma and a possibility" to the women. Do these words mean that Tanner is afraid of marriage, of coitus? Not exactly. He fears, rather, being seen by others as a man who surrendered to his desires. He has written in the handbook that "marriage is popular because it combines the maximum of temptation with the maximum of opportunity," and he does not want to be looked on as a man who took advantage of these maxima, who appeared to need coitus, that unsupermanly whim. It may well be this sexual vanity that has convinced him he has the makings of a Superman.

How well does Tanner's dramatic alter ego, Don Juan, fill the Superman bill? The hell scene is described in the epistle as "a totally extraneous act," a "pleasantry," and "not the essence of the play," deprecations that are belied by the scene's pertinence to the four acts of the main plot at almost every stage of the debate, by its rounding-off of their meanings, and by its inclusion in the third act, separated from the remainder only by Mozart, darkness, and new costumes.

Certainly the scene is a metaphor. Hell is a place very like suburbia, especially as the commercial theatre sees it, an agreeable realm where nice folk have all the space they can pay for as they worship the body and drool over romantic art. Its opposite, heaven, nurtures Creative Evolution and should perhaps be known as Creative Heaven. It encourages self-contemplation leading to self-understanding, the cultivation and accumulation of brain power. Only a person who chooses this trail to self-realization can master the Life Force and cease to be a coward when confronted by death. Life in heaven, creatively speaking, requires effort, discipline, self-denial, until the brain can be tuned like a fine instrument, until it does not have to yield to the instincts. Such a brain will have an "idea" to latch on to, and an idea can make brave men of cowards. In heaven, Juan tells Ana, "you live and work instead of playing and pretending."

The hell scene as a quartet (Shaw had something of the same passion that Nietzsche had for music), dominated by two of the instruments, becomes an *agón* between the activism of Juan's clangorous brass and the passivity of Lucifer's mellifluous woodwind. At stake in the debate are three souls. Two of them waver, but at last the Statue is seduced by the Devil away from the tedium of heaven, and Ana is rescued by Juan from hell, for the Superman needs a Lilith, an ancestral mother. The third soul, Juan's, is also up for grabs. Until now he has remained undecided in hell. The Devil's homilies nauseate him with their leave-well-enough-alone, picked-over wisdom. He is ready to move.

Juan is not Tanner. He enjoys an advantage over Tanner because of his self-knowledge. He knows that he wanted women and ran away from them. For Juan the better life will come not from changing the system from within but from escaping and changing himself, an altogether more drastic experiment. At the end of the debate he does abandon the system, hell, and goes off in quest of his higher self. His rebellion is personal. Tanner's is merely political. As Tanner has written in his handbook, "The need for the Superman is, in its most imperative aspect, a political one." Accordingly, Shaw offers us the chance to compare the personal and the political would-be Supermen.

Tanner relies for his theory of the political Superman on the fortuitous appearance, once or twice in the history of every nation, of a man (not a woman) who breaks the rules and will eventually sire children who drive out ordinary, inferior folk. Thus he writes in the handbook: "Until there is an England in which every man is a Cromwell, a France in which every man is a Napoleon, a Rome in which every man is a Caesar, a Germany in which every man is a Luther plus a Goethe, the world will be no more improved by its heroes than a Brixton villa is improved by the Pyramid of Cheops. The production of such nations is the only real change possible to us." Failing the spontaneous growth of "such nations," man's spiritual and physical improvement must be given an artificial fillip: "The only fundamental and possible Socialism is the socialization of the selective breeding of Man." Tanner has not quite formed his plan: "As to the method, what can be said as yet except that where there is a will, there is a way?" Still, " if a woman can, by careful selection of a father, and nourishment of herself, produce a citizen with efficient senses, sound organs, and a good digestion, she should clearly be secured a sufficient reward for that natural service to make her willing to undergo and repeat it. . . . Even a joint stock human stud farm (piously disguised as a reformed Foundling Hospital or something of that sort) might well, under proper inspection and regulation, produce better results than our present reliance on promiscuous marriage." Therefore, "a conference on the subject is the next step needed." Such a conference "will be attended by men and women who, no longer believing that they can live for ever, are seeking for some immortal work into which they can build the best of themselves before their refuse is thrown into that arch dust destructor, the cremation furnace."

So ends Tanner's handbook, without suggesting how these delegates will be chosen, or by whom, and who will be the judge of a "citizen with efficient senses, sound organs, and a good digestion," so that his persevering mother can be awarded a bounty. Is Tanner joking? Not entirely, although he does hope to startle fuddy-duddies like Ramsden. Is Shaw joking? Not entirely. He is creating a figure named Jack Tanner whose thunderclap ends with vaporous banalities: Where there's a will, there's a way. Hand out subsidies. Call a conference.[12]

In his list of potential Supermen, Tanner includes the dictators Caesar, Cromwell, and Napoleon, but we notice that his German representatives are Luther the preacher and the poet Goethe. His handbook was written too early for Kaiser Wilhelm or Hitler, but if he had put Bismarck in, he would have given the game away, and so would his author. No wonder Shaw was vexed that Tanner had struck some people as "the Just Man made Perfect." Before tackling Tanner and Juan, Shaw had devised his own Napoleon and Caesar. Everybody recognizes that he has a talent for giving body, brain, and eloquence to stage figures who seem larger than life. But these protosupermen are flawed. What the playwright has done, always by means of comedy, is to bring them down to life size from time to time without really shrinking their stature.

Shaw kept writing about incipient Supermen to the end of his career.[13] He found them appealing—and often dangerous because of that appeal—in that they could impose drastic measures on a populace while avoiding the debilitating procedures of democratic government. His Caesar is wise and clement, the antithesis of Lucan's malicious portrait. But Shaw announces himself as a practical person and a skeptic, not a hero-worshiper. If we read Carlyle into him too intently we shrivel the comedy. The real Caesar was a murderer. So is Shaw's Caesar, and it is appropriate that he ringingly says, "To the end of history murder shall breed murder, always in the name of right and honor and peace, until the Gods are tired of blood and create a race that can understand." This same Caesar subsequently approves of Rufio's slaying of Ftatateeta on the grounds that she is an animal of prey and that you kill such an animal: you don't judge it or take revenge on it; you dispose of it before it disposes of you. Caesar may have his idealistic moments and seem like an annunciator (if not a forerunner) of the political Superman when he speaks of the gods' creating "a race that can understand." But this race will not come about until "the end of history," and you can't go much farther forward in time than that.

Don Juan's personal Superman is not socially dictatorial like Tanner's political one. Juan is going to begin the evolution of man from within himself. Unlike the Devil and his followers, who are content to drift, Juan has set his mind to improving his mind, so that he may cast out all remnants of the Life Force and grow "omnipotent, omniscient, infallible, and completely self-conscious." Here's another appealing program: do-it-to-yourself improvement. The Statue says reflectively, after he has rejected Juan and a heavenly domicile, that there is "something statuesque" about the conception of the Superman. Of course. There is something about the Superman that makes each of us see him in our own image. He is "me" raised to the nth power, the worship of the political hero turned inward. If Tanner's theory gets perverted in our own time into "inspirational" plays, books, films, and television specials about Churchill, Patton, or a king of the Mob—those mushy tributes to other lives boldly lived—Juan's ambitions turn the worship of the popular hero inward as they speak to the incipient hero in oneself. Juan is a formidable dialectician, but he is easily, if unwittingly, mimicked by hucksters who promise a serene temper through Yoga, a better technique in bridge bidding, more delicately tuned artistic sensibilities by direct mail, less or more of a body, or perfect report cards for one's children. These promises make a competitive spirit in us itch.

As a conclusion for the hell scene, Juan's new-blown personal creed, self-awareness, is twisted by his first convert into conventional religious dogma. Ana cries: "My work is not yet done. (*Crossing herself devoutly*) I believe in the Life to Come. (*Crying to the universe*) A father! A father for the Superman!" The thoughtlessly devout woman dreams of herself in Christ. She is Ana become Mary. Juan's Superman will be weaned on seventeenth-century Catholicism— and Spanish Catholicism, the least tolerant.

Did Shaw intend us to see flaws in both these "Supermen"? Well, he did put them into his play, and he is a playwright before he is a philosopher, and his play is a comedy before it is a philosophy. Further, his characters are all his characters, and all his spokesmen. In the epistle he says that they "are all right from their several points of view; and their points of view are, for the dramatic moment, mine also."[14] If Shaw is, then, biased from all sides, so to speak, we do well not to put aside too speedily Ramsden's censuring of Tanner. Or the Devil's strictures on Juan. For instance, this one, spoken to the Statue: "Beware of the pursuit of the Superhuman; it leads to an indiscriminate contempt for the Human. To a man, horses and dogs and cats are mere species, outside the moral world. Well, to the Superman, men and women are a mere species too, also outside the moral world. This Don Juan was kind to women and courteous to men as your daughter here was kind to her pet cats and dogs; but such kindness is a denial of the exclusively human character of the soul." This is the only time we are told that Juan is "kind to women and courteous to men," and in this respect too he is no mere projection of the imperious John Tanner. They both look on others, however, as being less than themselves. Their yearning upward starts from a superior foothold. But we do not have to take the Devil as Juan's final judge. He feels sore at losing two subjects, and in his mouth phrases like "the exclusively human character of the soul" turn wet, if not sticky. Yet something inhuman does attach itself to Juan, apart from his chilly resolution (not unlike that of a driven businessman's) to "live and work instead of playing and pretending." The nature of this inhumanity has to do with the dramatic character of the hell scene, especially with its place, time, and modality.

Its place is nowhere, a featureless void conjured up out of the Spanish Sierras by the melody from Mozart and the "heavenly music" of Mendoza's doggerel, a fantastic setting one twist out of focus from the world of the Spanish golden drama but kept down to earth by a firmly satiric and realistic dialogue that matches the colloquies between Molière's Don Juan and Sganarelle. Somewhere in the offstage distance lies Creative Heaven, abandoned by the Statue, who considers it a nest of insufferable intellectuals. The scene's time is an ambiguous seventeenth century, the period of Tirso de Molina or Juan's, Ana's, and the Commander's legendary deaths (Ana has just died), but blended into the early twentieth century, the era of their modern counterparts and the subject of their discussion. In concocting this time warp Shaw gives us his parallel between the two societies that the Don and Jack respectively rebel against. As for the modality, that is even more ambiguous. This hell is a dream, and that heaven lies beyond the dream. But who dreams it? Not Tanner alone, for Mendoza wakes at the end and asks, "Did you dream?" Tanner punningly replies, "Damnably. Did you?" Mendoza says, "Yes, I forget what. You were in it." Tanner responds, "So were you. Amazing." This is not the kind of dream life envisaged by Strindberg in *A Dream Play* (written in 1901, the same year that Shaw wrote *Man and Superman*), over which "a single consciousness holds sway . . . that of the Dreamer." It is a joint dream, in which the other two principals, Ann and Ramsden, do not take part. To qualify for the celestial or infernal regions, however, the quartet must be dead. This is a dream about four ghosts who are past the fears of, in Juan's words, death and degeneration.

If we keep in mind this poetic-fantastic treatment of time, place, and being in the hell scene, we must distinguish the nature of its roles (and especially that of Juan, who is sometimes said to be Shaw's approach to or delineation of the Superman) from the nature of the roles in the enclosing four-act comedy. Tanner has too many defects to stand in for the incipient Superman, but Juan, who has fewer disqualifications, is nevertheless an incorporeal spirit drawn from literature and plunked down in an otherworldly landscape. We could look on him as the potential ancestor of the Superman only if he were still a man. As Shaw presents him, he is not continuous with mankind but a comic vision of a sort of demigod. We can look on Molière's Juan as a preliminary sketch for the Superman, if only because of his contempt for the conventions of his day, for the supernatural (the Statue), and for the immediate prospect of death by hellfire. But Shaw's Juan is another matter. He, together with the scene that holds him, is a caustic mockery of the Superman.[15]

That Shaw subscribed personally to many of Juan's beliefs does not invalidate what I am saying here. He frequently propounded the evolutionary power of the individual will with a persuasiveness that might have surprised Lamarck. But in a number of prefaces and in his theatre, whether it be *Man and Superman* or *Back to Methuselah*, the playwright reveals his skepticism about the possibility of a Superman's coming into existence. The skepticism is, broadly speaking, threefold. First, mankind starts out with too heavy a handicap, too far to go. Second, as Ra states in the prologue to *Caesar and Cleopatra,* while the world may have changed in some outward features during its occupation by people, people themselves have not drastically altered. Through the millennia they have remained morally static, and this is the substance of Shaw's argument with the neo-Darwinians. Third, the fortuitous appearance from time to time of a Socrates, a Christ, an Augustine, or a Teresa of Avila is no cause for self-congratulation, since, when a Superman of a sort materializes, men and women do not acknowledge the superhuman qualities. They may even act with exceptional cruelty in the face of a superior being who shames them and shows up their pettiness.

In *Saint Joan* Shaw meditated twenty years later on a nonfiction candidate, a historical saint who can claim some nearly superhuman qualities without sacrificing her humanity. Joan does not fear death or torture, only a life in prison, which would be a mockery of life, especially for her, an evangelist. She is hampered by no sexual longings, no traces of the Life Force.[16] But after this saintly hermaphrodite has proved her credentials, men (and Shaw does indict *men* here) burn her. Five centuries later, when she is safely out of the way, a threat and an embarrassment to nobody, the church that persecuted and killed her canonizes her. If she could return to life, as in the epilogue another Shavian dream—men would burn her again, says the ghost of the Dauphin. In 1920, the year of her canonization, as in the year 2000, we could not stomach another Joan. But will the Superman turn up once more, if at all, as a Superwoman? And if she is a dedicated virgin like Joan, how will she breed in the manner ordained in Tanner's handbook?

In dismissing the male candidates I did not reckon with a Superwoman, any more than Tanner reckons in his handbook with a woman artist. In this play Miss Ramsden, Mrs. Whitehead, and Ann's younger sister, Rhoda, are women we can safely dismiss out of hand, mostly because they consist of tiny roles in this gigantic play. But how about Ann? And Violet? We can probably reject them as well. Despite Ann's final ordeal, whether it consists of psychological torture or orgasmic excitement, and despite Violet's determination and both women's will power, blazingly superior to that of the men, they both, as Shaw makes plain, live by (or only slightly above) what Alfred Doolittle, about a decade later, would call middle-class morality.

It may be objected that by calling some parts of the play ironic or satiric or comic and by stressing Shaw's skepticism, I am bending the meanings of *Man and Superman* to suit some thesis of my own. The objection would be a fair one. It is possible to prove any number of theses from this play and also to confirm one of Tanner's maxims: "The golden rule is that there are no golden rules."

From what we know of his life and personality, Shaw the man embodied one of Creative Evolution's more successful attempts to prefigure the Superman. Yet forty-plus years after his death, literate public opinion has fixed him in the image of an epigrammatist with a swarm of bees in his bonnet, some of which—vegetarianism and antivivisectionism, say—we are increasingly admitting into our own hives. Or he is taken to be an "optimist" or a "meliorist" who constructed an elaborate intellectual contraption out of *idées trouvées*.

Because of his sense of humor, the good-natured chaffing, many commentators have failed to appreciate that his wit reaches below the lines and situations and quirks of role: it saturates the play's very grain.[17] Underlying the jest is the grim superjest. *Man and Superman* surveys humanity's chances of self-transcendence with a wry mistrust—but without gloom. Thanks to God's gift to him of overflowing comedy, Shaw devastates one of our loftiest aspirations without rancor. Creative Heaven remains accessible only as a dream of afterdeath. What, then, is left? Is Shaw, horror of horrors, a "negative thinker"? Not at all. Just as he shared many of Juan's beliefs, so he shared many hopes that Tanner gives voice to in the dialogue and pen to in the handbook. In his multiple personae as political thinker, historian, economist, spokesman on current affairs, and vestryman—the most eloquent of the Fabians—Shaw was insistently the naturalistic artist, with modifications. He could probably not swallow Zola's proposition that environment determines personality (I doubt whether Zola could swallow it whole), but meanwhile there was work to do in society: improving the environment might give men a fighting chance to improve themselves, but even if it did not, social improvement was a first order of business. Insofar as Tanner imagines himself a Communist in his ideals, he is on the right track. Unfortunately, he is Tanner, with Tanner's shortcomings. In the past one hundred years, owing to power-mad autocrats who posed as Communists, we have often seen the road to heaven paved with bad intentions. Jack Tanner is not cut out to be a wholehearted reformer, let alone a revolutionist. The social system already has hooks into him. In act IV it will claim him wholly. Let him play the gadfly all he wants. In thirty years he will be Roebuck Ramsden, or possibly he will go into Parliament as a radical and end up a well-meaning, Asquithian liberal, especially if he comes by a peerage through Ann's intercession. What Tanner lacks is the initial unselfishness that would make him renounce his position in society instead of trying to laugh it off ("I am a gentleman: I live by robbing the poor"). That is why Shaw shows us that Tanner went into marriage all too willingly, protesting to the last but still only "talking," still finding his reward not in better social conditions for others but in winning Ann and a derisive burst of "universal laughter."

By the late 1920s the Superman had found his way into comics.

DEPENDENCE DAY
Ah, Wilderness! by Eugene O'Neill

Let us now reverse the picture, and look at the other side of it; let us put ourselves in the midst of a democracy not unprepared by old tradition and new culture to participate in mental pleasures.
ALEXIS DE TOQUEVILLE, *Democracy in America*

When the Circle in the Square Theatre in New York, which goes in for classics of all vintages and rewarms them without reheating them, revived *Ah, Wilderness!* (1932) one cold February, its advertising campaign called the play "O'Neill's Valentine to America," thereby wedding a positive image to a seasonal come-on. We do not as a rule associate O'Neill's theatre with tributes to this country, much less to the imminence of spring, and though I hate to come down—slightly—on the side of darkness and bleakness, what we end up with in this comedy is a bouquet of roses that sports at least as many thorns as blossoms. Or even, to liquefy the trope, a toxic nectar.

To start with the name of the play: the author adapted it from Fitzgerald's famous stanza in which all the nouns, as in German, lead off with capitals:

A Book of Verses, underneath the Bough,
A Jug of Wine, a Loaf of Bread—and Thou
Beside me singing in the Wilderness—
Oh, Wilderness were Paradise enow!

There is not much difference between *Oh, Wilderness!* and *Ah, Wilderness!* other than the one vowel and a pursed versus an elongated mouth, although the *Oh* could connote passion, the *Ah* a mood of reminiscence that might be cheerful or might not. A wilderness does not strike us as an upbeat topic for a play. We could assume the word carries some irony, but irony usually goes the other way: an upbeat word threatens or includes something else, as in Beckett's title *Happy Days*.

The play, set in New London, Connecticut, opens on the holiday of holidays, the Fourth of July, in the year 1906. Despite the screens, hot-weather flies buzz into the house the second anyone opens a door. Outside, eleven-year-old Tommy keeps setting off firecrackers that make everybody inside jump. Apart from these trivial irritants, the atmosphere in the home of the Miller family breathes serenity, time out from work, but not altogether from domestic routine. In the supposedly hallowed spirit of Independence Day, the dramatic temperature will, from the first scene on, remain mostly low.

O'Neill does insert climaxes into the first three acts and the first two scenes of act IV, such as a squabble between Nat Miller, the good-natured editor and paterfamilias, and a neighbor, Steve McComber, who sells "dry goods" and whose daughter, Muriel, has received wildly affectionate billets-doux from Nat's sixteen-year-old son, Richard. A drunken and funny outburst erupts from Uncle Sid about lobsters, love, and liquor. Muriel, who has met Richard on the beach, very nearly walks out on him. These and other moments of tension or excitement are, however, for the most part soft-pedaled. So is the last scene of the play, which turns into an anticlimax when Richard and his father launch a man-to-man talk of the kind that is almost unimaginable today, but Nat grows suddenly abashed and the scene subsides into a reconciliation as Richard kisses his dad good night. Then Richard steps outside, meditating and looking, according to his father, "like a statue of Love's Young Dream." His parents kiss and move out of the moonlight "into the darkness of the front parlor."

This is a tranquil ending. Or is it? The critical consensus tells us that we caught O'Neill here in a mellow, nostalgic state of soul that enabled him to compose a comedy, for a change, and to close in on a typical and benevolent New England family of yore, not a closetful of misbegotten haters. The mood evoked in this 1932 work resembles that of Thornton Wilder's *Our Town,* written several years later. I would submit, though, that by the close of that play too we have been exposed not to the idyll of small-town America so often reproduced in small-town America's theatres but to small-town America's constrictions.[1]

As the curtain falls we can look back and ruminate over some of what the action and the story told about the family and others. The final embrace of Nat and his wife, Essie, may bring them together, but they never moved far apart. Nat, whom another figure in the play calls "a good scout," has in his personality a touch of the poet that responds to his son's adolescent, poetasting fervor.[2] More enlightened than the average father of the time (insofar as we know anything about that fictitious entity) and certainly more understanding than the parents in *Spring's Awakening,* he appears eager to please his wife, that is, not to displease her, although he sometimes fails. He used to swim well; now he has become "rusty." If we regard swimming as what it was for the playwright, an act of liberation, we might say that Nat now confines himself to safe, familiar waters. His daughter, Mildred, does more or less the same. She remarks that she doesn't swim "so awful far" [out] and that she likes the water "wonderful and warm" when she dips into it.

Mother Essie, who is still bringing up the last three of six offspring, plays Nat as the heavy: "Wait till your father comes home." But she ascribes the children's misdoings, as she sees them, to his influence. A woman trapped in domestic chores and cares, she has to give vent to her anxieties by nagging at the rest of the family. When she shifts from her dislikes to her likes, one of her favorite adjectives is *nice*. *Nice* has negative meanings, such as not causing discomfort or worry. She lives up to the socially authorized standard of a wife and mother. She has hardened into a pattern of fussy domestication. If she feels any larger discontents, she would not think of voicing them. To do so would not be nice. It is hard to interpret the clinch between her and Nat in the fourth act as much more than resignation to more years of the same, even after Richard, Mildred, and Tommy have departed.

The play also offers two love affairs: the senior one between Lily and Sid, which, after some roller coasting, does go astray, and the junior romance between Richard and Muriel.

Lily and Sid are already in-laws, the younger siblings respectively of Nat and Essie and already fond of each other when the play starts. They are possibly drawn together by sensitivity to received opinions of the time that an unmarried man of forty-five must be a drifter, while an unmarried woman of forty-two must be, well, unmarriageable. Nat and Essie call Sid "a card" and "a case" and "a caution." Sid makes people laugh to ward off their contempt or ridicule, but his formidable sense of humor needs alcoholic lubrication before it goes into gear. Describing how lobsters make love, or saying he invented them, or marching around the living room to his own rendition of "In the Sweet By and By," he breaks everyone up. When he recovers from a drinking jag, though, he turns remorseful and reverts to the naughty boy who "was always getting punished— and see what a lot of good it did me!" Sid, a free spirit when under the influence, has no place in that society except as a drunken buffoon and a caution—a role he feels ashamed of when sober.[3] He cannot hold down jobs; he has no prospects. He and Lily may perhaps "meet on that beautiful shore" or "in the sky by and by," but not in this particular lifetime.

Lily looks at first glance like a typically prim schoolmarm who advises her niece against indulging in excessive loops and flourishes in her handwriting and advises her brother and sister-in-law against encouraging Sid's clownishness, but she proves herself to be, in her own fashion, a nonconformist. She will not marry for the sake of becoming a married woman in order to acquire that much respectability and to escape from people's pity for what was then called an old maid. Richard thinks she has driven his uncle to drink, but he misreads her. Lily, a proud woman, will wed only a man she can idealize. Sid has let her down too many times. As some consolation, she may act as substitute mother to her students and to her nephews and niece, but she feels more like the Millers' boarder than a family insider. She and Sid will not finally make a match, but they may well strike us as partners in unfulfillment, if not undeserved sterility.

In the teenage pair, Muriel and Richard, we find a marriage ordained by local assumptions. An assured income and an assured level in the urban hierarchy—these represent the summit of parents' ambitions for a young fellow like Richard near the beginning of the century, as they do for most middle-class parents toward the century's end.

Muriel's mother, Alice, does not appear in the action. Still, we learn that she was a good-looking girl, like Essie. She picks through her child's underwear for paper she considers forbidden—lush love letters from Richard—much as Essie scavenges for Richard's scandalous books. Essie, in other words, stands in for both mothers. It happens that Muriel resembles Essie in being short, plumpish, attractive, and a scold. For Richard, passing time with his sweetheart is much like passing time with his mother. Muriel is similarly shockable: she doesn't like even mild oaths or smoking or people who drink or get out of control. Her first lines when she sneaks out of doors to meet Richard on the beach consist of reproaches: "I'll bet you'd forgotten I was even coming. . . . You might think of me for a change." More reproaches punctuate her dialogue through the scene. She doesn't want to sit in the boat or gaze at the new moon ("That's not much to look at") or stay out long, for fear of being punished. When she hears that Richard had an encounter in a tavern with Belle, a good-time girl, she wishes him dead. When he remonstrates with her, she bites his hand and tries to run away. Actually Muriel does not come across as quite the sourpuss I have made her seem by selective quotation. Rather, she is a young woman any man could have married in 1906. She acquiesces without question in other people's plans for her and Richard. She doesn't want to muddy any waters. She is suppressed and oppressed and repressed. Richard himself observes that she is "afraid of life."

He isn't. Yet. Richard has just about reached the age of—significant word—independence. As he tries with youthful courage and enthusiasm and a certain Cyrano-like panache to break out of the mold that Lachesis is weaving around him, he discovers the era's new literature of "pure" feeling and "sheer" intellectualism and sloshes around in it as ungovernably as his uncle Sid does in liquor. They form a notable contrast, these two. If Sid reformed, he would very likely turn into another desperately repentant proselytizer like Hickey in *The Iceman Cometh*. As it is, he will probably decline slowly into the Jamie Tyrone of *Moon for the Misbegotten*. If Richard were never to reform according to the lights of his family and community, he would grow into the Con Melody of *A Touch of the Poet*, a full-time poseur. As it is, he will probably wind up as someone like the Marco Polo of *Marco Millions* or as a Billy Brown, the commercially successful hero of *The Great God Brown*—but a Billy who manages at an early age to repulse a soul-invasion by the aesthetic and ascetic Dion Anthony. Richard has two chances to assert his independence and model himself on Hedda Gabler's admirer, Eilert Løvborg. First, he might make a night of it with Belle in or near the tavern, for she will accept even underage "johns," but he cannot bring himself to do so. The inhibitions imposed by his upbringing win out and confirm his loyalty to Muriel. Later, on the beach, before Muriel's arrival for their tryst, he stares at the moon, communes with nature, and feels half in love with easeful death, but instead of rowing away in the boat and the moonlight to the great shore elsewhere, he and Muriel sit in the shadows and settle his future. Vine leaves in *his* unruly hair? Not a hope. She will buy him expensive pomade to tame it, to flatten fur into glossy leather. She would like him to follow his father and three older brothers through Yale. In after years, if he doesn't watch out, instead of taking over his father's newspaper, he may slide, under Muriel's pressure, into running his grumpy father-in-law's business. Dry goods all right. He has already come by some of them in the form of Muriel. The married couple will purchase a house and cram it with kids and furniture, as his parents have done.

We learn from the first stage direction that the "fairly large" sitting room that accommodates much of the action has two bookcases in it, two double doorways, a screen door, a sofa, a writing desk and its chair, four more chairs, a big round table, three rockers, and three armchairs. With that many obstacles, even a room of, say, seven hundred square feet (twenty by thirty-five) would know acute traffic holdups and maybe occasional gridlock. It's no wonder Nora the maid has trouble serving dinner.

At this time, as airline announcements repeatedly say, we must alter direction briefly to introduce the play's one Norwegian and two Irish godfathers, none other than Henrik Ibsen, Oscar Wilde, and Bernard Shaw. Various other literary names crop up in the text of *Ah, Wilderness!* from Kipling and Swinburne to Carlyle and, of course, the Fitzgeralded Omar Khayyam, but Ibsen, Wilde, and Shaw seem to recur pointedly. Richard calls *The Ballad of Reading Gaol* "one of the greatest poems ever written." Richard is not given to understatement and dotes on the word *greatest*, but seldom deploys it inaccurately. Ibsen is "the greatest playwright since Shakespeare," a judgment with which any critics who know the drama since Shakespeare would concur today (if the judgment has any value in the first place), although today's critics (and teachers and journalists) are fond of hedging their bets on superlatives by inserting a *perhaps* that will temper the claim: "Perhaps the greatest." Richard finds Shaw "the greatest living playwright," which in 1906 and in English he unquestionably was. Richard owns two books by, as Essie has it, "that awful Oscar Wilde they put in jail for heaven knows what wickedness." Arthur, the brother still at Yale, explains, "He committed bigamy." Sid "smothers a burst of ribald laughter."

Arthur would be too young to recall Wilde's trial and death, but in the family the memory would still be fresh of the recent New York productions of *Ghosts* and *Mrs. Warren's Profession*. *Ghosts* had a reception slightly less frozen than the one it had provoked in London. William Winter, a leading critic of the day in the United States, described it as "a gem of decadence," but Richard owns a copy of Shaw's *Quintessence of Ibsenism,* which cites the London reviews in some detail. As a devout reader he must know that Winter's coldness did not measure up to theirs, which went right off the temperature charts and plunged into indecency. The American reviewers made up for their reticence, however, when they greeted *Mrs. Warren's Profession.* That play, says Essie, the amateur critic, was a piece of theatre "so vile they wouldn't even let it play in New York." She is thinking back to the previous October (1905), when the single performance of *Mrs. Warren* by Arnold Daly's company and a single performance that preceded it nearer home, in New Haven, and has slipped Essie's mind, had both been shut down by the police.

As a nineteenth-century homosexual and a seditious author, Wilde had personified a challenge to the type of family life conducted by the Millers and their neighbors. In *Ghosts* and several plays that followed it, Ibsen had written of the frustrations, even neuroses, the scandalmongering and petty enmities, and the subjugation of the women in similar, if smaller, communities in Norway. As for Shaw, he permeates this play of O'Neill's, not only in that Richard views himself as a Eugene Marchbanks from *Candida* ("Out, then, into the night with me," he yells as he "stalks out, slamming the door behind him," after a tiff with his mother) but also because, whether by chance or design—Lachesis again—he and his mother have the same names as two of the characters in *The Devil's Disciple.* This last play, Shaw's only one set in New England, takes place during the War of Independence. Its eponymous hero, Richard Dudgeon, goads the people of Websterville, New Hampshire, into resisting the English as he contends with his puritanical mother and other relatives. An orphan girl named Essie, continually irked during the action by being asked whether she is "a good girl"—*good* meaning pretty much the same here as *nice*—represents the youthful impetus of the revolution, America's young independence. Treated as something of a colonial possession by the Dudgeon family, Essie finally becomes recognized as a person in her own right and is given the last spoken line of the play.

Is Richard Miller in *Ah, Wilderness!* really the young man Eugene O'Neill once said he wished he had been, a remark cited in practically every published commentary on the play? What, O'Neill, who spent his active career striving to retain his spiritual and social independence? If we reconsider Richard's progression through the four acts, we see that his aspirations are quashed, but in the most gentle, disarming manner. He didn't want to go to Yale, but thanks to his father's affable insistence, he will. He didn't want to toe the line or have to hide his books. He couldn't make up his mind about Muriel, unless she behaved like an acolyte, a willing receptacle for his feverish messages. O'Neill could never have dwindled, or wished to dwindle, into the accommodating Richard whom his mother, in one of her echoes of Shaw, calls "a good boy." But in the Richard of act I, even with his extravagant manners, we may well glimpse the young

O'Neill—the Richard, that is, who proclaims, "I don't believe in all this silly celebrating the Fourth of July—all this lying talk about liberty when there is no liberty! The Fourth of July is a stupid farce!" From that point on, *Ah, Wilderness!* instead of being a frolicsome exception to the O'Neill canon, belongs to it securely, harmonizing with the tones and themes found in *The Hairy Ape, The Great God Brown, Strange Interlude,* and *Mourning Becomes Electra,* through to his adumbrations for the unfinished play cycle "A Tale of Possessors, Self-Dispossessed"—the greed and covetousness, the anti-intellectual and parochial yearnings for respectability, the hovering ghosts of guilt, missed opportunities, and other preoccupations.

If Richard is decorously stifled, what happens to the other roles, especially the women? At the beginning of the holiday Essie and Lily have no plans. They are at the disposal of the men. Nat and Sid go off to a picnic booze-up, Nat as a small release from his work habits, Sid to drown his woes at becoming once again unemployed. The women sit home and wait, and wait, and fret about the children and do the usual housework and cooking. When Sid returns he will fall asleep and forget his promise to take Lily to see the fireworks display. The teenage girls will slip into the same pattern of frustration as their female elders. Mildred must cut out the flourishes and loops that adorn her handwriting. Muriel must be protected from literature, ideas, and intimations of sex. In the tavern scene the scornful treatment of Belle by a bartender and a salesman echoes this attitude toward women as lesser beings. The fortunately married ones like Essie are worker bees whom the men mollify by letting them assume the airs of queens.

Thus, if *Ah, Wilderness!* emblematizes any sort of a valentine, it pays its love and respects to the playwrights O'Neill wanted to feel worthy to follow—in particular, Bernard Shaw—not to small-town America. In New England, he tells us, prudery and coyness have overtaken the yearnings for independence. Puritanism has returned in a cushioned, twentieth-century form. But O'Neill keeps his moralizing at such a soft pitch that it is hardly detectable. He does so partly by mocking Richard's overblown theatricality as he voices his early sentiments of rebellion, partly by suggesting a genuine underlying warmth in the Millers' feelings toward one another and partly by dispelling the generation gap in the closing scene between Richard and his father. All the same, for those who stay in that enclave of genteel smothering, the wilderness is going to have to remain paradise enough.

SOCIETY AS A BROTHEL
The Balcony, by Jean Genet

VERONICA (Eric): *Hello, last week on "Party Hints" I showed you how to make a small plate of goulash go round twenty-six people, how to get the best out of your canapés, and how to unblock your loo. This week I'm going to tell you what to do if there is an armed communist uprising near your home when you're having a party.*
The Complete Monty Python's Flying Circus

The man in general's full-dress uniform lies suspended between two chairs. In front of the chair supporting his feet, a beautiful young woman with red hair whinnies and, without leaving the spot, begins to trot like a horse. The General is a client at a brothel, pretending to be a dead hero. The Girl is a whore with equine and narrative capabilities. She imitates the General's red-maned warhorse, a mare named Dove who hauls his bier. She also describes the scenery along the funeral route:

THE GIRL: The procession has begun . . . We're passing through the city . . .
    We're going along the river. I'm sad . . . The sky is overcast. The nation
    weeps for that splendid hero who died in battle . . .
THE GENERAL: (*starting*) Dove!
THE GIRL: (*turning around, in tears*) Sir?
THE GENERAL: Add that I died with my boots on.[1]

The mimesis has charm. It delivers one of the most memorable vignettes in this memorable play, and it burnished the reputations of Arnette and Salome Jens, the sisters who successively played the girl mare in the first New York production. But why does the General pretend to be dead? If the man gets his thrills from taking on the status of a high-level officer, why not a live one? Is this his way of spiting the ungrateful world, of asking it, "Are you certain you'll be glad when I'm gone?" Is it an expression of the death instinct, repeated with or without variations every time he pays a visit to the brothel?

The General is not the only role in *The Balcony* (Le Balcon, 1956) who flirts with death and looks on it as a consummation of sorts. In order to examine the motif of death in the action and roles, however, one must bypass much of the ornate criticism that clings to Jean Genet and makes his writing seem little more than self-indulgent pranks. For his plays, like Pirandello's, have become a treasure house for the rococo critical imagination. As visitors bask in the heady atmosphere—the mirrors, the screens, masks, grandiose costumes and cothurni, the role-playing, verbal efflorescence, and parodoxes—they may well start to burble about the undecipherable nature of levels, dimensions, contexts, multiple images, loci, ritualism, identities, and infinite reflections and counter-reflections.

I will not counter with a no-nonsense interpretation of *The Balcony*. It does deal with pretense. It does include dressing up and make-believe on subsidiary stages. Mirrors do figure in six of its nine scenes. At the same time, brothels with amenities like the ones in this play exist. So do masochistic deviants (or "kinkies") like the General, who unbottle their fantasies there; so do madams like its proprietor, the stately lesbian Irma; and so do prostitutes like her assistant, Carmen, who dreams of a wholesome country life *en famille*. These figures are all society's outsiders, as are most of the other roles created by Genet, but the territory "outside" the regular social order is as real as that within and may even act as its distorting mirror.

In some respects *The Balcony* represents a modern approach to the documentary theatre. It is much more mettlesome than some later examples of "theatre of fact," and more factual.[2] Genet's brothel may have no direct historical antecedents; one of its sources is his own novel *Querelle de Brest*. Nor does the revolution in the play reproduce any particular revolution in history. But the brothel and the revolution are no less "true" for not having literal referents. Genet treats them as two historical essences, social foes, which he sends into unwonted battle.

The conflict becomes apparent in the early scenes. Four clients, the Bishop, the Judge, the General, and the Beggar, are strenuously playing out their "scenarios" in different studios within the brothel, but the clatter of machine-gun fire outside is audible: the revolution has begun to penetrate the brothel's isolation. Then a bullet smacks through a window and kills its only male whore, a beefcake type named Arthur. The bullet serves as an introduction to the revolutionaries.

They are a mixed group who have taken over a café for their headquarters. Roger, a humorless, unimpressive, fortyish plumber, feels sure the revolution can carry the day only if it "despises make-believe and complacency." He has fallen in love with Chantal, one of the women from the brothel who is now in the café with him helping to bandage wounds but proving inept as a nurse. The other leaders decide to put Chantal to better use. She will become the symbol of the revolution, a sex symbol. Because she has "learned the art of shamming and acting," they will paint her image on a flag and "invent a Chantal who becomes more and more fabulous . . . Invent a historic statement signed Chantal . . . [with] her voice on [at?] all the barricades . . . Her face on all the billboards." These other rebels do not worry about what the revolution stands for, so long as it wins support from the people. They want to barge into power, not to reform society. They offer their followers, not ideals and principles, but banners, battle cries, entertainment. The revolution turns into a sexual release: "Without the people's anger there'd be no revolt, and anger is a carnival . . . Let them have their fling. I've never seen such excitement: one hand on the trigger, the other on the fly. They shoot and screw." But this carnival depends on carnage. In its name people are killed in the streets. It grows so boisterous we could almost imagine that a client has staged it in one of Irma's studios.

Before the revolution begins to go downhill, it does make some headway against the state. Then the state allies itself with the brothel. An envoy comes from the court to see Irma and asks her and three of her clients to impersonate the Queen, the Bishop, the Attorney General, and the General, who have fled or been killed in the revolution or have otherwise vanished. Irma and her cohorts agree to do so under protest. When the time comes, though, they acquit themselves well in public. The people feel reassured about the stability of the state. Chantal is shot. The revolution slumps with her, its symbol, and dies. The brothel has won out over its antagonist.

By the end of the play, when Irma closes up for the night, another revolution has begun in the streets. The first one is only a memory, and the second will surely fare no better than its predecessor. Thanks to hindsight, we can understand why the first had to go under. Trying to compete with the brothel as a sex carnival, it found itself hopelessly outclassed. Roger, the one sincere revolutionary leader, the one man who despised the brothel, was himself corrupted by it from the start when he filched one of its women, Chantal.

The brothel, a capably run institution, is indeed a birthplace for make-believe, what Irma grandiosely calls "a house of illusions." But if that were all it meant to the kinkies who patronized it, they might as well have joined the revolution and indulged their kinks without monetary payment. In this case, Irma would have had to shut up shop, and the revolution would have won. But the kinkies know what they want, and only the brothel can supply it. This particular evening they take big risks going there. The streets crackle with rioting and shots, but bullets will not deter these gentlemen. They must have their couple of hours in a studio to capture the orgasm that eludes them at home.

Genet does not give us their case histories (except to say that the one who plays the Bishop is a gas man by profession), nor does he need to. All we have to know is that they risked their lives for a perverse orgasm. According to Wilhelm Stekel, such aberrants seek their satisfaction with an almost pious fervor. The piety is not surprising. Stekel associates the aberrations among his patients with religious constraint during their upbringing and with an excessive fear of God. He says that they "throw the conventions overboard, and create a conventional religion of their own which gives their sexual expression plenty of elbow room." He adds that fetishists, for example, are "seekers of God. They approach God by dark and devious routes."[3] The dark and devious routes include death. In the opening speech of the action, the man dressed up as the Bishop talks bluntly of "a skillful, vigorous heading toward Absence. Toward Death. God?" Here God is a conscious objective, if an equivocal one (that question mark), by way of death.

In his celebrated work on masochism, Theodor Reik similarly argues for a religious propensity in his patients: "I wonder how anybody can speak of [the masochist's] weakness, helplessness, and the effort to renounce [his] own personality. That would seem to be like denying courage to a martyr, who would rather burn than abjure his creed."[4] Much as the masochist will undergo all kinds of physical pain to achieve orgasm, so a zealot, who is what Reik calls a "social" masochist, will undergo torture and extreme humiliation for a cause he believes will fulfill him. Reik sees a streak, if not a backbone, of social masochism in the temperaments of saints and martyrs.

Genet takes for granted this confusion between sexual and social obsessions. In the brothel's studios the devotees abandon themselves to sexual consecration. The house of pleasure is a house of worship. In it each man finds a contrary, double satisfaction: he acquires a feeling of potency from the clothes and the role he puts on, and at the same time he debases himself in that role. Or rather, he debases the role and its garb in order that they may serve his sexual satisfaction. In other words, when swathed in the role's pretensions, he looks comic; debasing himself, he voluntarily undergoes agony. There is then an element of masochism in each of the aberrants' personalities. The Bishop likes to hear a recitation of sins that will discomfit him. The Judge licks the feet of the Thief he is supposed to be trying. The General glorifies and punishes himself simultaneously by enacting a scene in which he is dead and being drawn through the streets to his grave. The Beggar wears filthy clothes, a louse-ridden wig, and an abject expression while he is being whipped. But because they simultaneously abuse themselves *and* their assumed roles, we can detect an element of, if not sadism, at least defiance, in their patronage of the brothel.

From the first Genet commingles sexual and religious ceremonies. The opening scene sets the tone by introducing us to the Bishop in a studio set that represents a sacristy. He wears robes of exaggerated size so that he looks larger than human, like a principal in a Greek tragedy. He has stayed beyond the two hours he paid for. Now he pleads with Irma to be left by himself briefly without any extra charge. When she goes, he parades his episcopal image in front of a mirror and rejoices that he doesn't carry the responsibilities of a preconized bishop. He salutes his garments: "Rigid cope, you make it possible for the most tender and luminous sweetness to ripen in warmth and darkness. My charity, a charity that will flood the world—it was under this carapace that I distilled it." Beneath the cope he is masturbating, consummating, ending his ecclesiasticism with the flourish of an ejaculation.

Although we are led to believe that this Bishop is played by a gas man, we never see the gas man, whatever a gas man is (a meter reader? a clerical or some other minor employee of a gas company, as the pioneering director Antoine famously was for a time?). We see only the Bishop. There may be a shadowy gas man in the story, but there is none in the action; if a gas man in bishop's apparel differs graphically from a bishop in bishop's apparel, Genet declines to show us the difference. If we insist that this is a gas man metaphorically wearing a bishop's mask, that mask then has the same lineaments as the face behind it—or else it is transparent—or it is not a mask any longer but has become a face.[5] This figure looks like a bishop. He performs like a bishop. He talks like a bishop, sometimes flaunting an episcopal *we* in place of *I*. Even when he loses his temper and shouts, "Fuck the function!" or "For Christ's sake leave me alone. Get the hell out!" we wonder if bishops do not occasionally unbend in this manner.

An actor playing the Bishop has to play nothing but a bishop. Even if he perversely sets his heart on letting a gas man peep through in performance, the action will not support him. Much the same is true of the other patrons of the brothel. They seem to assume roles the way some tribesmen don charms, as a plea to heaven for virility and safety. But Genet shows us only the assumed roles, which are *the* roles. When the Judge crawls across the floor to kiss the feet of a very good-looking young woman, we are not reminded of the run-of-the-mill tight-lipped person on the bench. Still, this Judge is called Your Honor and correctly costumed.

The third client, the General, is a more complicated case. This time we see the character as a "timid-looking gentleman" before he dresses up. The woman who plays his aide (and later his mare) removes his civilian clothes and helps him into his uniform: "When he is completely dressed, he will be seen to have taken on gigantic proportions, by means of trick effects: invisible foot-gear, broadened shoulders, excessive make-up." This time we have watched the role being transformed. We must then ask Transformed from what? Previously he was a "timid-looking gentleman." Yet many true-blue commissioned generals, however fearsome on the battlefield (or more likely at the command post), are timid-looking when in mufti. Since he talked like a general from the start, he has transformed himself from a timid-looking general to a bellicose-looking general. He was a general all the time.

Similarly, in another scene we see a "little old man" put on a grimy wig. His act of gratification involves playing a beggar who is flogged. But what his non-beggarly existence consists of during the rest of the day we never discover. He could be another gas man. Or a bishop, a judge, a general.

In Pirandello's *Six Characters in Search of an Author* the six characters are actually in search of an audience.[6] An author may dream up the Father (or any of the other five), but it takes a spectator to recognize and acknowledge the actor in that role. The other actors do what they can to facilitate this recognition. The actor playing the Director treats the actor playing the Father *as* the Father, and the actor playing the Father reciprocates. Unless the acting is unusually poor, the spectators then follow the actors' leads: they recognize both the Director and the Father.

Genet introduces something like this reciprocity into the action of *The Balcony*. The Bishop's role needs an "opposite," somebody who will confess to him and whose sins he will absolve, somebody who will give him the opportunity to carry out his episcopal functions, somebody, therefore, who certifies him as the Bishop: a penitent. The Judge needs a criminal, the Thief, a young woman on whom he can sit in judgment—as he explains, he wants only to judge her, not condemn her—while the Beggar needs an oppressor with a whip, and the General requires his mare. But if the obligation of the opposites is to take the kinkies seriously and attribute roles to them, the young women playing those opposites seem unable to take themselves seriously as opposites. They keep breaking out of their parts and virtually winking at the audience: in the Judge's scene the Executioner does "exchange a wink with the Thief." These young women's roles never amount to anything but whore-playing.

Later in the play the opposites become dispensable. When the Envoy asks the kinkies to drive through the city in a coach as the "real" Bishop, "real" Attorney General, and "real" General, they feel nervous about abandoning their brothel scenarios and translating themselves from private images in Irma's studios into public images (which must be improvised, at that) in the world at large. But their squeamishness does not make them less "real," for any officially endorsed figure very likely feels nervous about appearing in public during riots. Their stage fright—for that is what it amounts to—is not at all unreal. When their public performance begins, the only doubt that arises is whether they will sustain their high ranks convincingly or look like kinkies.

In the absence of the brothel girls, the task of being a collective "opposite" or role-confirmer for these purported officials falls to the general public. We do not see this public, but we do learn subsequently that it accepted the Bishop, Judge, and General as real, without question. Possibly this public (in the story) was blinded by the "gold and glitter" that are said to have surrounded the dignitaries. In any event, it responded favorably, throwing flowers and cheers at them. It even blew them kisses. And why not? We, the other general public, have already attributed these roles to the kinkies: to us they have become what they pretended to be. Even if we wanted to, we could not interpret them as anything but bishop, judge, and general, because the playwright has given us nothing further to go on. When they appear in public, they do not change; they are the outgrowth of what they were from the beginning of the action. They have merely enriched their roles and presented them to a new, offstage audience, the new opposites.

Irma is another case in point. The Envoy asks her to stand in for the missing queen. She does, and successfully, assisted by her "splendid head, sturdy thighs, solid shoulders." More than successfully: she makes a better queen than the original queen evidently did because she is better-looking. Good looks enhance majesty. She does not, strictly speaking, however, transform herself into the queen by changing her role, nor does she need to. Even as a madam she has a queenly presence and authority, whereas the missing queen was a figurehead who spent her days, the Envoy explains, embroidering invisible handkerchiefs (like an actress in an uninventively directed play), sleeping, drying dishes, and picking her nose. Irma is not impersonating the queen but slightly extending her own personality. She is playing herself, and the Envoy, who later says she made a first-rate queen, serves as her opposite. As though to underscore this observation, at a certain place in the text Genet stops using Irma's name and starts to call her the Queen. It is the most natural thing in the world for this procuress to assume royalty.

What does Genet mean by this demonstration? That life is all pretext, appearances, theatre? I think he is driving us toward a narrower, sharper, and more satiric conclusion: bishops, judges, and generals are kinkies, queens are procuresses, opposites (the public) who take these figures at their dressed-up value and serve them are whores, revolutionary slogans and symbols (Chantal) are whoremongering. The author likens this state of affairs to the performance of a play. But Irma's final speech, which compares her brothel to a theatre, has come in for frequent, tortured misinterpretation: "In a little while, I'll have to start all over again . . . put all the lights on again . . . dress up . . . (*A cock crows*) Dress up . . . ah, the disguises! Distribute roles again . . . assume my own . . . (*She stops in the middle of the stage, facing the audience*) . . . Prepare yours . . . judges, generals, bishops, chamberlains, rebels who allow the revolt to congeal, I'm going to prepare my costumes and studios for tomorrow . . . You must now go home, where everything—you can be quite sure—will be even falser than here." She is not saying that life is less "real" than Genet's theatre (or her brothel) is. To claim this on her behalf would be to deny the play its application to life. She is insisting that there are more disguises and pretense in life than in the theatre and that in life the disguises are harder to penetrate. A play can show us, more clearly than a scrutiny of life can, what life is really about. It can reveals kinks and sham for what they are. It can do a sorting job, bring life into focus. It can make us laugh at these roles, until we realize we are laughing at ourselves. For if we have accepted what the play says, we are the people who make bishops, judges, and generals out of kinkies and queens out of whore-mistresses.[7]

Most of the criticism of *The Balcony* fastens onto other aspects of it, in particular the rituals, disguises, and mirrors, which are constantly held up as prima facie evidence of Genet's contempt for reality: his masks beneath masks, reflections within reflections, screens behind screens, and other infinite recessions.

Such critical sophistry makes the play look like literate escapism. Stagings based on such writing—and I have seen several—become intolerably mannered. The actors lose touch with the specific content of the action, wallow in their supposed roles-within-roles, devote themselves to portraying Genet as the champion of high camp, and, worst of all, fail to reckon with the boiling disappointments that underlie the comedy, an acute dyspepsia that darkens the play throughout and helps turn it into a dystopia.

For many critics Genet could be summed up in Sempronius's description in *The Apple Cart* of his late father: "He was a Ritualist by profession, a Ritualist in politics, a Ritualist in religion: a raging emotional Die Hard Ritualist right down to his boots." What is a ritual? It's a prearranged ceremony. A church service is a ritual; so is a public parade. So is taking a bath or sweeping a floor, so long as it goes according to plan and according to form. In a ritual, there are no hitches, no divergences from the timetable or program. If a horse in a parade kicks an onlooker or if one of the ceremonial figures passes out, that part of the ritual resembles theatre. But ritual is the opposite of theatre, just as the young woman who plays the Penitent is the opposite of the Bishop. She defines him, and ritual defines theatre. It marks one of theatre's boundaries by being what theatre is not: predictable, self-contained, formal.

Sometimes the theatre will introduce an imitation of a ritual, as happens in one scene of *The Balcony*. Shortly before the coach parade, the Bishop, the General, the Judge, the Police Chief, and Irma appear briefly on the balcony of the brothel: they "simply show themselves" to the populace in their ceremonial garments. The Beggar stands nearby. He has the only spoken line in the scene: "Long live the Queen!" Chantal comes into sight. We hear a shot; she falls and is carried off dead. The Bishop later reveals that he had her killed and then canonized, her image blazoned on the flag. Since the shooting was prearranged, the scene constitutes an imitation of a ritual sacrifice.

But the scenes in the studios do not imitate rituals; the kinkies cannot follow their standard scenarios. Irma keeps looking in (the Bishop has run twenty minutes overtime). Startling noises, such as a scream, break in from other studios. The principal conflict of the action—between the brothel and the revolution—cuts into each scenario with gunfire from outside.

Imitations of ritual in the theatre became voguish in the 1960s, and some critics elected Genet to lead the ritual contingents. He has said that he does not create "characters," by which he evidently means stage figures whose behavior accords with a limited quantity of background information. As for the screens, disguises, and mirrors, these are part of a device that Genet uses theatrically, not ritualistically. Far from telling us that nothing is real, they tell us that in the brothel, as in the playhouse, everything is adaptable. The screens, for instance—bloodred in the Bishop's studio, brown in the Judge's, green in the General's—

simplify the setting, characterize it, and close off the rest of the studio from view, while reminding us that it is a studio. The distortedly large clothes reinforce each kinky's impression that he is what he pretends to be. He can gauge the effects of the clothes on his opposite, or he can look down at his chest and shoulders and knees and drink in reassurance.

Or he can stare at himself in a mirror. Irma thoughtfully provides a mirror for each studio. The bishop gazes into his and is smitten with his image. Before he masturbates, he says to the reflection: "In order to destroy all function, I want to cause a scandal and feel you up, you slut, you bitch, you trollop, you tramp." Until now he has not tasted the power of being a bishop. He uses the image in the mirror for erotic stimulation, yet even as he does, he appeases his power-lust by profaning the robes and "destroying" their "function."

The Judge, too, has a mirror available to him, but he does not use it. Instead he looks at bulgy Arthur, the male whore, and talks lovingly to him as though to an idealized version of himself, heavy with tangible musculature: "Masterly mountain of meat, hunk of beef that's set in motion at a word from me! (*He pretends to look at himself in* [*Arthur*].) Mirror that glorifies me! Image that I can touch, I love you . . . You're all there, my huge arm, too heavy for me, too big, too fat for my shoulder, walking at my side all by itself! Arm, hundredweight of meat, without you I'd be nothing." The "mirror" is again an opportunity for self-love. In the Bishop's scene the self-love affects to be desire for a woman ("You slut, you bitch"); in this scene it masquerades as homosexuality.

The mirror in the General's studio has the same purpose. Admiring his image in it, the General sees shining back at him a historical validation: he is the hero of Austerlitz, Napoleon vanquishing the Austrians. Unlike Napoleon, however, he has no Moscow, Waterloo, and St. Helena in his future. He is dead and going gloriously to eternity without a defeat. He is the model of a modern general, an untainted victor, because he is dead: "What is now speaking, and so beautifully, is Example. I am now only the image of my former self." Before the "cortege" sets off, "he bows to his image in the mirror." This is the necrophiliac version of self-love. As in the two previous scenes, the kinky loves his image in the mirror because what he sees there is himself transfigured.

As an element in the stage design, the mirrors have a further purpose: suspense. Each one is angled to reflect to the audience part of Irma's room. We will not see that room until scene v, but the mirrors forecast it. They alert us to Irma's omnipresence as the brothel's grandmistress, and they hint at the immensity of the premises.[8] The mirrors, then, do not scatter the effects. Nor do they, as some critics maintain, reduce the play to "nothingness," whatever that is.[9] They do the opposite. By reflecting the studios and Irma's room to each other, they enlarge the brothel and unify the scenes. They also enlarge the studios: mirrors make a room look artificially more spacious.

Genet's language serves as another agent of enlargement and ratification. The Bishop says, "We must use words that magnify." Most of the roles do. Their speeches move effortlessly out of conversation and into clusters of imagery. Genet sometimes handles images the way Shaw handles logic, with comic hyperbole. By exalting the dialogue, raising it beyond simple meanings, he frees it from the constraints of everyday banter and attains a sumptuousness, a verbosity that can impound complicated states of consciousness. One example is Irma's long speech about her brothel. She sees it as a universal refuge, each client's respite from each day's boredom, his glimpse of self-fulfillment, his hoped-for reality, and perhaps a quicker outlet to death and its attendant glories. Irma inaugurated the brothel, and she will reinaugurate it every day, but it does not exactly belong to her. Her clients make it what it is, real estate she does not quite control. It is unreal estate. To Carmen, she says:

I'm only the manager. Each individual, when he rings the bell and enters, brings his own scenario, perfectly thought out. My job is merely to rent the hall and furnish the props, actors, and actresses. My dear, I've succeeded in lifting it from the ground—do you see what I mean? I unloosed it long ago and it's flying. I cut the moorings. It's flying. Or if you like, it's sailing in the sky, and I with it . . .

Darling, the house really does take off, leaves the earth, sails in the sky when, in the secrecy of my heart, I call myself, but with great precision, a keeper of a bawdy house . . . When secretly, in silence, I repeat to myself, "You're a bawd, boss of a whore-house," darling, everything (*suddenly lyrical*)—everything flies off—chandeliers, mirrors, carpets, pianos, caryatids, and my studios, my famous studios: the studio known as the Hay Studio, hung with rustic scenes, the Studio of the Hangings, spattered with blood and tears, the Throne-room Studio, draped in velvet with a fleur-de-lys pattern, the Studio of Mirrors, the Studio of State, the Studio of the Perfumed Fountains, the Urinal Studio, the Amphitrite Studio, everything flies off: studios—Oh! I was forgetting the studio of the beggars, of the tramps, where filth and poverty are magnified. To continue: studios, girls, crystals, laces, balconies, everything takes it on the lam, rises up and carries me off!

It is as if Irma wants to regard her property as a merchandising operation, a department store of sex anchored in familiar surroundings, but it defies her and becomes airborne, a balcony absurdly hanging in the high atmosphere, like the General absurdly hanging between his chairs or a moon spinning independently and mocking the earth below. And it really does turn. As a scene in one studio finishes, a turntable carries the setting off to the right and brings on the next, shaped like a pie slice, from the left, while "the same chandelier" reappears over every scene.

In all, the brothel has thirty-eight studios, "every one of them gilded, and all . . . rigged up with machinery so as to be able to fit into and combine with each other." Irma's office or room has immediate access to each studio. The brothel thus seems to resemble a vast, rotating movie lot with the sound stages distributed around the hub of Irma's office.[10] Genet does not provide a full list of the studios, but if we visualize each "slice of the pie" as a miniature of some activity outside the theatre and brothel, the brothel is a miniature of society as a whole. The mirrors in each scene reflect the miniworld to itself.

In the accompanying diagram, I have not included anything like all the thirty-eight divisions within the circle that represents the brothel but have only tried to show how each studio stands for, or at least subtends, a segment of society on the outside. The studios, identified in the inner circle surrounding Irma's office, reflect segments of social activity, indicated in the outer circle: the Bishop and Penitent's studio, for instance, represents officially sanctioned religions, whereas the General and the Mare's studio depicts defense ministries and armies. The twenty-three other studios not explicitly identified on the diagram comprise the Rose Garden Studio, reflecting parks and tourist attractions, the Chamber of the Sands, representing exile, and twenty-one unnamed studios, portraying industry;

sport, domesticity—you name it. The reader is invited not to accept my equivalents of these segments of society but to feel free to reinterpret each one with the aid of personal biases.

As a satire of society *The Balcony* laughs at men in authority as they seek for images of themselves that they can love. It laughs more bitterly at men without authority who defer to those images (attribute them) and even worship them. Both groups are taking part in a game. X names himself a judge or bishop or general. He drapes himself in an awesome outfit, grows confident from the feeling of being dressed up (literally suited) for his role and from the sight of magnified reflections that enlarge him spuriously in the eyes of other men. His old self or personality fades away.

The games are what gives the play its thematic continuity, games such as I'll-be-bishop-and-you-be-penitent. But they are games played in earnest, games propelled by desperate intent, games that are liable, because of their peculiarities, to invoke the unexpected, games of life and death. The Bishop begins by masturbating or "playing" with himself; he ends by wishing to play with other men's lives, to move them about like chess pieces: "Instead of blessing and blessing and blessing until I've had my fill, I'm going to sign decrees and appoint priests."

As an arena for games, theatre plays by heightening its effects.[11] In his playhouse-brothel Genet takes this heightening to a personal extreme. He pours into his drama a sumptuous language, bulks out his conceptually big roles with padded costumes, and seizes other theatrical opportunities, such as keeping visible that token of the post-Renaissance indoor theatre, the chandelier.

As part of the heightening procedure he plants contradictions in the characters' desires: they feel pulled between playing games of sex (the mastery of themselves, themselves as analogues of musical instruments) and games of authority (the mastery of others, others as "played" instruments). Genet unites the contradictions, without trying to resolve them, in an ingenious way. He implies that power over oneself and power over others can be achieved simultaneously by playing games of death. In the early scenes he seems to show us the brothel as a theatricalization of life, of real life, with a real bishop, judge, and general giving rein to their all-too-real kinks in order to live at the top of their bent. But there are plenty of hints that death is a more attractive game for them to play than life is. The General mimics it. The Bishop speaks of it. So does the Judge, when he reminds the Thief that she could annihilate him if she wished: "You need only refuse—but you'd better not!—need only refuse to be who you are—what you are, therefore who you are—for me to cease to be . . . to vanish, evaporated. Burst. Volatized. Denied." All three kinkies will later be photographed in official poses, wearing official grimaces. They do not need to circulate in public now that they have established themselves as living beings; they can die or disappear, and the photographs will move around in their place.

The others expire too. Beefy Arthur has already gone. He took a bullet in the brain and is now a corpse, "truer than life," lying in splendor on a black fake-marble slab. He was, as the Envoy says, "meant for grandeur," grandeur in death. Chantal had to die in order to be apotheosized: out of an image of whoredom and revolutionary vulgarity, she has metamorphosed into a saint blazoned on the national flag. Irma, even, has "died," at least her personal self has. In becoming the Queen she finds that her being is made rigid, imprisoned by her public function.

THE QUEEN: Nothing will ever again relate to my person alone? Nothing concerning me will ever again be able to happen to others?
THE ENVOY: (*curtly*) Quite.
THE QUEEN: Every event of my life—my blood that trickles if I scratch myself . . .
THE ENVOY: Quite, Madame. Each event will be written with a capital. And now . . .
THE QUEEN: But that's Death?
THE ENVOY: It is indeed.

At last the turn comes for the gaudiest figure in *The Balcony* to play the game of death. He is the Police Chief, Georges by name, the ultimate provenience of power in the state. He is also Irma's intimate, her ally, Pericles to her Aspasia. Georges wishes to make himself immemorial, to discover—as the Bishop, Judge, and General have already done—an image of himself that he can love. He has been advised to let one image of himself as an executioner be promulgated, and another circulated in the form of "a gigantic phallus" as tall as himself. The first, the executioner, could be said to represent his power of death over others; the second, his power of death over himself, since the six-foot organ is detached, lifeless. In alarm Irma objects to the phallus: "Although my house is reputed for its imaginativeness, it's known for its decency, and for a certain tone."

Genet's exquisite irony intensifies. Georges decides that his ideal memorial, his death-in-life, would be for somebody to impersonate him in the brothel. While the impersonator mimics him, he will mimic death by disappearing to "wait out the regulation two thousand years," the equivalent of the Christian era—so far. The two millennia will sanctify him, much as the church (the Bishop), the law (the Judge), and the military (the General) have been sanctified by the two millennia since the death of Christ and the decline of Rome. He will, we assume, mimic resurrection as well when he feels like it, and reemerge as top dog in the state.

There is one handicap. Who voluntarily imitates police chiefs? As Irma points out, "My dear, your function isn't noble enough to offer dreamers an image that would enshrine them. Perhaps because it lacks illustrious ancestors?" This is true. We remember certain bishops, judges, and generals, often the cruelest ones, and we certainly remember many queens and whores. But how many police chiefs do we find in history books? The policeman has to yield, when it comes to glory, to the master detective or the master criminal—or the person who contrives to be both, such as Vidocq, whom Balzac celebrated as Vautrin. Fortunately for Georges, Roger, the defeated revolutionary, comes into the brothel expressly to impersonate him. No sooner is he inside a studio (which is got up to look like a mausoleum) than Roger is awarded his opposite, a slave, to attribute to him the role of police chief. But Roger is still secretly a rebel. And in him the revolution twitches its final, futile defiance.

He ends his scenario by making "the gesture of castrating himself." With this gesture he hopes to mutilate the image of the Police Chief as a man of power. Roger then goes off, having bloodied Irma's mausoleum carpet. The idiot has performed his task by denaturing himself. For the purposes of the play he is dead. And his gesture has gone askew. Trying to discredit Georges, he has succeeded only in becoming Georges's opposite, an impotent, and in confirming Georges as a man of power. What looked like Georges's peripeteia is actually Roger's. Georges could not be happier. His impersonator finally came. His image will be enshrined in history as a man so potent that somebody felt it necessary to geld him in effigy. Better yet, he is physically untouched: "Well played. He thought he had me. (*He places his hand on his fly, very visibly feels his balls and, reassured, heaves a sigh.*) Mine are here. So which of us is washed up? He or I? Though my image be castrated in every brothel in the world, I remain intact."

Georges, Genet's most savage portrait in the play, is so unmanned that he cannot play out his own fantasies. He must wait until somebody does the job for him by proxy—anybody, no matter who, an avowed revolutionary if necessary, just so long as *he* doesn't get hurt. Now he can retreat into his two-thousand-year hibernation. A studio has been prepared, a mock-up of a tremendous lump of architecture still in the planning stage. It incorporates law courts, opera houses, railroad stations, pagodas, monuments. It will consist of one mountain on top of another, and that on top of a third, and on the peak, "a tiny diamond sentry-box." The Envoy says: "He who gets it will be there—dead—for eternity. The world will center about it. About it will rotate the planets. It will no doubt be the most imposing funeral-pile in the universe. From a secret point of the third mountain will run a road that will lead, after many and many a complication, to a room where mirrors will reflect to infinity—I say to infinity!—the image of the dead man. To infinity—and for eternity—in the depths of a vault." The triple mention of "infinity" has sent some commentators into their own infinities. But this edifice is no less than a magnification of the brothel, right down to the mirrors. Like the brothel, a floating balcony, it will "sail in the sky" on top of its mountains. Here Georges's image will live on with its wound, while he plays the game of death in a brothel mausoleum. The image will evoke the images we retain of other symbolically castrated heroes: the shorn Samson, the blinded Oedipus, Philoctetes and his rotting foot, Christ crucified.

A magnified image in a magnified brothel—like all official statuary, ludicrous. So much, says Genet, for your saints and heroes.

DIONYSOS IN SUSSEX
The Norman Conquests, by Alan Ayckbourn

A long furlough, a real holiday, and a wholesome, simple way of life will do wonders.
TH. D. VAN DE VELDE, M.D., *Fertility and Sterility in Marriage*

A principal if passive player in Ayckbourn's trilogy *The Norman Conquests (Living Together, Table Manners,* and *Round and Round the Garden,* 1973) is the home, viewed from the outside at the opening of *Round and Round the Garden* as "a Victorian country vicarage-type house with terrace and doors leading directly into the sitting room."[1] The grounds at the back, "once obviously well laid out," are "now wildly overgrown," thanks to the neglect of an aged gardener. Situated in Sussex, probably on the chalky topography of the Weald, an hour or so by car south of London and a shorter distance north of the Channel, it betrays none of the remote, stylized chill of the house in *Desire under the Elms* or the antique friendliness of the thatched Surrey cottage in *Mrs. Warren's Profession.* Its "vicarage-type" aspect lends it a primness that sorts ill with the former personality of its owner, a widow who now lies inert in an upstairs bedroom but whose alert life "was centred around men. . . . When they lost interest in her, she lost interest in herself." She once picked up a sailor on the beach at Weston-Super-Mare and a Polish rear gunner while her husband was away in the armed forces during World War II. Now—the year is 1973—she spends chunks of her waking life absorbing novels of exquisite banality that she insists on having read aloud.

This unnamed matron with a possibly psychosomatic ailment has three offspring. Her oldest, Reg, an estate agent, or realtor, who loves games, riddles, and jokes, married Sarah, who is devoid of any sense of fun and whom the old lady never liked. Sarah strives to repay the dislike by behaving like a correctly affectionate, if not quite devoted, daughter-in-law: she has an entertainingly perverse sense of duty and, with Reg's cooperation, two children, aged seven and five. The older of Reg's sisters, Ruth, a successful business executive, is the best-looking person in the family, according to Reg, but she will not compromise her looks by wearing glasses to correct her nearsightedness. She has a sharp wit and needs it to counterattack the philandering and other predations of Norman Dewers, whom she married five years earlier. Norman, a latter-day Dionysos, masquerades as a "gigolo and assistant librarian." During his and Ruth's previous visit to the house over the Christmas holiday, seven months before, Norman was found rolling on a rug, making love to Annie, the younger sister of Reg and Ruth. Annie lives in the house all year. Like the youngest child of tradition, she has become the aged parent's slave, feeding her, "lugging her in and out of bed, single-handed, day in day out" for the past five years (since Ruth's marriage, which seems to have coincided with the mother's collapse?), and tending to her mother's other wants, including the reading of spicy gobbets from romantic fiction without the option of lowering her voice in embarrassment.

The sixth of the trilogy's characters is Tom, a veterinarian slow of speech and slower on the uptake. He lives nearby and continually visits the house on the pretext of treating the resident cat's ailments but actually to keep Annie company and let her serve him meals.

Five of the six roles appear at first to be straightforward, comic-farcical types loaned—virtually cloned—from familiar theatrical forebears. Sarah looks like a nagging and exacting hausfrau, Reg a downtrodden spouse, Ruth an icy career woman, Annie a frumpish virgin, and Tom a dimwitted rustic, an updating of the "looby" from Molière and the Restoration. Norman, less scrutable to start with, remains a shifty soul. He initiates the play's action. His Christmas romp on the rug encouraged him to tempt Annie into an assignation. They would spend a "sordid weekend" on their own in Hastings, where—we recall the magic number 1066 and all that—William the Conqueror defeated King Harold and began the original Norman conquest. The sextet, five of whom begin as cartoons, take on surprisingly protean shapes as they interact in the warren of subplots.

In Ayckbourn's other experiments with form, such as the three acts of *Absurd Person Singular*, which take place in different kitchens on three successive Christmases, we watch him manipulating time (and unavoidably space, because of the nature of the time manipulations) consciously and with dazzling ingenuity.[2] With *The Norman Conquests* "I decided," he explains in a preface, "to write them crosswise. That is to say, I started with Scene One of *Round and Round the Garden*, then the Scene One's of the other two plays and so on through the Scene Two's." The spectator remains in the dining room for the whole of *Table Manners*, some of which takes place at mealtimes, in the sitting room for *Living Together*, and out of doors for *Round and Round the Garden*.[3] The author specifies the time for each scene, breaks each play into two acts, and breaks each act into two scenes. In combining the scene equivalents with the "crosswise" or lateral design of his construction, we can visualize his scenic arrangement for the entire trilogy (see table). Because certain of the scenes overlap in time or even coincide on the clock (10A and 10B), an actor who leaves the stage usually walks into another play.

Ayckbourn wrote for audiences who consisted mostly of summer visitors to Scarborough's seaside lures:

When I first considered the trilogy, I was aware that it would be optimistic to expect an

ACT AND SCENE	TABLE MANNERS	LIVING TOGETHER	ROUND AND ROUND
I.i	Saturday, 6:00 P.M.(2)	Saturday, 6:30 P.M.(3)	Saturday, 5:30 P.M.(1)
I.ii	Sunday, 9:00 A.M.(6)	Saturday, 8:00 P.M.(4)	Saturday, 9:00 P.M.(5)
II.i	Sunday, 8:00 P.M.(8)	Sunday, 9:00 P.M.(9)	Sunday, 11:00 A.M.(7)
II.ii	Monday, 8:00 A.M.(10A)	Monday, 8:00 A.M.(10B)	Monday, 9:00 A.M.(11)

Note: The numbers in parentheses indicate the overall chronological order of the scenes.

audience like this necessarily to be able to give up three nights of their holiday to come to our one theatre. Any suggestion that it was essential to see all three plays to appreciate any one of them would probably result in no audience. . . . Similarly, were the plays clearly labelled Parts One, Two and Three, any holidaymaker determined to play Bingo on Monday would probably give up the whole idea as a bad job. The plays would therefore have to be able to stand independently—yet not so much that people's curiosity as to what was happening on the other two nights wasn't a little aroused. Second . . . it should be possible to see them in any order. Third, since we could afford only six actors, they should have that number of characters. Fourth, ideally they should only have two stage entrances since that's the way our temporary Library Theatre set-up is arranged (but then this is common to all my plays).

He did finish with three self-contained plays, and they certainly make dramatic sense seen in any order. I am not sure I could differentiate them satisfactorily, except by referring to emphases on certain roles (Ruth and Tom put on theatrical weight in *Round and Round the Garden*). Ayckbourn himself, with the hindsight of repeat performances, discerns "a distinct atmosphere" developed in each one.

The schematic elements, always present in Ayckbourn's theatre, here include four scenes for each play, a three-day weekend that tightens as it rolls forward (five scenes for Saturday, four for Sunday, three for Monday), a balance of three male and three female roles, and a dramatic logic that is nigh on tragic (or farcical) in its finality. The schematics offer us the reassurances of traditional form. But the total work has an organic progression because the schematics do not become tediously repetitive and predictable, as happens often in plays and novels that have a large cast individually and instantly identified by tag lines, speech patterns, stances, idiosyncrasies of dress, physical peculiarities, or mannerisms. Even with characters who verge on being types, Ayckbourn's plotting engages them in encounters that seem spontaneous, rather than calculated, and blithely confound our expectations.

In any case, because they mesh so neatly, the three plays lend themselves to interpretation as parts of a single superwork that came into being because the playwright evidently found himself with too much material on his hands to compress into one digestible or quaffable absorption. It's likely that in the two decades since *The Norman Conquests* was written some enterprising producers have followed the example set in New York in 1975 when selected performances unfolded the entire work in one matinee-into-evening—as has similarly happened from time to time with *Man and Superman* and *Strange Interlude* and with Peter Brook's version of the *Mahabharata*. I for one feel convinced that, given an ergonomic seat, clear sightlines, a feverish technical crew, meal breaks, and coffee intermissions, one could get more out of such a one-shot exposure than out of the three-part split.

The dominant genre of this triple-threat work is rueful comedy, which benignly mocks the characters as they reveal themselves. Seldom does this comedy froth up and spill over into farce, as happens in some other Ayckbourn plays. Fragments of comic substance derive from lines aimed with intentional wit by Ruth ("Other people's marriages are invariably a source of amazement") and Norman ("Is this lettuce leaf all for me? I can hardly believe my good fortune"), although when Norman ventures into ecstasies of self-pity they too become laughable, whether or not he means them to be—and he probably does. Reg tries to arouse laughter with his gags, but the punch lines have a way of turning soggy as they fall on uncomprehending ears, such as Tom's. The most appreciative response Reg probably wins is a strained smile. Tom suddenly remembers the one joke he knows, but he tells it so uncompellingly that the others continue their conversations across his snatches of recollection, and he never gets to complete it. Sarah indulges in sarcasm, much of it aimed at her mate. It never goes beyond melodrama toward a startling home truth. Annie doesn't come across as an object of laughter, either when she is a victim, a guise in which the other women have cast her, or when her rage loosens under stress and she lets unwonted insults fly.

Annie's role, which occupies more stage time than any one of the other five does, seems the tamest in the trilogy, lengthy gray stretches relieved by bursts of passion, but it incorporates several transformations, one of them a treat for the audience when she swaps her "very old sweater, button-up and too large, jeans and gum boots" for a dress and puts on makeup—a variant on the Hollywood secretary or store assistant who takes off her glasses. Norman, like a Hollywood beau, spots the change instantly, because he always realized she could be beautiful, if not sexy, though it leaves Tom pondering why she looks different. But if she is to hold her own against the exaggerations built into the rest of the dramatis personae, the role of Annie needs great helpings of brio as well as some bravura backing by the others in the cast.[4]

Still, as I have already argued, this is less a study of isolated and perhaps forlorn individuals than a comedy of interplay. It has something of the charged but laconic vernacular of Pinter (especially the unanswered questions) and N. F. Simpson and, before them, the fizz of the French well-made plays of nineteenth-century middle-class drama and their British derivatives, as well as the antisentimentality of Goldsmith and Molière and reminders of the checkered dialogue and comic agony of Chekhov. Here and elsewhere, Ayckbourn takes his time uncovering plaintive depths in the relationships as well as in the individual souls, while never soaking them in eye-brine.

The following discussions of the interplay among the three couples may imply here and there that residues of the roles carry over from one scene to the next in which they appear (as they often do), and that each role hovers intact over the entire play (as it does not). I do not subscribe to the overall psychologizing of parts, and any sentences in these chapters that seem to do so come from the inescapable generalizing or even flattening entailed in order to avoid writing a promptbook. If pressed, I would insist that one can make almost no deductions about the roles other than what is said and done, scene by scene, in the action, plus what is alluded to in the story.

That apologia duly entered, I begin with Sarah and Reg, the two who have been together longest—eight years—citing some of what goes on between them. Norman meditates about what doesn't go on between them:

NORMAN: What's inside you, Reg? Apart from twelve bowls of cornflakes? What do you feel with Sarah? Do you sometimes feel like saying to her, no this is me. The real me. Look at me . . . (*Reg finishes his cornflakes.*)
REG: I'll tell you something, Norman. You're a nice bloke. You've got your faults but you're a nice bloke but I think you must be the last person in the world I ever want to have breakfast with again.

It seems safe to say that Reg finishes his cornflakes before replying because he means to offer a studied nonreply. Does he, on reflection, have the disquieting feelings Norman mentions or anything like them? If he does, he surely refuses them admittance to his surface consciousness; he would not dare entertain them, much less splash about in them, as Norman might do. Reg tells Sarah nothing personal. At best he puts up with her, obeys when she tells him to wipe the dishes or bring suitcases into the house or go into another room and collect any object he sees there for no reason that makes sense to him. At worst he rebels mildly. She yells at him; he yells back; she hurls a tin of water biscuits at him. He hurls nothing back, not even an affront. He flees. After she behaves coldly toward Norman, Reg warns him: "Got a long memory has Sarah. It'll be a few months before you're back in favour." Norman answers lightly: "Ah well. I'll try and win her round."

REG: No chance. You'll be told when you're forgiven and not before. She doesn't talk to me for days on end sometimes. Amazing how she remembers to keep it up. I mean, if I have a row in the morning, when I come home in the evening I've forgotten all about it. Until I open the front door. Then it hits you straightaway. Atmosphere like a rolling pin. Know what I mean? She's got great emotional stamina, my wife.

NORMAN: So have I.

REG: You'll need it. Good luck.

Several pages later Sarah bids Norman a warm good-bye. A perplexed Reg notices: "She's forgiven you very quickly, hasn't she?" But as we know from a corresponding scene in another play, or will learn if we see the trilogy in a different order, Norman "won her round" when he cheered her up, kissed her, and promised her a weekend in Bournemouth, a resort west of and slightly upscale from Hastings. When did it occur to Reg to take Sarah to Bournemouth—or any other seaside spot? Not since before their marriage, when they visited Hastings. He would accept at face value her complaint about being too busy with the home and catering to him and the other two children.

Reg has a love of play that extends to inventing board games. If they are four-handed, like his current one, an elaborate crime pursuit (two cops, two crooks, and a police superintendent who can see around corners), the games arouse among the other three players sensations that range between yawning tolerance and passionate apathy. After the game founders on Saturday evening when the others become preoccupied with hating one another, Reg utters the bewailing curtain line: "Won't anybody play with me? Please." This is a game that "took me months to make," but after the Saturday fiasco he confides to Sarah he has dreamed up a liberating improvement: "I think I've adapted it now so I can play it on my own."

Sarah doesn't give a hoot about the game—nor about Reg, an observer would think. Here is one relationship that remains fixed through the trilogy, at least from Sarah's point of view: Reg exists to service her in one way and another. She cannot be bothered to answer his remark about his precious game. The reason may be that she craves to get home as fast as possible. Why? To spend what is sometimes called quality time with the children? No: to spend Monday going over "the house from top to bottom" in preparation for Tuesday's visit from the cleaning woman. Elsewhere she speaks of "that dreary little house of ours," which is far from shopping and doesn't offer a glimpse of "a tree once in a while" in what must be a built-up section of London, as she wonders how her realtor husband could not find them a congenial place to live. Yet Reg, who takes playing with the utmost gravity, and Sarah, a confirmed houseworkaholic, are inseparably matched opposites. It was Sarah's idea that they go away this weekend in order to free Annie: in other words, so that Sarah might have the pleasure of freeing herself from housework at home in order to take over as many domestic chores here as she can uncover, from popping periodic medication into the old lady with callous efficiency to cooking, washing dishes, and determining places at table.

The next couple, Ruth and Norman, go through bouts of acute possessiveness and jealousy (both initiated by him), followed by forgiving and indifference.

RUTH: Norman, what is going on here? What are you up to?
NORMAN: Since when have you cared what I'm up to?
RUTH: Well, I don't normally. You know you're perfectly free to come and go. Not that I could stop you. But I do object to having my Saturday nights ruined.

Ruth, we notice, returns Norman poor satisfaction to his petulant question whether she cares what he does. The Saturday night that he has ruined she would have dedicated not to rest or pleasure but to work—along with the Sunday and Monday to follow. She claims she has reports to submit to the firm or she will be fired, and he agrees that her salary pays the household expenses: "All right, I'm a kept man. A married ponce." But he comes "bursting into my office when I'm seeing clients," she says, and behaves "abominably when I bring business friends home to dinner," and even scrawls "obscenities over my business papers"—all of these misdemeanors performed, according to him, because he loves her.

Norman's impudence has few bounds. He implies that Ruth is to blame because he, the neglected waif, was so starved for company that he made a date to take her sister away for this weekend. In their earliest exchanges he misses no opening for a rebuke. She asks Reg about his family and Norman points out that Reg has left the room:

RUTH: Oh. Well, I was only being polite. I haven't seen him for ages . . .
NORMAN: You haven't seen anyone for ages. Why don't you wear your glasses?

Or after she mildly suggests terminating their marriage if Norman is as miserable as he claims, he pounces on the legalistic word *terminating* and launches into hyperbole.

NORMAN: Is that how you've seen us for five years? a legal contract? Some marriage. No confetti, please—just throw sealing wax and red tape. Do you take this woman, hereinafter called the licensee of the first part . . .
RUTH: Norman, I can't go into all this now. Is there any sugar on this table?

NORMAN: And this man hereinafter called the donor and sole giver.

When Norman informs her that he had intended to go off for the weekend with Annie not to Hastings, where no rooms were available for booking, but to East Grinstead, Ruth, instead of breaking out in scandalized jealousy as Sarah would do in similar circumstances, laughs freely.[5] Yet precisely twelve hours later the two of them will snuggle on the very rug where Norman snuggled with Annie, make love, and then sleep together for the night, thanks in large part to Norman's wiles. (Whether because of his sexual friskiness, heavy drinking, or a relaxable temperament, Norman is the only figure in the play who sleeps well.) Although Ruth has gone into business and, from the sound of it, into its least risky area, accounting, she was once the adventuress of the family. Maybe she still is. Despite her casual breakfast talk about terminating the five-year marriage, she goes along with it and tolerates Norman's attentions to her sister and sister-in-law without undue grinding of teeth. She was the child who distanced herself from the family: she could not (and still cannot) abide her mother, "that evil woman upstairs"; resolutely walked out of this outer-suburban home, which is "like a brown museum. A very dirty brown museum"; and has remained childless by choice. Norman, by contrast, appears bent on keeping his affections within the circle of in-laws. Neither emotionally nor intellectually has he anything in common with them, and he goes to some trouble to establish that they are mentally inferior to him. Yet he returns to a family he is not related to by blood as deliberately as Ruth escapes it and, at the same time, suffers him to become her strongest link to it. In certain respects they suit one another down to the—well, to the rug.

The third couple, the unconsummated one, quivers with questions. Will Tom or won't he? Should he after three years say something committal to Annie? Should he even ask her if she wanted him to invite himself to go with her to Hastings? How exactly will he phrase whatever it is he decides to say in order to counter what he well understands to be his verbal ineptitude? On Saturday evening, when he first learns that she is going away for the weekend but doesn't yet know with whom, Tom offers to drive her to the village bus stop. But after a conversation with Norman, who advises him to adopt a disdainful loftiness, stop letting her take advantage of him, and even give her "a bit of the old boot . . . the metaphorical boot"—not the caveman treatment—and then after she tells him, "You're boring, slow-witted, dull, and utterly stupid," Tom responds with synthetic fury.

TOM: The next time you're planning holidays for two, if you want me along,
    perhaps you'd be good enough to be polite enough to ask me.
ANNIE: You've got a hell of a nerve.

TOM: And anyway, if you want to be seen with me, you'd better smarten your-self up a bit. You're a mess, you know. You look like something that's fall-en off a Post van.

ANNIE: I beg your pardon? . . .

TOM: I'm going home. I'm fed up. Just count yourself lucky I don't belt you one and give you rabies.

And he strides out. Can these two bumblers catch hold of a happy ending? For a while, it looks out of the question, But even after two outbursts, the breach may be closable. Annie says: "I don't know why I'm so mean to him sometimes. It's just when you're fond of someone—you worry what other people think of them. You want them to be something they're not capable of being. Which is very unfair on them really. I mean, he's Tom, isn't he? That's one of the best things about him. He's always Tom. He never pretends. He never puts on an act for anybody." Tom is certainly "not capable of being" someone who rises to hints, even seductive ones. When they have a little interlude together at the end of the weekend and Annie confesses gingerly that she will have to sell the house some-time and move to a smaller one in Essex or Norfolk or Northumberland, he remarks, "Bit off the beaten track," which Northumberland assuredly is. The best consolation he can afford is "Well, if you do sell it, give me first refusal, won't you?" He watches "curiously" while she smashes a plate in methodical rage.

After his excruciating hesitations and her heavy promptings, Tom does final-ly propose: "Would you like me to marry you? I would. Like me to marry you. May I? I want to," whereupon Annie finds she doesn't know. He will have to wait until she has "had a chance to—go away somewhere. And think about it." Norman has just renewed his pledge of a weekend together; she may as well see how that pans out before making up her mind about Tom. Besides, now that Tom has actually asked, she may be having an attack of the shivers at the prospect of living with him. When he proposes, he comes onto the stage "laden with a very heavy coil of rope." Does that weighty rope say something to her about their joint future?[6] Are marriage's proprietary rights, if any, worth a close life with this fond plodder, this obtuse teddy bear? As the deferred proposal comes almost at the end of the third play (if we take them in the usual order), the snatch of con-versation leaves Annie and Tom in kinetic balance. Their "relationship"—a word that became in the 1970s a synonym for an unmarried couple—will continue unaltered for the indefinite present. In such a state they are, if not quite compat-ible, not quite mismatched, either.

Of the fifteen duets that are possible between these six figures, twelve take place across the three pairs to supply some of the most heated scenes and beats. In gen-eral, the three women antagonize one another more than the three men do. At first Tom and Reg both say they like Norman. But when Tom suspects that Norman is being impolite to Annie, he threatens him with bodily harm, and when he hears Norman say Ruth is as dried out as an old tea bag, he thinks Norman is talking about Annie and takes a poke at him. There is a neat touch of irony here. Most of the time Norman gets away with sneering at the other two men, confident they will not realize he is patronizing or demeaning them. At times he appears to be asking for trouble and escapes reprisal only because his targets are too dense to take offense. Then Tom socks him for the wrong reason.

Tom, the only nonrelative, has come to be accepted by the others, partly out of deference to Annie, as a fixture in and around the house. He is handy, paints the ceilings, fixes a car, and has a knowledge of medicine. Sarah, who finds him "a trifle ponderous," reminds him to exert some initiative, and he nods as if he knows what she means. Ruth calls him "that limp man." But they both hope he will stop dithering and bestow a firm pledge upon Annie. Norman resents Tom for getting in the way of the weekend affair. But then almost everyone gets in Norman's way, Norman included. Out of those twelve possible duets I have picked five that galvanize some of Ayckbourn's more vivid scenes, all of them executed with dramatic concision. They consist of subplots between Annie and Sarah, Ruth and Tom, Norman and Sarah, Norman and Annie, and Norman and Reg. Norman comes in for the most attention because he not only jolts the play forward but also periodically stirs it up and elicits someone's disapproval.

If Annie does not feel desperate about securing a husband, Sarah oozes desperation on Annie's behalf, busying herself to seclude Annie and Tom as often as possible. Sarah considers an unmarried woman like Annie or a married and childless woman like Ruth an anomaly that may somehow discredit her own upbringing and existence. Sarah's fussiness and her determination to rule, to assert order, and to secure peace (however hard she has to fight for it) bother her sisters-in-law.[7] Annie is less openly unsympathetic than Ruth; she would probably never call Sarah "Mother Doom," as Ruth does when Sarah goes into one of her sulking fits. On the first evening, and in the play's most sustained duet, Annie lets Sarah pump her for information. Sarah strives to be understanding and au courant. She knows Annie is off on "a nice dirty weekend somewhere," which "we all need now and then, don't we?" But she assumes Annie's partner will be Tom. Annie warns her:

ANNIE: It's awfully sordid. You're sure you want to hear?
SARAH: Of course I want to hear.
ANNIE: It'll shock you.
SARAH: My dear, I've been married for eight years. I've had two children. I think I've just about seen everything there is to see. I defy you to shock me. I honestly defy you.

With this last speech Ayckbourn sets Sarah up. She is asking to have her bravado challenged: she becomes a Falstaff, a miles gloriosus. We expect the shock to overwhelm her all at once, but the author introduces it by degrees: she is deflated slowly as Annie, giggling with mixed shame and delight, tells her first about Christmas on the floor ("It was just wham, thump, and there we both were on the rug") and then about East Grinstead with Norman, not Tom. In an indignant explosion Sarah vents the shock she expected not to feel. She yammers about "all the trouble" she has gone to disposing of the children for the weekend and "delegating responsibility for the 'Bring and Buy Sale' which I'm sure will be a disaster because I'm the only one among them with any sort of organizing ability. And Reg has had to cancel his golf." The shock, we imagine, is complete. But the kicker, the real windup for this scene, will be withheld until Sarah finds Annie and Norman embracing. She screams, "Deceitful little whore!" and "You're just like your mother" and "Dirty little slut . . . slut, slut."

The Ruth-Tom duet hinges on a misunderstanding, that old standby of comedy and farce. Tom proves to be the source or the object of nearly every misunderstanding in the trilogy. He finds Ruth sitting on the side of a folding chair, instead of on its seat.[8] The truth is, she cannot see the chair properly to figure out how to unfold it, and she refuses to put on her glasses not merely because of vanity but also because she claims they "press on [her] sinus passages" and make her sneeze. Tom, ever polite, sits on the side of another chair. Before long, he gets to asking about Annie, fearing that he may be "in her bad books," because the previous evening he "told her to straighten up," said "she looked a mess," and "threatened to belt her."

TOM: I haven't slept a wink. Do you think I've damaged my chances?
RUTH: Chances of what?
TOM: I don't know. Just general chances.
RUTH: Well. Some women do respond awfully well to that sort of treatment. They enjoy tremendously being told they look a mess. And they actually thrill to the threat of physical violence. I've never met one that does, mind you, but they probably do exist. In books. By men.

After Tom mentions that he likes her appearance better when she wears her glasses, Ruth borrows her husband's technique to unburden herself of some of the frustrations of conversing with the well-meaning, tactless oaf. She seeks a spontaneous reaction. What would he say if she told him she hates him? that she loves him? if she were to strip and dance naked (keeping her glasses on) and flash "messages of passion and desire," and "hurl you to the ground, rip off your clothes and we would roll over and over making mad, torrid, steaming love together. How does that grab you, Tom?" Tom, flabbergasted, takes the sarcastic supposition as a literal recital from Ruth: she has been "carrying a torch" for him. A few minutes later, when he sees Norman and Annie kissing, he takes his revenge on Annie and, as he believes, reciprocates Ruth's crazed love for him by seizing and kissing her to assure her that he loves her. Reg stands by, "greatly amused" at the two hugging pairs. Sarah enters with a tray, drops it in horror and cries out, "Stop them. Somebody stop them."

If Tom has no inkling how to approach a woman, let alone court her persuasively—he amounts to a bucolic Englishman's nightmare reflection of himself—then Norman, prey to an unrelenting sexual hunger, has developed a seductive technique the other sex finds hard to resist. Through his vessels there courses the blood of Don Juan and numberless other seducers. The women in the trilogy, Ruth among them, disapprove of Norman, but he repeatedly quells their misgivings with two magic spells from his repertory: "I want to make you happy" and "I love you," that last one the age-old plea of men, especially in films and television drama, to the women they are deceiving.

His duets with Sarah start out frostily. As soon as she finds out about his projected tryst in East Grinstead, she urges him to leave Annie alone and to go home. On Sunday morning at breakfast she, Annie, and Reg decline to speak to him because of his wild behavior on Saturday night after he imbibed most of a bottle of "rather lethal" dandelion wine, and he has to exercise his ingenuity to trick them into answering him—an excuse for the author to show off this hero-villain, after a delayed entrance, as an inventive and unfazable monologist. One scene and two hours later, when she comes upon Norman embracing Annie while Ruth fights off Tom, Sarah lets fall her tray and composure. By the next scene in the trilogy, which takes place on Sunday evening, she begs him not to act up because she has had "a lot of nervous trouble in the past" and she gets "these rashes up the insides of my arms."[9] She is ready to appeal to Norman's better nature, in case he has one, and he is ready to exploit their shared experience as the two in-laws of the family.

NORMAN: Your trouble is you're over-emotional.
SARAH: Very possibly.
NORMAN: You're like me.
SARAH: Are you sure I am?
NORMAN: We feel. We've got nerve-endings sticking out of our heads. We've no cynicism or scepticism to act as shock absorbers. Everything that is, that happens becomes part of us. We're probably a new race. Had you thought of that? Born too early.
SARAH: All I'm saying is, if there's too much noise, I get these headaches.

Norman makes his next move on Monday morning, when, between slices of "cold and flabby" toast and jam, he volunteers to take Sarah to Bournemouth, where "I'd give you a great time."

SARAH: I can just see us going.
NORMAN: I'd very much like to make you happy.
SARAH: Pass the jam, would you?

Between pensive mouthfuls of jammy toast, Sarah inquires, "Were you thinking about my health? . . . When you mentioned about this holiday? Did you want to take me away just for my health?"

NORMAN: Well, that came into it. There might be any number of reasons.
    I'm easy. (*He smiles.*)
SARAH: So long as I know. (*She smiles.*)

With Annie, too, Norman plays the game of pretending they are the only two people in the family (perhaps in the world) who truly understand each other. He proclaims himself an old-style romantic when she calls him quaint, but he clearly is at least as much an exponent of physical love as of chivalric, hands-off devotion. Annie savors his physicality when she tells Sarah, "He says it was uncontrollable animal lust" that drew him and Ruth together, but "it's died out now. They are like two empty husks." Ayckbourn deliberately makes fun of Norman's tropes, but I believe we are supposed to see, as in Tom Conti's television performance, that Norman speaks to the three women, and especially to Annie, with a fervor that will not be gainsaid.[10] But how can he be sincere if he speaks to all three women with fervor? The answer: he plays each moment with as genuine an emotional stake in his pleas as that of the actor assigned to him. He can beg Ruth to take the day off to spend with him, and after she consents, he can sneak a last minute with Annie to promise her he will phone her for a new date, and within minutes, he can cause the car accident that will strand him at the house for at least another day with Ruth and Annie and Sarah—as if to vindicate his boast to Reg: "That's what I'm like inside. That's my appetite. That's me. I'm a three a day man." He means what he says when he says it. He may even mean what he says when he intentionally lies.[11] The dramatist does not take sides or play favorites. Norman's passion is real—and comic.

NORMAN: You'd be happy with me, wouldn't you? You'd be happy?
ANNIE: Yes.
NORMAN: (*moving to embrace her*) Oh, Annie . . . Oh God. (*He is entangled
    in the brambles.*)

His comic agony flows freely when he drunkenly confides in Reg, who has no idea what he is getting at and who makes Norman look as laughable as the brambles do when they have the chance. "On a night such as this," Norman says, all the "old base instincts of primitive man, the hunter, come flooding up. You long to be away—free—filled with the urge to rape and pillage and conquer."[12]

NORMAN: It's suddenly come to me, this tremendous idea. It's terrific. Let's all of us—you, me, Tom—let's take a couple of weeks and just go. . . .
REG: Where were you thinking of going?
NORMAN: Everywhere. Let's see everywhere. Let's be able to say—we have seen and experienced everything.
REG: We'd have to be going some to do that in two weeks, wouldn't we?
NORMAN: I've never really looked before, you know, Reg. These kids today, you know, they've got the right ideas. This world is my world and I'm going to wrap my arms right round it and hug it to me.

For the time being, he wraps his arms around Reg: "I love you, Reg. I'm not ashamed to say that to my brother." Reg shakily fends him off with "That's good news, Norman, yes."

Ayckbourn has extruded laughter from leaning three yearning women against three men with arrested development. Annie feeds Tom; Ruth puts up the money to sustain her alliance with "the slob I married"; Sarah keeps Reg and their family in order (or nervous disorder) and has whipped Reg into shape as a home helper. Ruth yearns less than the other women, although her adoption of the orphanlike Norman suggests a taste for the unorthodox that sorts ill with her stern career. The women cannot do much for one another, but there is some purposefulness in their choices. They may even have made more fated matches, for better or for worse, than Katherina did with Petruchio and Juliet did with Romeo.

The Norman Conquests gives us less thoroughgoing a vision of modern man and woman as implacable adversaries who cannot escape each other, who cannot—but must and do—live together than we find in the subsequent *Bedroom Farce*. But the trilogy evokes comparable guilt, accusations, and disappointments over lives that should have yielded more fulfillment. Every one of the roles reveals flashes of suspicion that life, somewhere out there, has more to explore if only one took the trouble to track it down and find out where "somewhere out there" is. Ayckbourn conceives of another of his middle-income, lower-middlebrow households and into it injects a spirit of mischief, of appetite, of spontaneity, a figure who is, to coin an awkward word, "abnorman." In spite of his occasional earthiness, Norman grows unfathomable, as a Dionysian creature should be:

NORMAN: I love you.
ANNIE: Oh, Norman . . . When you look like that, I almost believe you. You
  look like a—what are those things . . ?
NORMAN: Greek gods.
ANNIE: Old English sheepdogs.

What is such an extraordinary creature doing plunked down amid these five ordinaries? They do not comprehend what they are dealing with, and the enacter of the role should not seem to show them by exceeding the bounds of decent unself-consciousness, for in the end they will spurn him.[13] He engineers an indefinite postponement in everyone's departure by smashing his car into Reg's.

RUTH: If I didn't know you better, I'd say you did all that deliberately. . . .
NORMAN: Give me one good reason why I'd do a thing like that?
RUTH: Offhand, I can think of three.

The point of her casual "if I didn't know you better" is that she doesn't. If this book-bred Dionysos had come along a generation earlier, he might have teamed up with the now-prostrate mother, who was his counterpart. But the three women in the action, whose defenses evaporated in the face of his offensives, carry their assortment of agonies over the present and future, over work, home, marriage, and nonmarriage, away from him—into the house and another, unwritten play. They would not believe him even if they had stayed to listen to his, and the trilogy's, final line: "I only wanted to make you happy." The monotony of their existence does not allow for happiness, only for dreams of happiness, its nonpursuit.

SUMMARY
Pain in Hiding

If the plays in the first segment illustrate tragedies and melodramas that conceal comic potential, then the ones in this second segment illustrate wit—some boisterous, some gentle, some satiric, some bitter—that conceals, or doesn't quite conceal, the experiences of agony. To this foursome we could add Anouilh's *Ring Round the Moon*, Benavente's *The Bonds of Interest*, De Filippo's *Filumena Marturano*, Guare's *The House of Blue Leaves*, Horváth's *Tales of the Vienna Woods*, Mamet's *Glengarry Glen Ross*, Pinter's *Old Times* and *The Homecoming*, Rostand's *Cyrano de Bergerac*, Sartre's *Kean*, Schnitzler's *Reigen* and Bentley's reworking of it as *Stage 2*, Stoppard's *Jumpers*, Synge's *The Playboy of the Western World*, Thomas's *Under Milk Wood*, and almost all of Shaw's full-length plays, especially *Captain Brassbound's Conversion* and *Heartbreak House*.[1]

Some of these plays could comfortably follow one of the recipes for tragicomedy: they are overwhelmingly comic in tone through to just before the end, and then they turn serious, if not grave. Examples would be *House of Blue Leaves*, *Cyrano*, and *Playboy*. I have allied them with this species of the comic agony under the influence of recent productions, in which the directors interwove the comedy and melodrama throughout.

If this class of play is not easily distinguished from a tragicomedy, it is also a cousin of straight comedy, in which the roles unfurl their wit at the expense of others and in the form of wisecracks. In the comic agony, though, the roles are liable to broadcast, sometimes painfully, sometimes continually, their own deficiencies and to turn their wit back into themselves. Or they may venture into comic admissions of guilt, not to arouse pity but to rake themselves as mercilessly as they do the rest of the world. I mentioned satiric and bitter wit: these are allied with the practice of concealment. When wit aims at social targets, rather than people, it may boil up from indignation, usually over folly or injustice or both, and its release acts as a pain reliever to the speaker while it exacerbates bad relations with the listeners, as it was meant to do. This class of comic agony (in Shaw, Brecht, Genet, Sartre, Osborne, and a score of Latin American and British playwrights of the sixties and seventies) is heavily populated by society's human scourges, contemporary Don Juans and Alcestes. These operate in direct contrast to the leading figures of the next segment, who are victims.

As with straight comedy again, in this class of plays the roles generally end on a note of reconciliation or, at worst, with the acceptance of a bad deal. They still bear hereditary marks of the comedy of rejoicing, the celebration of fertility and community, but the reconciliation and the joy are restricted. Not every figure on stage shares in them.

PART III
Howling at Farce

MALE HEROINE
The Breasts of Tiresias, by Guillaume Apollinaire

The age demanded an image
Of its accelerated grimace
Something for the modern stage,
Not, at any rate, an Attic grace.

EZRA POUND, *"Ode pour l'élection de son sépulchre"*

The Breasts of Tiresias (Les Mamelles de Tirésias, 1917) is the most famous unknown play of the century. When Apollinaire subtitled it "a surrealist drama," he secured it an entry in the index of every textbook about the modern theatre and made his own name a stepping-stone in the history of the French avant-garde set down between Jarry and Ionesco. But the play itself is infrequently discussed and even more infrequently performed, an unfair fate for a work that predates almost every dramatic innovation of the later 1900s, from nonpsychological roles and the reversal of sexes to satire on our upstart civilization and on traditional forms of theatre.

To start with, the hero is a woman. Her name is Thérèse. She walks onstage wearing a long blue dress and a blue face. The print on the dress (monkeys and painted fruit) could be a comment on the play's tropical, pre-Tanzanian setting, the island of Zanzibar. The blue face could denote several things—anemia, a low temperature, the cosmetic smeared on by some Arab women to proclaim their modesty (Zanzibar was an eighteenth-century center of a flourishing slave trade conducted by Arab merchants), or even the blue dye, woad. Thérèse would like to become, without further delay, a warrior like that blue-hued British terror of antiquity, Boadicea, as the opening lines declare:

No Mister husband
You won't make me do what you want

(*In a hushing voice*)
I am a feminist and I do not recognize the authority of men

(*In a hushing voice*)
Besides I want to do as I please
Men have been doing what they like long enough
After all I too want to go and fight the enemy

143

I want to be a soldier hup two hup two
I want to make war (*Thunder*) and not make children
No Mister husband you won't give me orders.[1]

Between sneezes, cackles, a fit of hysterics, the noise of broken dishes, and her imitation of the chugging of a train, Thérèse recites a list of further resolutions. Her ambitions include becoming a parliamentary deputy, a lawyer, a senator, a cabinet minister, and president of the state. In 1917, when the play was first staged, none of these positions could be seriously entertained in France, Zanzibar, or anywhere else by a woman.

Thérèse, however, is not going to remain a woman. She opens her blouse. Her breasts fly out. One is red, the other blue to match her face. They float upward like balloons but are attached to her by strings. She pulls the strings to make them dance. Then she explodes them with a lighter. To take her transsexual conversion a step further, she sprouts an instant beard and mustache. So, after all, her blue face denotes her rebirth: blue for a boy.

The unnamed Husband, a baker, is heard offstage asking for lard. "Listen to him," says Thérèse, "he only thinks of love." Coming into view, the Husband mistakes the mustached and bearded Thérèse for a man who has killed his wife and put on her clothes. "They fight," decrees a stage direction, "and she overpowers him." She tells him she is leaving him and taking with her a chamber pot, a basin, and a urinal, which he understands to be, respectively, a piano, a violin, and a butter dish. One could speculate at length on the significance of these objects as Thérèse or the Husband or both identify them, but Apollinaire may be plucking random items and associations out of his unconscious.[2] She thereupon hurls herself on him and "takes off his trousers, undresses herself, hands him her skirt, ties him up, puts on the trousers, cuts her hair, and puts on a top hat." Now she has completed the transition:

The baker of Zanzibar
Has a wife who changes her skin
She carries a joke too far.

Too far? Or not yet far enough. The "joke" has hardly begun, for the Husband follows her lead. When a woman steps out of her femininity and insists on making war, not babies, making babies is up to the man. The Husband breaks out of his bonds and sex: in less than a day he becomes the mother of 40,050 children which he fabricates out of ink, paper, and glue. He does this for his nation and its survival; he undertakes a personal program of repopulation for the sake of which he is willing to go through agony and self-denial. But lo, he prospers. One female child immediately marries a rich man in order to divorce him and collect alimony. Another child pumps out best-selling novels, just like that. A third coughs up curdled milk, enough to float him into large-scale retailing. The Husband has reason to feel pleased. He has satisfied his patriotic sentiments, has kept pace with his creative urges by making children in place of baking loaves, and has turned a nice profit, since his only outlay was for ink, paper, and glue. With mixed pride and scorn he asks:

Who are those idiotic economists
Who've made us believe that the child
Means poverty
Whereas it's just the opposite.

During twelve packed hours (this action, running for less than a day, has a unity of time), while the Husband becomes famous for his mass rearing of remunerative offspring, Thérèse becomes famous as the general of the Zanzibar army and a deputy in the legislature. The same evening she returns from her labors disguised as a fortuneteller whose skull is lit from within by electricity. She praises the Husband and informs him that he will be "a millionaire ten times over." She literally tells fortunes. Then she rips off the disguise: she is the original Thérèse, only a Thérèse on top of her luck, a Thérèse who has seen the light and has a craniumful of electricity to prove it. Light has gone to her head, and success to her heart. She has brought home the chamber pot, the basin, and the urinal, as well as a new conviction that "we've got to love or I'll die." This belief reconciles her with the Husband, who was asking at the start for nothing but lard/love. She now flirts with the spectators by throwing balls and balloons at them. The play ends with a chorus, of which the last lines are

Luck is a game win or lose
Just keep your eye on the play.

But keeping one's eye on this particular play is not a straightforward act. A pioneering drama, it contains sixteen scenes that assail us with varied and frisky wonders. Two men named Presto and Lacouf put in brief appearances. If Thérèse and the Husband are interchangeable opposites, Presto and Lacouf are undifferentiated. A director might elect to have them performed by contrasting buffo actors—fat and thin, tall and short, timid and aggressive—but Apollinaire gives no hints. From the dialogue we gather that Lacouf has won at a game of cards; Presto has lost. Are they gamblers? Is one lucky and the other reckless? The play doesn't say. It presents them engaging in a short argument over whether they are in Zanzibar or Paris. The argument ends when they produce cardboard revolvers, fire at one another, are both killed, and both come back to life. During the action they will shoot one another dead three times and three times doggedly revive. What are Presto the loser and Lacouf the winner all about?

Well, Zanzibar is not only the location of the play. It is also the name of a French game of chance, the card game Presto and Lacouf have been playing. Lacouf, who maintains that they are in Paris, is a winner and cannot be wrong. This particular Zanzibar is Paris. They are playing a Parisian scene in a game of chance. Since a performance in a playhouse, no matter how diligently rehearsed, is also a game of chance, Apollinaire's nonsense begins to look less nonsensical.

The four roles—one can hardly regard them as semblances of human beings—of Thérèse-Tiresias, the male-female Husband, Presto, and Lacouf are even less defined than the "types" are in a nineteenth-century farce or melodrama. By "less defined" I mean not only less realized but also less restricted. Whatever they do or say we must accept as plausible (or reject the whole work), and we must credit them with being capable of anything. No story from the past lurks behind the action to govern their future. But in the drama, as in life, a vacuum becomes abhorrent. What will take the place of human traits? The answer: animated objects, which in nineteenth-century farce grow almost as necessary to the action as the roles are. In *The Breasts of Tiresias* objects have a kind of humanity. The most conspicuous object, a newsstand, remains on display throughout. Interpreted by an actress, this Newsstand sings, dances, and even speaks a few ruminative lines—more than can be said for another objectlike role, called the People of Zanzibar, played by one actor. He is speechless but entrusted with all the sound effects, such as revolver shots, thunder, drums, the breaking of dishes, and the crying of the Husband's newborn children. The People of Zanzibar is a collective, animated object.

The play also comes equipped with a prologue, spoken by someone called the Director, a written preface, and verses (bouquets, really) addressed to the actors of the first production. Like the dedicatory letter to *Man and Superman,* together with "The Revolutionist's Handbook," these additional elements help us to understand what the playwright is getting at by elaborating on his attitude toward his work. Apollinaire seems to be constructing a theoretical plinth out of women's liberation and the failure of the French population to multiply. The preface says, "We don't make children any more in France because we don't make love often enough," a poisoned barb when aimed at Frenchmen. But repopulation and equality of the sexes are not the only social questions raised by the play. A third has to do with the destructiveness of war, which Apollinaire connects to the other two.[3]

The Breasts of Tiresias had its first production during World War I. Apollinaire himself had been invalided out of the army after a head wound and a trepanning operation. (He was to die two days before the Armistice in 1918.) The so-called Director (a role, as distinct from the play's *metteur en scène*) appears only in the prologue, not in the action, as an army officer just home from the front, like the author. After having lived through the heavy bombardments in the trenches, which "put out the stars" and "even murdered the constellations," he hopes the audience

Will be inclined to profit
From all the lessons that the play contains
And so that the earth will be starred with the glances of infants
Even more numerous than the twinkling stars
Hear O Frenchmen the lesson of war
And make children you that made few before.

The play can therefore be construed as a dramatization of these three questions of the time, as of our time. It can also be construed as a warning. France's population will dwindle if Frenchwomen keep pressing for equal (or better than equal) rights, instead of renouncing them as Thérèse does when she returns to the Husband and says, "We [France] have got to love or I [France] will die." The same will happen if France keeps going to war.

Apollinaire says with apt understatement that *The Breasts of Tiresias* has a "less somber style" than that of the drawing-room problem play, which had dominated the French stage for three-quarters of a century. It demonstrates how topical material can be presented in the theatre with farcical effects and imaginative mockery, but without ever losing sight of the main themes. These boil down to the lapel slogan Make love, not war.

But how much notice are we supposed to take of the farcical, mocking tone? Does it compromise the themes? In his preface Apollinaire writes, "I cannot possibly decide if this drama is serious or not. Its aim is to interest and entertain. That is the aim of every dramatic work." We can readily see why he feels doubtful whether his play is or is not serious. It has a thesis, that the fertile shall inherit the earth. Its antiwar sentiments correspond in some particulars to those of the *Lysistrata*.[4] And yet, trying to persuade people to stop making war and start making children, however virtuous an endeavor for a playwright, seems unlikely to bring results when he fools around with the questions in so many ways. Apollinaire was an art critic of long standing and, like Shaw, the most discerning critic of his time in his chosen field. As with Shaw, we can skate hurriedly across the theory and stop to examine the measures the play proposes. "It is up to the authorities to act," says the preface, "to facilitate marriages, to encourage fruitful love above all else; the other important questions such as that of child labor will then be easily resolved for the good and honor of the country." This is blatant irony. The authorities are "to encourage fruitful love," and "the other important questions" will be "easily resolved." Apollinaire is making social proposals and laughing up his sleeve at those proposals, acting as the critic of his own work.

In the preface and subtitle to this play Apollinaire coined the word *surrealist*.[5] The prologue goes on to tell us that surrealism can "bring forth life itself in all its truth," as against ordinary realism, which photographs "the so-called slice of life." By means of surrealism the theatre can start

connecting in unseen ways as in life
Sounds gestures colors cries tumults
Music painting acrobatics poetry painting
Choruses actions and multiple sets.

Apollinaire's text "connects" these varied nouns visually by omitting punctuation. Acrobatics, painting, and the rest of them will team up with objects to fill the vacuum created by the depersonalizing of the roles. The new surrealist theatre will also incorporate

Changes of scene from pathos to burlesque
And the reasonable use of the improbable
And actors who may be collective or not
Not necessarily taken from mankind
But from the universe.

Given such innovations as "actors who may be collective" (the People of Zanzibar played by one performer) "or not" (Thérèse, the Husband, Presto, and Lacouf), and others "not necessarily taken from mankind" (the humanized Newsstand), surrealist theatre can proceed to deal with the population shortage, women's liberation, the failure of the French to make love often enough, or any other crisis, possibly at the cost of losing a serious, clear-cut thesis, but never at the cost of losing its theatricality. Apollinaire has joined in the twentieth-century quest for a theatre that is inherently theatrical.

The quest typifies not theatre alone but most of the arts during the first two-thirds of this century. Music wanted to be a pure form of sound, or even almost pure percussion created by previously nonpercussive instruments like woodwinds and strings. Painting strove to become paint on a surface, or off a surface—bas relief. Sculpture turned into volume or the absence of volume—bounded space, holes. The dance after Isadora Duncan consisted of successive, separated movements in time. Poetry broke down into discrete words, fiction into independent subplots and sometimes fractured sentences. Filmmakers sought the essence of sequential (and nonsequential) moving and still images with contrapuntal sound.

Not until playwrights understand the theatre's limitations, proposed Apollinaire, can they surmount them and explore what he calls the "infinite possibilities" by the "reasonable use of the improbable." In the play he shows that the limitations have not as yet been approached (in 1917) and that destruction must precede the rebuilding. The technique he employs for the destruction and rebuilding is the miracle—sudden mutation.

He gives us many examples of the miracle in the theatre. Thérèse turns into Tiresias, her breasts into disposable balloons, her husband into a mother, Zanzibar into Paris, a newsstand into a figure with moving arms and a talent for dance, song, and speech. The chamber pot, basin, and urinal are said to be (and therefore become) a piano, a violin, and a butter dish. Paper, ink, and glue are transformed into children, while children are said to be (and therefore become) cash assets, not liabilities. The population of Zanzibar is, by a miracle of reduction, one actor. The voices, relayed through a microphone, become mechanical sounds dissociated from the actors who own them. Several dead figures miraculously resurrect themselves.

Apollinaire tears down such conventions of the realistic theatre as boundaries between the sexes, between life and death, between species and numbers. The unity of place, which he adopts, is a joke if the audience can be in three places at once—Paris, Zanzibar, and the playhouse. The unity of time is also a joke if, between a sunrise and a sunset, Thérèse and the Husband can rise to the top of the politico-military heap and repopulate Zanzibar-France. The author wants these convention-smashing miracles to look casual, like the game of chance called Zanzibar, but he does not intend to relinquish control at any moment. The dramatist remains the play's deity. The prologue explains that

His universe is his stage
Within it he is the creating god.

Amid the flux of novelties supplied by this magnanimous god we find one strange item, the Newsstand. Why does he give it prominence by keeping it/her onstage throughout? It is "decorated with a mirror on the side facing the stage," so that it reflects the events and becomes a metonym for an instant newspaper. In addition, more than half of the second act occupies itself with the news or the newspaper world: a Reporter interviews the Husband, the Husband uses newsprint to manufacture his children, the 40,050th child turns out to be a journalist, "radio placards" enter at one point with news headlines written on them, and so forth. Now the newspaper format can be regarded as one model for many forms of twentieth-century art, especially theatre. Each page of news is a mosaic. The components of this mosaic scream for the attention of one pair of eyes. A political announcement sits cheek by jowl with a gossip column. Reports of landslides, revolutions, wars, train disasters, are interrupted by panels of "human interest" stories that the editors play up campily: postman bites dog, dog paints gouaches.

And the variety of typefaces! Even if they belong to the same family, we find some set in capitals, some in upper and lower case, some in roman face, some in italics, others in bold. One photograph has human faces bigger than the sky-scrapers in another photo. Advertising carries its own halftones, typefaces, decorative borders, drawings, and blocks of empty white space that set off the messages. It is absurd to talk of the design, sense, order, or relatedness of a newspaper page. The most that can be managed is a hopeless clapping together of fragments. Strangely enough, the fragments do not melt into the overall jumble. Each one, by contrasting with the others, stubbornly remains itself, sometimes even becomes enlivened as itself because it fights with what surrounds it.

We find a not dissimilar structure in *The Breasts of Tiresias*. Each of its sixteen scenes exists in its own right and has an enlivened identity because of the contrast with the scenes that precede and follow it. In this kind of dramatic progression the narrative is suppressed; so are all climaxes. Strictly speaking, the play has no "big" scenes, only a succession of small ones. It creates no special expectations in the people who see it, no powerful desire to know what will happen. Instead, they are asked to concentrate on what is happening, on what is "new" or "news." Hence a line is repeated as if for emphasis: "Just keep your eye on the play." Meaning: this was a play you should have been watching second by second. If we do watch, we notice that Apollinaire has not only, by a theatrical miracle, converted a thesis play into a travesty of itself, an antithesis farce, but has also, like Thérèse liberating herself from the balloons, liberated himself from constraints that date back to the well-made play.[6]

There remains one transformation to notice, Apollinaire's treatment of Tiresias. The old sage, variously depicted, appears in a number of Greek and Greek-derived plays in which he performs secondary functions as a foreteller of doom. A few poets have also cast him in their work, among them Ovid, Tennyson, and Eliot. As a prototype, Tiresias has accumulated a number of attributes, though not all of them show up in every play:

He is bisexual. According to one myth, when he was a young man out walking through a wood one day, he saw two serpents intertwined in the act of love. Tiresias impulsively thrust his stick between them, a gesture that today would be considered a Freudian interference. Ovid, the source of this account, does not record what happened to the serpents, but the effect on Tiresias was momentous: he suddenly turned into a woman and remained a woman. Walking in the same vicinity more than seven years later, Tiresias saw the same two snakes and wondered aloud what would happen if she thrust her stick between them again. She risked it and turned back into a man.

He is blind. Since Tiresias had been both man and woman and had experienced love as both sexes, Zeus called on him to settle a quarrel. The monarch of the gods had angered his consort, Hera, by claiming that women enjoy the sex act more than men do: men are too busy working at sex to enjoy it. Tiresias, now a man again, supported Zeus's male point of contention. Hera, violently offended by Tiresias's reply, struck him blind.

He has prophetic gifts. Zeus took pity on Tiresias and probably felt indirectly responsible for the blinding. By way of compensation, he conferred on Tiresias a supernatural vision. In time Tiresias became the most famous seer in Greece, although his predictions always had to do with coming misfortunes and catastrophes.

He is a Theban. Tiresias plays a part in most of the tragedies that make up the two strings of Theban myth: the defeat of the young prince Pentheus by his godly cousin Dionysos (Pentheus's death and dismemberment at the hands of a horde of women led by his mother, Agave) and the House of Labdacus, the myth of which includes the unmasking and expulsion of Oedipus, the deaths of Jocasta, Antigone, Polyneices, and Eteocles, and the murder of Creon's daughter Megara, as well as her three sons, by her husband, Heracles, during the fit of insane violence imposed on him by the gods. Tiresias foretells most of these horrors, but he enters the action of each play (always briefly) as an impartial presence, almost otherworldly, an understudy for Apollo.

Tiresias thus bodies forth an ideal, an evolutionary step past humanity and in the direction of the superhuman. He combines earthly knowing culled over an exceptionally long lifetime with unearthly seeing, which includes the arts of foresight and the black arts of sorcery. He is the spiritual father needed by a community because of his three roles: as a priest he interprets the will of the gods, as an elder and revered statesman-citizen he has earned a temporal authority that may challenge the will of kings like Oedipus, Pentheus, or Creon, as a man-plus-woman he provides incomparably experienced counsel. Such a fatherly ideal has persisted through history, and not only in Western cultures. Joseph Campbell mentions an Asian analogy when he observes that Tiresias's eyes "were closed to the broken forms of the light-world of the pairs of opposites, yet he saw in his own interior darkness the destiny of Oedipus. Shiva appears united in a single body with Shakti, his spouse—he the right side, she the left—in the manifestation known as Ardhanarisha, 'The Half-Woman Lord.'"[7]

In Apollinaire's hands Tiresias, that mythical remnant, undergoes drastic revision. If Tiresias was successively man, woman, man, Thérèse is successively woman, man, woman. Tiresias was old: Thérèse is young. Tiresias came from Thebes, one of the cradles of European culture; Thérèse comes from Zanzibar, an island outpost of Africa—but a Zanzibar with Parisian seasoning. Tiresias was an impartial observer and seer; Thérèse is a doer, a participant and mainspring of the action. Tiresias was a mantic, but seldom a moral, force, a man who said what was bound to happen but rarely ventured an opinion on whether it was for the best or the worst; Thérèse also acquires mantic powers of a sort when she plays the fortuneteller, but she is partial. She reverts to womanhood with a personal undertaking: "We've got to love or I'll die."

The reasons for these mutations of the venerable prophet seem to me to lie in Apollinaire's subversiveness, his resolve to undercut the dignity of the myth, to belittle the lofty ideal. As a fictitious figure, a literary concept, Tiresias is all very well. As a human being he would be insufferable, politically and morally neutral, so confident of his foresight, so complacent about his superior function and other people's miseries that he would never stick his neck out. He is a preacher who has no stake in the life around him, only a faith in the inexorability of fate. He has belonged to both sexes; now he transcends sex, which is like saying that he transcends living. In the new version of him, Apollinaire substitutes jocosity for prophecy, as when Thérèse returns as the fortuneteller whose head is lit up. By the play's end Apollinaire has elbowed the old prig off his pedestal.

Shaw does something similar with John Tanner and his alter ego, Don Juan. It may be only coincidence that *Man and Superman* was written a year before *The Breasts of Tiresias*, but Shaw's play also debunks the ideal of a superman, instead of endorsing it.

As for Thérèse, I have no idea whether Apollinaire had that galvanic woman St. Teresa of Avila in mind as a model (or antimodel) for his hero-heroine, but one of the saint's confessors wrote to a fellow cleric, "You deceived me in saying she was a woman. She is a bearded man." Apollinaire's Thérèse is not a version of Tiresias but a retort to him. Giving up her masculine ambitions constitutes a positive gesture, not a sexist surrender to woman's oppressed role as a mere hanger-on of a wife. She is making the conventional dramatic choice between love and duty and saying that duty is worthless without love. But even then the play is laughing at itself. When Thérèse tosses balloons and balls into the auditorium, what she is doing in effigy is flinging at spectators a free supply of sexual equipment. When we watch her gesture of farcical abandon, can we forget that during the first performance of the play Apollinaire was in mortal pain from one of the wounds of war?

TIMID EXHIBITIONIST
Professor Taranne, by Arthur Adamov

As though intoxicated by contempt for my own self, I purposely subjected myself to all sorts of petty humiliations. The servants passed me by at table; I was met coldly and haughtily; at last they took no notice of me at all.

IVAN TURGENEV, *A Prince Hamlet of Shchigrov District*

Arthur Adamov became visible in the blaze of experiment that rekindled French and international drama soon after World War II. In November 1950, when Adamov had his first two productions (of *The Big and the Little Maneuver* and *The Invasion*), which opened within three days of each other, Sartre had established himself as a writer of world rank, and Camus, De Beauvoir, Tardieu, Genet, Vian, and Ionesco had started to rattle the traditional barricades. Less than two years later Adamov's *The Parody* was staged by Roger Blin (who had starred in *Maneuver*), beginning seven months to the day before that director unleashed the Paris premiere of *Waiting for Godot.*

During the fifties Adamov confirmed his reputation as an innovator to watch with a succession of short and full-length dramas, among them *All against All* and *Ping Pong*. By the time he completed the latter, he had turned to an explicitly left-wing theatre. In those same years he wrote superb translations in French of Kleist, Büchner, Gogol, Dostoevsky, Chekhov, Strindberg, and Gorki. Besides Blin, his directors included Jean Vilar, Roger Planchon, Jean-Marie Serreau, Jacques Mauclair, and other pioneers of that questing golden age of French theatre.

Despite Adamov's renown at home, few of his plays made the transition into English, much less found performances in the United States. In 1959 three leading New York newspaper reviewers walked out during intermission on the first night of *Ping Pong*. The off-Broadway producers capitulated, probably never contemplating that the play might deal more cogently and suggestively with American than with French business practices. The play closed after one more showing.[1]

Adamov often works a vein of comic agony, although his comic elements are less broad than those of his contemporaries, Vian and Ionesco. His heroes yearn to be taken into serious account, but their yearning succeeds only in making them into laughingstocks or in driving others from them.

In earlier, more conventional drama than Adamov's, a character uses language to state a case, to explain his plight, to attack or defend, to display eloquence—to make himself, in a word, understood. For such a figure language is a handicap, the prime cause of misunderstandings and unintelligibility. He would be better off dumb than loquacious. The priest Malagrida may have sagely remarked in the eighteenth century that "speech was given to man to enable him to hide his thoughts."[2] The speech of Adamov's creations does not enable them to hide their thoughts; it prevents them from expressing their fears and wishes. Their own words undo them. In the two scenes of the single act of *Professor Taranne* (1951) Adamov demonstrates how speech can be a form of self-betrayal.[3] The action sets off echoes that are anything but nostalgic in the memory of a reader or spectator who has ever said the wrong thing and then hopelessly compounded the error by elaborating, clarifying, apologizing, or sinking into other patterns of irresolution.

According to Adamov, the play is "a faithful transcription of a dream."[4] Its dreamlike atmosphere does wear away the impression that the hero has control over what he says, as well as what he does. In both scenes he is humiliated, subjected to one rebuff after another, and isolated from the rest of the figures. Both scenes, then, explore the same thematic content. It is as if the dream is dreamed twice, only with different antagonists and with bleaker implications the second time around.

The first scene takes place in a police station, that purgatorial domain between freedom and imprisonment. Taranne, a fussy college professor—we are not told what he teaches: theatre, perhaps?—stands before the desk of a chief inspector. In the story he was arrested for undressing on a beach in front of some children. He now protests his innocence. The Chief Inspector appears less interested in investigating than in correctly completing his official statement. A young male employee and an old female employee watch and listen but take no other part in the interrogation.

Taranne opens the action with a long, blustering monologue. He reminds the Chief Inspector that he is a famous scholar. He ridicules the charge that he exposed himself but keeps getting caught up in his own divagations: "What man would stand naked in this cold? (*Laughing*) I don't want to become ill, and have to go to bed for weeks; like all great workers I am miserly with my time." As for the strange children who reported him, why, children are notoriously unreliable. His sister has a little girl "who wants, who is determined, to be taken seriously." He describes her: "She makes you listen to her all the time. I'm very fond of her otherwise. I can say I'm fond of all children. But that doesn't mean I believe everything they say." He is talking fast and breathlessly, not giving the Chief Inspector an opportunity to answer or butt in. As he speaks he keeps backing away from the offense of having been a "flasher," yet he cannot avoid returning to it over and over.[5] Of the children who claim to have seen him undressing he says, "They were encircling me. And then more of them started to come, from everywhere at the same time. They came toward me. So I started to run away. I don't know why I ran." But is running away from children a crime? "Look at me," he pleads, "do I look like a man who has dressed in a hurry?"

The Chief Inspector's reply to the monologue introduces an opinionless tone, a neutrality that will dull the speech and behavior of all the other roles: "I am sorry. But the report I am looking at does not bear out anything you say." The report speaks for him. A document, a sheet of paper. There is more than one copy of it. This is French bureaucracy, the most intimidating of all uncivil services. Taranne presses on with his defense: "I have given numerous lectures abroad. My last ones were in Belgium where I enjoyed an unprecedented success. The young men fought to get into my courses and to have a sheet of paper with my handwriting on it."

The situation comes right out of a farce: to be caught in public with one's pants down. Adamov has an insidious comic touch, but the wry humor points up Taranne's fearfulness, and the farce belongs to a nightmare. The Chief Inspector does not, however, behave threateningly. All he wants, in order to "clear this matter up," is to impose a light fine and file a signed statement, an admission of inadvertent guilt, "in which you admit you were surprised in a naked condition, by some children, as night was falling. You can add that you didn't know you were being watched." Being watched! The casual remark sends Taranne off on a paranoiac sidetrack: "I know only too well that I am being watched and probed, that everybody has his eyes on me. Why am I being stared at like this? I never stare at anybody. Usually I lower my eyes. Sometimes I even close them, almost." He invites his interlocutor to call witnesses who will, as he puts it, testify to his morality and renown. As if waiting for him to say this, six people enter the station—a lady journalist, a society woman, and two pairs of men who are evidently politicians and prospering academics. They seem to know each other (one of them remarks, "It's a small world"), but not one of them recognizes Taranne at a time when he craves recognition. The society woman raises his hopes: she does know him! But no, she has taken him for his rival, Professor Menard. Afterward she doesn't know why she made the mistake because—veiled insult—she realizes that Menard, after all, is larger and stronger-looking. Who are these six characters in search of a function? A cross-section of the world? Of Taranne's world? None of them has anything to do with the police station or with Taranne's case. They enter, meet, and discreetly snub him. Like the two silent employees, they are strangers, each an additional pair of eyes and ears to assist at his humiliation.

As adventitiously as they entered the nightmare, they file out of it. We will not see them again. If this were a literal trial scene, instead of a metaphorical one, they would be neither hostile nor friendly witnesses. All they would do is hurt the defendant's credibility. By the time they go, the Chief Inspector and the two employees have also sidled out. Taranne stands alone and discredited, with nobody to turn to. He runs outside into the corridor. Where is everybody? He was supposed to sign a declaration. He was supposed to pay a fine. Then he would have endured the necessary penalty and gone free.

While he is out in the limbo of the corridor, a hotel manageress appears, makes a few swift changes in the props, and converts the stage into the office of a hotel, a spot as public (and therefore impersonal) as the police station. She vanishes just as Taranne comes back to find himself somewhere new.[6] A hotel. No, not new. He knows it. He lives in this hotel. But when he explores the key rack, his number has disappeared, even though the rack is full of keys. He wonders if any mail has arrived for him, any word from the outside world. But there is no sign of the Manageress, no sign of anybody, until two nondescript policemen walk in. They ask for Taranne by name without giving his title. Once again he goes on the attack in his defensive way: "I haven't done anything wrong to anybody. (*Laughing*) I have a conscience." Those last four words are the understatement of the play.

The policemen say nothing about the original charge, his public nakedness, but Taranne feels compelled to bring it up and to lie about it: "I've just come from the police station. I signed the necessary papers. The witnesses have testified to my good behavior; everything is settled." The policemen could not care less. They have called on him in connection with a different charge, not a grave one, no more than "a breach of our regulations," a mere "minor offense." Taranne left papers in the bathing cabins on the beach. This ominous-sounding delinquency with its overtones of espionage is, like most minor offenses, nonsense. But Taranne again overreacts, making himself appear guilty by the vehemence of his protests. When the policemen produce a notebook, Taranne starts to contradict himself. He acknowledges the notebook as his, but he cannot decipher the handwriting, which he admits is his own. He says the book is full of notes, but after the policemen let him examine it, he agrees with them that it is almost empty. He says that he never repeats himself when he lectures. But he also says, "At the beginning of each lecture I sum up what I said the last time."

The policemen do not persecute Taranne, any more than the Chief Inspector did. They tell him charitably that all he has to do is sign a disclaimer: he was never inside any bathing cabin. But Taranne is bent on making himself sound credible. He tries to do this by bringing up peripheral matters, such as his lectures, and thereby strains his credibility further. At the point where he has practically incriminated himself, the policemen walk out. He starts to panic, instead of feeling relieved, because they have not given him a statement to sign. The nightmare is playing variations on itself. Now the scene narrows in on the peripheral matters, which, as we see, are not peripheral at all but the core of the play.

The Manageress returns with an "immense roll of paper," which "some-body" has left for Taranne. He unrolls it and finds the plan of a ship's dining room. He has the place of honor at the center of the head table, but he doesn't remember booking a place on a ship. Nevertheless, he feels he should have booked one. He has more cause for self-condemnation.

Taranne is trying to figure out what the plan could mean, when his sister, like everybody else in the play, enters unexpectedly. Possibly she is the sister he mentioned earlier, the one with an oppressive little daughter. Her name is Jeanne. She is a "young brunette" with "regular features" and "an even voice." Scanning the drab vacuum of a hotel office, she says colorlessly, "It's nice here." This averaged-out soul has a letter addressed to Taranne. First she withholds it. Then she lets him take it from her. Then he gives it back and asks her to read it aloud.

The letter methodically chops away at Taranne's professional qualifications. Jeanne reads it in "a flat voice," as if reciting its accusations on a witness stand. But Taranne has imagined these accusations. It makes little difference whether he reads the letter himself or has it read to him, for Jeanne is another version of Taranne, a conscience figure (to coin a term that had better be allowed to lapse after this one use), as we can tell from her name, an ellipsis in French of "I, Taranne": *Je . . . anne.*[7]

A dean at a university in Belgium wrote the letter. At that same university, Taranne has said, he enjoyed an unprecedented success. According to the letter, Taranne has been inconsiderate, if not worse. He forgot to ask after the health of the dean's wife. He disrupted the lecture schedules by talking too long and neglecting to inform the administration of the times of each lecture. He bored his students, one of a teacher's two worst fears. He plagiarized from Professor Menard, his rival, and was detected, the other most turbulent fear. He will not receive an invitation for a return visit.

As he listens, Taranne berates and belittles the writer. He gets hot, he shouts, and he begins to make a speech about what he would have told those peo-ple in Belgium if they had only had "the courage to stand up and say the things to my face instead of whispering them like cowards." Then, with the paranoia glaring on him like a rash, he concedes to every one of the letter's charges: boring students, thoughtlessness, plagiarism—all of it.

Jeanne goes out. She has not reacted to his admission of guilt. For he has at last made a confession. The Manageress comes in, clears the room of furniture, and goes out. She has not looked at Taranne.

Alone again, Taranne searches for a hook. He finds one, high up on a wall, and with difficulty hangs the ship's plan. The sheet unrolls. It has "a large, gray surface, uniformly and absolutely blank." Anything imagined on it would have been an excuse on which Taranne could "hang" his fears. As a plan of a ship's dining room it evoked his dread of going back to Belgium to be shown up and of going by sea (from France to Belgium!), so that he would have all the more time to worry during the voyage while he tried to live up to the place of honor at every meal.

The stage is now empty but for Taranne, the letter from Belgium, the almost empty notebook, and the empty roll of gray paper. He has been undone by paper, from the report the Chief Inspector had of his undressing and the statements he was never given to sign to the telltale pages of his notebook and the plan of the ship. Even when he boasts of his success in Belgium, early in the play, what does he adduce as the token of that success? "The young men fought to get into my courses and to have a sheet of paper with my handwriting on it." We now comprehend that Taranne is so guilt-drenched that he sees himself being persecuted not even by people but by words, written and unwritten. Plainly, he even dreamed up the charge that he had exposed himself in public. All he did was to change on the beach in order to save paying for a cabin. We smile tolerantly. It was all a nightmare, nothing more. At that moment, he "turns his back on the audience" and "very slowly begins to undress. Curtain."

Adamov once called the state of ignominy "the unnameable."[8] In this play his hero submits to the unnameable fears of ignominy by performing a gesture of resignation, undressing. Taranne is an exhibitionist. The charges leveled against him, by others or by himself, induce him to "exhibit" his hidden self. During the action he reveals that there is more to him than a timid pedagogue: there is also a timid exhibitionist. He feels bound to preserve a front as a dignified celebrity but cannot uphold this public image of himself. He finally displays his private image, his body, but even then feels ashamed and turns his back to the audience.

Previously he has shown himself to children, who probably will feel too bewildered to take reprisals and may be more impressed by his "size" than adults would be. But the children do take reprisals. Before they go to the police they buzz about him menacingly like the flies that torture Io in *Prometheus Bound* or the furies that pursue Orestes: "They were encircling me. And then more of them started to come, from everywhere at the same time. They came toward me. So I started to run away.... They were running and all shouting together. As if someone had told them to." They tormented him with their cries: "'You'll see. You'll see.' But see what? I've done nothing wrong."

When he fails to uphold the front, it is not a grand or life-shaking failure. Taranne is no Oedipus, no monster, not even a daring crook who makes away with a hefty haul. The best he can manage in the way of antisocial activity is to breach some petty regulations. The inner Taranne is small, ludicrous, and pathetic.

As an infrequent exhibitionist—probably when the pressures from within grow exorbitant—Taranne is a performer. Philip Weissman drew an analogy between acting and exhibitionism:

The actor has some of the characteristics and the modus operandi of the sexual exhibitionist. The exhibitionist has the need to show himself (his penis). He constantly struggles to restrict and control his exhibitionistic urges for fear of being caught, incriminated, and punished. The need to allay his anxiety at times is so intense that the perversion must be carried out at any cost, no matter what the social or legal consequences might be. The exhibitionist, like the actor, may also costume himself in either the clothing of the opposite sex, or in the costumes of the same sex, in order to deny the unconscious fear of having been castrated. The exhibitionist and the actor are repetitively compelled to enact another identity which produces a temporary reduction of their identity.[9]

Weissman is saying that the actor is a sort of exhibitionist. I am getting at something different: that Taranne's exhibitionism is a form of acting. He plays the part of the celebrated scholar. His performance is carefully graded throughout the text. It begins with his confidence in his histrionics during the opening monologue. As the action proceeds his doubts show through more clearly. His last protest is more shrill and patently hollow than anything he has said before. As if to underline the sham, Adamov has couched the line in the conditional: "I'd have raised myself to my full height and I would have said (*with an oratorical gesture, raising his voice*): 'Gentlemen . . .'" That is as far as he gets with his remonstrances. His voice peters out. He has reached the end of his duplicity.

Why does Taranne elect to put on this performance? He is not, after all, a good actor, and seems aware of the deficiency. The most likely answer is that acting is one means—not the most efficacious one for him, only the one that occurs to him—of trying to make others feel what he feels. The play demonstrates "the absence of communication." Adamov himself first used this phrase in a note to a subsequent play, in 1953. Whether it originated with him I can't say. But since 1953 it has swollen tremendously in meanings and applications, has become a standby of critical writing, in the social sciences as well as the arts. The phrase has grown so bloated that it seems to explain and at the same time obviate the need for explanation.[10] In its most vague and banal usage it is taken to mean that people cannot get facts and opinions across to each other. But they can, if defectively at times. Adamov is dealing with something more specific: the inability of one figure to communicate his anguish.

Communication, we are constantly being told, is a two-way process. Taranne tries to transmit his anguish for it to be received. The others do not receive it. They don't attribute to him the role of public celebrity, and if he debases his image they don't worry about that, either. They are an audience left cold by his acting. Only sheets of paper answer him, words recorded and unrecorded against him in perpetuity. His anguish goes out into space like a lost radio signal and dies there. The others pick up only his nuisance value. To Taranne as a human being they remain apathetic. One after the other they walk out on him. Their apathy darkens and embitters the comic agony of his fate, for as he more desperately strives to alter that fate by talking it out, the more surely he brings it to pass.

But then, if the play really is a dream, and not reality in the guise of a dream, Taranne may after all be the celebrity he claims, whose writings and research (plundered by the charlatan Menard who tried to take credit for them) will give a place in history to their originator, an academic giant idolized at the university in Belgium and other centers of learning where he overwhelms faculty and students alike with his lectures. Why, in that case, should Taranne undergo so horrible a dream—that he had turned into a despised version of Professor Serebryakov from *Uncle Vanya*? Very likely because the summit is a precarious position to occupy—one can easily topple or be pushed or shot down from that conspicuous peak by deserving or undeserving rivals—and because dreams specialize in such fears of loss and displacement. They deny the dreamer the absolution he craves. Finally, unanswerably, Taranne dreams because he, for all his fidgetings, posturing, and other pointers to his comic agony, cannot wake up.

ANYTHING BUT ABSURD
Jacques and *The Chairs*, by Eugène Ionesco

The headlong race between his misfortunes and his dreams was at that moment reaching the finish line.
GABRIEL GARCIA MARQUEZ, *The General in His Labyrinth*

In the grand old farces of a century ago, the stage, with its doors and windows all over, is Pandora's box. Lift the curtain, and trouble breaks out. People hurl themselves in and out of drawing rooms, swing on chandeliers, grab a table for a shield, don drapes for camouflage, fly into a wardrobe for a fallback position. Ionesco has immeasurably extended the cubic volume of nineteenth-century farce. In *Victims of Duty* Choubert climbs on a chair, which stands on a table, in order to advance (or retreat) into the farthest reaches of his memory. A corpse in *Amédée* visibly grows out of the window and expands down the street. Furniture in *The New Tenant* clogs up an apartment, then the entrance stairway, the street outside, the city, the world.

In Ionesco's theatre of hyperbolic strain the protagonists must often surrender to three-dimensional novelties, which act as impersonal forces and allow the playwright, like the nineteenth-century farceur, to play a god who plays solitaire with his universe, along the lines suggested by Apollinaire. But the protagonists must also contend with opposing internal forces, contrary impulses within themselves, so that the roles take on colorings of pathos. These are not the old, merry farces, although they seem no less funny (for a time) than those forebears. Instead, they consist of farces with a new twist, a twist of the knife, the twist of tragedy in which much of the injury becomes self-inflicted.

Jacques: or, The Submission: A Naturalistic Comedy (Jacques, ou la soumission, 1950) is very nearly that, the tale of a submission by a young man named Jacques. The author narrates it, however, as a parody of a family comedy in a style not remotely "naturalistic." As the son of the family, Jacques has, of course, the same name as the other members of it, but the same given name, not the same surname. There are Father and Mother Jacques, Grandfather and Grandmother Jacques, and, to relieve the uniformity, a sister Jacqueline.[1] By means of this simple name reversal, Ionesco makes the rest of the family appear like projections of the hero.

The opening scene offers that staple sitcom situation: Mom, Pop, and other family members berate Junior for his selfishness and remind him of what he owes them. Mother Jacques entreats: "Remember, my son, remember that I gave you suck at the bottle. I let your diapers dry on you. . . . I have been more than a mother to you, I've been a true sweetheart, a husband, a sailor, a buddy, a goose. . . . I held you on my knees and pulled out your cute little baby teeth, and tore off your toenails." [2] Does he appreciate her sacrifices? Not a bit. She has "brought a mononster into the world; a mononster, that's what you are!" Father Jacques takes another customary domestic tack: "You're not worthy of my ancestors. You resemble your mother and the idiots and imbeciles in her family." As loftily as Molière's Don Louis addressing his son, Don Juan, he recalls the obligations of Jacques to the family name and standing: "Impeccably brought up, like an aristocrant, in a family of veritable leeches, of authentic torpedoes, with all the regard due to your rank, to your sex, to the talent that you possess, to the hot blood that can express—if you only wanted it to, all this that your blood itself could but suggest with imperfect words." In these "imperfect words" we hear the tone of the heartbroken paterfamilias who, by posing proudly on his dignity, squashes it. To sister Jacqueline, Jacques is the idolized big brother gone bad: "In spite of all the immense love I have for you, which swells my heart to the breaking point, I detest you. . . . Never again will I bring over my little playmates so that you can watch them make peepee."

Exactly as, in sitcoms, a grandparent displays more understanding of youth than a parent does, Grandfather Jacques sings a ditty about a youngster of eighteen who believed children should be left alone. They have plenty of time to run after girls. The song is in effect a defense of Jacques, for the others in the family want him to marry and consider him ungrateful when he will not "submit" to their wishes. Nobody takes any notice of Grandfather Jacques's ditty except Grandmother Jacques, who smashes her husband over the head with her eighty-year-old fist.

Most stage living rooms display the last word in high style; so do the costumes. In *Jacques* the decor looks grubby and the costuming shabby. Most heroes spend their opening scene appearing handsome and athletic and insouciant as they bat wisecracks to the back of the balcony. Jacques sits morosely in his drab setting and listens to five pages of abuse without saying a word. Then his opening line is: "Let's pretend I've said nothing." The others troop out—as far as the doorway, where they stop, take cover, and eavesdrop on Jacques as he asks himself, "What do they want of me?" a question that has already occurred to the audience. Ionesco does not answer it openly but continues to disguise the aim of the action.

Jacqueline sneaks back into the room. She tells her brother he is "chronometrable." Then she creeps back to the doorway. Jacques is badly shaken. Chronometrable—that must mean something hideous, inconceivably frightful. He repeats the word over and over, undergoes "a mute debate with his conscience," and then "worn out, in a loud voice," he makes a confession: "Oh well, yes, yes, na, I adore hashed brown potatoes!" The others in the family rush all the way back from the door, overjoyed. Can it be? He adores hashed brown potatoes! They pardon him, welcome him back to the family bosom, and promise to reintegrate him with his ancestors.

Again Ionesco is disguising the action. Jacques has taken the first step in his "submission." Jacqueline's neologism *chronometrable* tells him his life is ticking away. He has only an appointed span. He must make the big decision now. And he does. When he replies that he adores hashed brown potatoes, he accepts what goes with potatoes. Meat.

The meat is a bride. She has waited outside with her parents, who brought her for a meat inspection. As a potential fiancée, this young lady, Roberte, creates a sensation when she appears. No ordinary hunk of meat, Roberte is a walking delicatessen. She has feet that are "truffled" and "armpits for turnspits," as well as "a tongue the color of tomato sauce, pan-browned square shoulders, and all the meat needed to merit the highest commendation," as her father points out. This is a fair list of accomplishments. Your average bride can offer only pedestrian talents such as washing socks or ripping off Chopin minuets by moonlight or producing certification that she has passed an evening course in decorating interiors. Roberte is solid meat, high and low. As a meaty bonus she has succeeded in growing two noses.

The question then arises: Is Jacques carnivorous? Apparently he is. He is even gluttonous. Roberte will not do. He wants, he says, a bride with at least three noses. Roberte's father, unfazed, hurries this, his only daughter, offstage and returns with his "second only daughter." The second Roberte, played by the same actress, has hastily donned a third nose. But Jacques remains unappeased. The second, triple-snouted Roberte is "not ugly enough." At this, the Jacques family and the Robert family walk out in high dudgeon and on tiptoe, hoping that Roberte II will bring Jacques to heel.

She tries. The last third of the play amounts to a seduction scene in which the traditional roles slip into reverse: Roberte, like Ann in *Man and Superman*, takes the apparent initiative in the wooing. During this sequence the play changes character. It forsakes the farce and broad comedy and becomes a grotesque fable. Roberte wins Jacques's interest by telling him a story. In her bathtub under the surface, she saw a male guinea pig in hiding. It had "two dark spots" on its forehead. The spots swelled and turned into "two very tiny guinea pigs, wet and soft, his little ones that were coming out there." Jacques answers "coldly" that the guinea pig was cancer. Roberte agrees with him. Encouraged by her friendliness, he tells her, "I feel I can trust you," and goes on to make his only long speech. In it he explains that he has felt lonely and trapped, ever since he was fourteen, when he first began to "understand" his life.

Having thawed him out and drawn him out, Roberte tells him a second story. It concerns an old miller with weak eyes. He meant to drown two puppies in a pond, but by mistake he drowned two foals. Jacques smiles (for the first time) at this tale. She continues it. The miller found he had not drowned the foals, or the puppies, but his own child. After this "the miller went mad. Killed his wife. Destroyed everything. Set fire to it. Hanged himself." Jacques, "very satisfied with this story," exclaims, "What a tragic error. A sublime error!"

She is capturing him. She follows up with a third and longer story, which Jacques in his mounting excitement cannot help interrupting at the end of almost every sentence. A horse gallops into a "city in the Sahara desert." He whinnies frantically with fear. There is a spark in his mane. He is on fire: "The more he gallops, the more the flame spreads. He is mad, he's terrified, he's in pain, he's sick, he's afraid, he's in pain . . . The flames are coming out of his ears and his nostrils, and thick smoke . . . How beautiful he is, he's turning all pink, like an enormous lampshade. He wants to fly . . . Through his transparent hide, we see the fire burning inside him . . . He's a living torch . . . He's only a handful of cinders . . . He's no more, but we still hear in the distance the echo of his cries reverberating and weakening."

During this sequence, the stage directions tell us that "the rhythm intensifies progressively, then slows down toward the end." It's the rhythm of a sexual climax. As the foreplay to this climax Roberte told about the guinea pig that gave birth. The next stage, the intimacy, comprises the story about the unfortunate miller, which makes Jacques laugh and leaves him "very satisfied." In the last stage, the stallion story, Jacques becomes more and more excited. At one point he cries, "He's burning too fast . . . Make the fire last." When it is over he feels "parched" and "exhausted."

Roberte then utters a string of images having to do with flowing, with a wetness that will quench his "fire." That is to say, her orgasm has begun: "My necklace is made of mud, my breasts are dissolving, my pelvis is wet, I've got water in my crevasses . . . In my belly there are pools, swamps . . . Everything trickles, the sky trickles down, the stars run."

By way of postlude or afterplay, Jacques and Roberte drift into a game, questions and answers that begin with the word *cat* (in French, the sound of *chat*: *chameau, chagrin, château, charrue,* and so on). They agree that from now on they will use the one word *cat* to designate everything they want to talk about.

While this dramatic climax mimics a sexual climax, its four animal episodes (and others referred to but not spelled out) give it the quality of a four-part fable: the story of the guinea pig; the miller's foals, puppies, and son; the burning stallion; and the cat game. At the same time, all four episodes apply to Jacques himself. He resembles the guinea pig trapped under water, and the two tiny guinea pigs, born out of his forehead, are cancerous thoughts breeding in his mind. As if to emphasize the identity between Jacques and the guinea pig, the lighting turns "greenish" and "aquatic," almost as if the setting were of a piece with the attic in that earlier fable, *The Wild Duck*. Roberte seems to be warning him (rather as his sister warned him earlier) that by shutting himself off from the world and thinking "cancerously" he is destroying himself. He picks up her meaning; he realizes the guinea pig is cancer. This meaning becomes more explicit in the story of the miller, who accidentally killed what he loved best, his son, then "cancerously" took revenge on himself by destroying everything he had, killing his wife, and putting his head in a noose.

The flaming stallion's fate, death by fire, offers Jacques an alternative, a transfiguration: the horse expires in blazing heat. As happens to Jacques, an internal fire conquers and consumes him. In the middle of this story, says a stage direction, "a blazing horse's mane crosses from one end of the stage to the other," as if to tell us this drawing room is Jacques's "desert." But Roberte's wetness will quench his burning. For the penultimate stage in this metaphorical submission Jacques and Roberte will restrict their expressiveness as human beings to one word. He will shut himself up in a narrow marriage. Roberte sums up their future: "In the cellar of my castle, everything is cat." One word. It implies sex.[3]

Yet throughout the seduction scene the two of them remain seated apart. The stage directions do not call for them to touch or approach each other. Jacques is seduced by words and finally reduced to one word. This is a fate he seems to have foreseen early in the action when he says, out of the blue, "Oh words, what crimes are committed in your name!"

Animals do not need words. Therefore, near the end, Ionesco shows us that these two young people are not human, after all. Jacques removes his hat (*chapeau*, a play in French on "cat skin") for the first time. His hair is green. The three-nosed Roberte takes her left hand out from under her gown, also for the first time. The hand has nine fingers on it. Noticing them, Jacques makes up his mind and completes his submission. He says, "You're rich, I'll marry you," as though they had stepped out of the parody and into a theatrical *mariage de convenance*. They embrace "very awkwardly."

The Jacques family and the Robert parents reenter to celebrate the union with an animal dance and animal noises, a caricature of a wedding party. They utter "vague meows" and "bizarre moans" and "croakings." Then they disappear, and the stage blackens. Out of the darkness comes a thin gray light. It shows us the upshot of the submission. Roberte squats alone on the stage, her three noses quivering "and her nine fingers moving like snakes." She is an impure human being, an impure animal, what Mother Jacques would call a "mononster."

Was this a true submission? Did Jacques bend, or was he twisted? If his family guided him and Roberte charmed him, they are the agents of his "downfall" into marriage and acceptance of the corrupt world's rule. But a submission is voluntary, an act of the will, unlike a seduction, which involves coercion. I am trying to make a distinction between pure and mixed forms. Older farces were, relatively speaking, pure, although there were plenty of exceptions. In a pure farce the roles have no responsibility (or a negligible responsibility) for their own fate and for the fate of the others. The events in the action buffet them about. Not their will but the will of the godlike dramatist determines what happens to them, whether they end up on a higher or lower rung of fortune's ladder or at about the same level.

In *Jacques* we have an impure farce. The action seems to remain at the disposition of the playwright. But behind the farcical facade Jacques does control the action. He submits, stage by stage, to certain pressures. These pressures come from within, not from without. He wants to submit. But why? The clue rests in his one long speech. It seems like a series of garbled reflections but is actually his confession. He tells Roberte he did not know how to break out of this isolation from the rest of the world. He speaks of some "others" (other than his family) who paid attention to his plight. They "said they would take useful measures. They implored me to hope, they appealed to my understanding, to all my feelings, to my love, to my pity. This couldn't go on for long, not for too long a time." Who were these others? The authorities, the gods? More likely they were Jacques's inner voices. Since they assured him that "it" (his isolation) could not go on "for too long a time," he looked and waited for a sign. That sign came when Jacqueline told him he was chronometrable. Time was running short. He had to make a move, search for an outlet. But "they've boarded up the doors, the windows with nothing, they've taken away the stairs," and "the attic" is blocked up. He has "been told," however, that "they've left a few trapdoors all over the place." Failing the attic, he says, "there's always the cellar" for an exit. Roberte replies, "Oh yes, the cellar . . . I know all the trapdoors." (Later she will speak of that "cellar of my castle, where everything is cat.") The only exit for Jacques takes him through a trapdoor into the cellar, the basement of his instincts, where he will become a slave to lust, to Roberte, to "meat." Even this late in the game, the grave dialogue is liable to merge into nonsense: "I absolutely want to go away . . . It would be better to go out down there than to be here. Anything is preferable to my present situation. Even a new one." He "absolutely" wants to go away because if he remains in his "present situation" of being shut off he may kill himself. He has told "the others" that he "preferred to withdraw," and they "replied that they would find it hard to do without me."

Jacques is faced with tragic alternatives. He can "withdraw"—commit suicide. He can remain in an intolerable state of suspension waiting for the sign (as Vladimir and Estragon wait in *Waiting for Godot*). But how will he recognize the sign if it comes to him? Or he can escape through "the cellar." He wants to live. He seeks an excuse, an opportunity. Roberte provides that opportunity with her "cellar where everything is cat."

By the end of his confession we have encountered a youth who turned against the world's orthodoxies and dreamed of escaping into a different future. But his desire not to be alone, not to feel incarcerated, undercuts the ambition. Roberte, what with her three noses and nine fingers and her seductive skill as a narrator, is a different future from the one he envisaged. So he chooses her. The final image sums up his choice: a decline into animality. There squats Roberte, her fingers squirming like Medusa's tresses. The parody finishes. Boy gets girl, plus "all the meat needed to merit the highest commendation."

The action of *Jacques* leads up to the beginning of a marriage. *The Chairs* (Les Chaises), written the following year, 1951, tells of the end of a marriage. Its principals, an Old Man and his wife, an Old Woman, are respectively ninety-five and ninety-four years old. As in *Jacques*, the action rises steadily to a climactic close.

The Old Man and the Old Woman talk about the past and look eagerly forward to a big event in the near future, the arrival that evening of a crowd of distinguished guests and an Orator who will address them, as the Old Man says, "in my name." The guests will all be people of consequence: "the intellectuals and the proprietors."

The old people speak of the building they are in as their house, but it seems more like a tower or lighthouse and is surrounded by stagnant water: the shape of a phallus, the environment of a womb. The stage represents about one-half of this structure's interior. Instead of a rear wall it has a semicircular cyclorama at the back, a construction that supports a row of ten doors and two windows, an ample number of exits and entrances for the most door-slamming of in-and-out farces, precisely what the action will turn into. The rest of the stage is sparsely furnished. The playwright asks for stools by the two windows, a blackboard and dais for the Orator, when he comes, two chairs for the old folk, and a gas lamp that gives out a green light, like the "aquatic" one in *Jacques*.

Under this light the old people relive their "green" years. She asks him to "imitate the month of February," and he "scratches his head like Stan Laurel." February—the second month—childhood—when he saw Laurel and Hardy movies? This assumption would put the time of the action at around A.D. 2000, looking back to the 1920s and 1930s. This memory leads them into adolescence, when they were married, and she urges him on: "Tell me the story, you know, *the* story. . . . It's also mine; what is yours is mine! Then at last we arrived." They arrived, he says, eighty years before, at "a big fence." But "they wouldn't let us in." It was a village called Paris, which "must have existed because it collapsed . . . it was the city of light, but it has been extinguished, extinguished, for four hundred thousand years." Stan Laurel as the February of the Old Man's life doesn't square with the collapse of Paris four hundred thousand years before. But this play is anything but literal. The Old Man is dribbling disconnected fragments of memory by free association. They come to him from all over his life. He has retreated from second childhood to babyhood and back to birth, letting words and assonances guide him: "At last we arrived, we laughed till we cried, the story was so idiotic . . . the idiot arrived full speed, bare-bellied, the idiot was pot-bellied . . . he arrived with a trunk chock full of rice; the rice spilled out on the ground . . . the idiot on the ground, too, belly to the ground." He is simultaneously a decrepit figure, almost a century old, and a baby ("the pot-bellied idiot") crying for his mother: "I want my mamma. I'm an orphan, dworfan." The Old Woman reassures him: "You have great qualities . . . dry your tears; the guests are sure to come this evening and they mustn't see you this way . . . you'll tell them everything, you will explain, you have a message." But she also recalls what he could have been—head admiral, head cabinetmaker, head orchestra conductor, head orator—if only he had "got along with other people, like other people do."

He sits on her lap, gets off, goes back. She is his mother; she isn't; she is. He is ruminating about the guests he has invited to listen to his message when "we hear the sound of a boat gliding through the water," then the ring of the doorbell. A lady enters, followed by a colonel, a woman named Belle with whom the Old Man was in love when they were young, a photoengraver, and more and more people. All these guests are invisible and mute. The Old Man and Old Woman, standing back to back, engage them in separate "conversations," or what Ionesco might call anticonversations. But the conversations break off as more guests pour in, and the Old Man and Old Woman dash back and forth between the doors and the stage, ushering in new visitors, introducing them, and bringing on more chairs from outside. Before long the stage fills up with chairs and disembodied guests.

Their influx speeds up the activity to a carnival of manic movement and sound. Boats splash through the water outside; the doorbell rings continually; the old folk scamper in and out bringing new chairs and arranging the old ones to make room. They hand out programs; they sell Eskimo pies; they shriek instructions at each other. Finally the crowd of invisible people and visible chairs separates them. They can catch sight of each other only by standing precariously on the stools next to the two windows. Ionesco fills a stage to bursting with two actors, furniture, noise, lighting, and the audience's fantasies.

From somewhere outside a fanfare tops the noise. The center door crashes open, and "a very powerful light floods onto the stage." His Majesty the Emperor has come. His invisible majesty. The Old Man weeps with pleasure and pride and calls out from his position by the window: "Your Majesty! I'm here, your most faithful servant! . . . Your servant, your slave, your dog, arf, arf." When he cannot break through the mob of guests, he balances on his stool and yells, while the Old Woman echoes his words: "I'm only a simple general factotum . . . I am a general, I might have been at the imperial court, I have only a little court here

to take care of . . . Your Majesty . . . I . . . Your Majesty, I have difficulty expressing myself." He begins to snivel. He tells the nonexistent emperor how he has
been humiliated, persecuted, never able to take his revenge. He has been
clubbed, knifed, supplanted, robbed, assassinated, refused a passport. He has had
scabies and been "kicked in the ass." His parents married him off while he was
still a child (shades of *Jacques*), but "fortunately, my wife has been both father and
mother to me." But all will soon be righted. The Orator is coming.

The Orator comes. He is dressed like a nineteenth-century poet or painter
and "very histrionic in manner, conceited; just as the invisible people must be as
real as possible, the Orator must appear unreal." While the Orator prepares himself for his address and "signs and distributes numberless autographs," the Old
Man thanks his guests, the organizers of the meeting, the owners of the building,
the architect, the "technicians, machinists, electrocutioners," the persons who
printed, manufactured, edited, and proofread the programs. He thanks the
emperor and the state. He thanks his "faithful helpmeet" and himself. He thanks
the Orator. Then he breaks into eight lines of rhyming verse in which he hopes
that he and his wife might have died together, been buried in the same grave, and
rotted in unison.

With cries of "Adieu!" and "Long live the Emperor!" the old people throw
confetti and paper streamers across the room and throw themselves out of the
separated windows. We hear "the sea-green noises of bodies falling into the
water." They have gone. Now it is time for the message.

The Orator stands alone on the stage, on the dais, before his audience of
chairs. He tries to speak but can only "make the signs of a deaf-mute," and gasp
out guttural sounds. He has an idea: turning to the blackboard he writes on it
one word, ANGELFOOD (which is what the old people have turned into, if they are
lucky), and a few broken words, some of which are corruptions of the old couple's
cry, "Adieu." Despite his impressive manner, the Orator has turned out to be the
deformed simpleton from the old farces, the laughingstock with a cleft palate or
a stammer. But the play at this point has abruptly changed character. At different stagings I have seen, the audience, after the big buildup to his entrance, was
always thunderstruck by his struggle to speak. It wanted to laugh but could not,
dared not. No one seems able to laugh even after he leaves, offended. Then "we
hear for the first time the human noises of the invisible crowd: these are bursts of
laughter, murmurs, shh's, ironical coughs; weak at the beginning, these noises
grow louder, then, again progressively, they become weaker. All this should last
long enough for the audience—the real and visible audience—to leave with this
ending firmly impressed on its mind."

If "the real and visible audience" does feels uncomfortable, the cause of the
discomfort may arise in part from the setting. There is an unexpressed, geomet-
ric continuity between the semicircular cyclorama on the stage and the auditori-

um, a completed circle formed by the stage chairs and the theatre seats, between the invisible audience on stage and that "real and visible audience" watching. The latter has been involuntarily co-opted into the action. Ionesco has attempted to transfer the feelings and memories of the Old Man and the Old Woman across the proscenium edge so that they awaken feelings and memories in the spectators. How well he succeeds will, as always, depend on the quality of the production.

The Chairs is a memory play, the memory of a life and a marriage. But whose memory? In the text the Old Woman has virtually no independent life, no story, of her own: "Tell me the story. . . . It's also mine; what is yours is mine." Her recollections do no more than support or counteract his. Together they relive snatches of *his* life. She reflects and refracts him back to himself. When, as an "orphan," he cries for his mother, she substitutes for his mother. When he blames life for its knocks, she substitutes for his conscience and reminds him of his own faults: he "never got along with other people, like other people do," and he could have been all sorts of high-ranking semi-supermen—an admiral, a general, a court official—if he had set his mind to it. While he woos the lady named Belle with exquisite chivalry, his wife is playing up to a male guest and revealing "her hidden personality," that is, his hidden personality: "She shows her thick red stockings, raises her many petticoats, shows an underskirt full of holes, exposes her old breast; then, her hands on her hips, throws her head back, makes little erotic cries, projects her pelvis, her legs spread apart; she laughs like an old prostitute." While he tells one guest that he and his wife never had a child, she tells another guest that their child ran away from home because he considered his parents cruel. While he tells a romantic story about letting his mother "die all alone in a ditch," his wife says his parents "died in his arms" and called him "a perfect son." The contradictions here may mean that the Old Man did his duty by his mother and father and bitterly resents his son's uncaring treatment of him and the Old Woman. As they reach the climactic sequences with the emperor and the Orator, she echoes his words, occasionally distorting them slightly, as if to stress their hollowness.

OLD MAN: For I have absolute certainty!
OLD WOMAN: He has absolute certainty!
OLD MAN: Never . . .
OLD WOMAN: Ever and ever . . .

Before handing over command of the occasion to the Orator, he reaches the limits of self-delusion. He becomes exultant, says he counts these moments as precious, as an apotheosis. He claims his "mission is accomplished" and he "will not have lived in vain." The Old Woman is meanwhile crying and sobbing. The sobs cut away at the optimism and conviction he voices. She stands for his doubts, fears, instinctual drives, his sense of his failings and his failure in life, all those parts of him that traduce his higher self.

This married couple is a single person. It must die whole, united, as the Old Man's rhyming verse suggests when it speaks of their lying, dying, and rotting together.

If the Old Woman represents the Old Man's baser self (his biblical Eve or the equivalent of Roberte and her "cellar" through which Jacques must pass), the other live role, the Orator, stands for his higher self, the source of his message to humanity. But the Orator "must appear unreal." This higher self is self-deceit, the Old Man's dream of himself magnified and elevated on a dais. The Old Man "has difficulty expressing" himself, but he can at least speak. The Orator cannot echo his words even as well as the Old Woman does; hence he distorts one of the most common words in the French language, *adieu,* when, like the old couple, he helplessly consigns everything "to God."

The three visible roles in *The Chairs* are one. But the guests, those unseen and unspeaking presences, also belong to the one. They are the Old Man's past accusing his present, compelling him to answer the big question: What have you made of your life since we occupied it? The question is not posed verbally, nor is it verbally answered. Rather, the Old Man spars with it. At different times he says to the room at large: "I believe in progress, uninterrupted progress, with some jolts, nonetheless." "As I've always said, pure logic does not exist; all we've got is an imitation." "At least, let's try to save face. Dignity is only skin deep." "I've invited you . . . in order to explain to you that the individual and the person are one and the same." "I am not myself. I am another. I am the one in the other." He speaks of "uninterrupted progress, with some jolts," and "an imitation" of "pure logic": these are empty semantics, evasions, like Professor Taranne's in that other nightmare. The Old Man has achieved nothing. He has intently wanted nothing, while these distinguished guests have all made "something" of their lives since the times he knew them. They have shamed him, a loser, a Stan Laurel whom life rewarded with perpetual ass kicks, all the way through that life to this ineffectual culmination, a ceremony that is an incisive skit on all those ceremonies we in the audience have sat through with their maddeningly tedious rituals of thanks and tributes.

Then there is the most distinguished of the guests, the emperor. He is even more a figment of the Old Man's crumbling mind than the Orator is. He amounts to a blurred and blinding vision of God. When the invisible emperor first enters, "the light reaches its maximum intensity, through the open door and through the windows; but the light is cold, empty." This empty God provides yet another excuse for the Old Man's wasted life, another justification: "I might have been something, if I could have been sure of the support of Your Majesty." Just as the semicircular setting and its chairs breach the boundaries between the stage and the auditorium, so the unification of visible and invisible roles destroys the boundary between what is real and unreal on the stage and helps us to understand the not-quite-hidden metaphor of the play.

The Chairs is a portrait of a death. Its action lengthens out to about an hour the last few seconds before the Old Man's death, which culminates in his suicide.[4] As the invisible presences, the memories, flow into the room in dribs and drabs, and then in overwhelming numbers, the past returns to him in a trickle that turns into a flood. The Old Man not only calls back his memories while he is dying; he also insists on inhabiting again those pockets of his life that cause him pain in retrospect. They show him to himself as a failure when he is on the rim of death and it is too late for him to remedy the failure. He summons an audience and a god to listen to his rationalizations—when he says farewell he also asks for God's mercy (*à Dieu*: may God dispose!)—and he summons his higher self to orate to them, but the Orator only confirms his failure. He has had an abnormally long life, what every person longs for—longevity is next to immortality—but his ninety-five years have gone misused, wasted. He did not even get to be one hundred.

The agitation mounts as the guests invade the tower, the emperor makes his "cold, empty" entrance, the Orator arrives, the old couple leap from their windows, and the Orator delivers his speech-which-is-not-a-speech—this fivefold climax is the spurt of final consciousness as the Old Man's life rallies its weakening forces before it evaporates. The last image of *The Chairs* is of life departed: "The stage remains empty with only the chairs, the dais, the floor covered with streamers and confetti. The main door is wide open onto darkness."

The feature of Ionesco's work that has given rise to most critical discussion, and most misunderstanding, is his verbal idiosyncrasy. The bastardized and dissected words. The neologisms. The antilogic. The frolicsome, contorted references that are not quite as lighthearted as they appeared at first glance. Some of these practices go back at least as far as Shakespeare. We could take a remark of the Old Woman's, "I haven't got thirty-three hands, you know, I'm not a cow," or some lines spoken by Father Jacques, "Your descendants will never see the light of day for they'll prefer to let themselves be killed before they ever come into being. . . . When I think that I had the unfortunate idea of wishing for a son and not a red poppy," and find them comparable to nonsense uttered by Dogberry, Holofernes, and Bottom.[5] In Ionesco, however, such lines are liable to emerge from any of the roles, not only from one who has been established as a clown or muttonhead. Some critics have therefore assumed that this playwright finds words meaningless. To say this is to deny him his comic gifts. His plays show us how words can be used without regard for meaning and often are. He demonstrates their power and powerlessness, their might and fragility, their incantatory and somniferous properties.[6] We notice that they can defy sense, adapt their meanings to varied settings, and take on new identities. When words are repeatedly intoned, they can acquire a life of their own that may not match any verbal definition. They can be raised to the status of objects, just as objects can be raised to the status of human beings in theatre. And like objects, words can become enemies, intimate acquaintances turning against the mouth that gives them life. Words, literacy's supreme token, can be made to sound illiterate.[7]

In both these plays the unspoken intention of the male "heroes" is to escape from a clinging childhood, from the time of preliteracy when their fears first took ineffable form. Jacques will escape by marrying into animality; the Old Man, more definitively by dying. In both plays the struggle to escape comes out of the opposition of a profoundly troubled person to an impersonal celebration: a wedding, a social gathering.

The conflict this author detects within one person between a social adult and a presocial, preliterate child gives rise to an antisocial being who is not at home in society and yet cannot use instincts properly. They have become defective assets, liabilities. Such a being will inevitably fall into conflict with the setting chosen by the playwright. The outcome in Ionesco, given his debts to an earlier theatre, will be farcical. But the farce is of the kind that encourages laughter and then chokes it off in midthroat.

ALMIGHTY GOAD

Act without Words I and *Act without Words II*,
by Samuel Beckett

Noticing that he had gone rather yellow, he suspected liver infection, and asked himself: "Do I have any pain?" And finished by having some.
GUSTAVE FLAUBERT, *Bouvard and Pécuchet*

From numerous accounts Samuel Beckett appears to have been a considerate, reticent gentleman whom renown (and notoriety) took by surprise, perhaps by storm.[1] Beckett's art, though, invites us to contemplate him as the theatre despot of the century, constricting the doings and sayings of the roles on his stages with the dedication of a whip-wielder in a galley. To this observation two conditions need to be attached: his captives do not protest about their psychic straitjackets; and out of Beckett's constraints there emerges some of the purest writing ever penned—not crystalline, no, far from that, but toiled at and boiled down to a breathtakingly limpid suggestiveness.[2]

Before deploring or admiring how he has trapped them in a mini-world of words (or, as Linda Ben-Zvi has suggested, of mere phonemes) in both their lines and his stage directions, one cannot help looking with some compassion on their confinement in the spaces.[3] Beckett's stage pictures give us Clov locked in a cell and in servitude to Hamm, who sits blind and hardly self-manipulative in his wheelchair while his parents, Nell and Nagg, bob into sight from the recesses of adjoining garbage cans; Winnie in *Happy Days* up to her ribcage in dirt and later up to her neck; Krapp transfixed by his tape recorder, unable to break quite into or quite out of the shell of his past; the nameless trio of *Play*, W1, W2, and M, in their "three identical grey urns . . . about one yard high," each one's "neck held fast in the urn's mouth," as though the urn-monsters have devoured all but the heads. Or the stage vista may be so boundless that it offers an infinite choice of routes for escape—that is, no choice at all: Didi and Gogo forever occupying a stretch of open roadway in *Waiting for Godot*; Henry in the radio play *Embers*, wandering along the shingle and his memories beside an open sea.

Certain unfortunates in Beckett's theatre have virtually no power to animate themselves. They want the equivalent of a switch to bring them to stage life. An extreme example occurs in *Play*: each "toneless" voice is "provoked" into speech by a spotlight that leaps through the "almost complete darkness" from face to face. Krapp seems scarcely to exist when he moves beyond the pool of light focused on the table that supports his tape recorder. The male figure in the television play *Eh Joe* has been sentenced to listen to the woman's voice that lashes him with reproaches and memories, while the heroine of *Rockaby* is spurred into speaking by the rocking of her chair.

In his experiments with two dialogueless playlets, the author was evidently inspired by vaudeville, the circus, pantomime, silent film farces, and their common ancestor, the commedia dell'arte. He posits a featureless male role, the mime of *Act without Words I* (1957), responding to beeps of a whistle from an unidentified source, a discontinuous vocal mirage in the desert where he finds himself, until its repeated calls have deceived him so often that "he does not move" but "stares at his hands," driven into immobility. In the partner work, *Act without Words II* (1957), a pair of players or clowns are pricked into activity: they quit the sacks they inhabit and perform a waking-up routine when poked at by a "goad," which approaches them on a "strictly horizontal" plane—a goad that is their incitement to life.

In all these cases Beckett has gone to the heart of theatre as a medium. His work has frequently been called minimal or minimalist because it seems pared down to essentials, devoid of many common, empty transitions of speech, those actors' leaning or hitching posts, which have been replaced by pauses that demand dramatic filling. A more apt adjective for this verbal concentration might be *elemental*. Critics have argued with some heat and less justification that Beckett's artistry is dehumanized, because the roles in his plays resemble men and women only skeletally. True, all right, but more than almost any roles conceived before or since, they are creatures of the stage, theatrical essences. When their turns come, they respond to cues, if only with expressive silences or expressionless faces.[4]

In his autobiography, Alan Schneider, who introduced Beckett's plays to the United States, directed almost all of them, and became the playwright's friend, pays tribute to Beckett's open-mindedness, as though to dispel the notion that Beckett could ever have been dictatorial other than on paper: "People always assume him to be unyielding, but when the chips are down, on specifics—here [on the set of *Film*] as well as in all his stage productions—he is completely understanding, flexible, and pragmatic. Far from blaming anything on the limitations and mistakes of those around him, he blamed his own material, himself. . . . He was even prepared to eliminate an important segment of his film."[5] In these sentences, Schneider anticipates the ruckus several years later (after his death) over JoAnne Akalaitis's production of *Endgame* laid in the New York subway. He defends Beckett from the criticism that he obstinately rejected production details that differed from what he asked for in his stage directions. Protests that arose over localizing the setting, giving up its deliberate nonspecifics and so refusing to respect the integrity of his drama, seemed to originate with Barney

Rosset, his publisher and "representative" in the United States, for the author, aged over eighty, lived in Paris at the time of the Akalaitis dispute. Schneider, who scrupulously observed Beckett's written directives as a rule, paid further tribute to Beckett's open-mindedness (at least, in dealing with interpreters he trusted): "After he's delivered me in his rusty tin buggy of a Citroën to the Invalides terminal or the Gare du Nord, he always has sent me homeward with the same farewell: 'Do it anny way you like, Alan, anny way you like.'"[6]

Ruby Cohn, though, who has described Beckett's stagings of his own plays, especially at the theatre in Ulm, writes that he "has imposed increasing restrictions upon his actors. His *Regiebuch* meticulously, almost maniacally, delineates such restrictions. Beckett's hope is that severely imposed limits will demand more of the actor, intensifying his emotional expression, rather than inhibiting it. Though he does not use Grotowski's word 'score' for his texts, he is a musician who appreciates his instrumentalists."[7]

In his writings Beckett has put the roles through paces as cruel as those ordered by the most heartless farceur—Feydeau, say. *Act without Words I*, with its three-word set description, "desert. Dazzling light," permits its single role, defined only as "the man," no egress into the "desert"—deeper into the stage—or off into the wings; and all the while he remains oppressed by his visibility, the embarrassment, of being dazzlingly lit. He first appears "flung backwards on stage from right wing." When a whistle invites him to return to the right wing and then try the left wing, he finds himself both times "immediately flung back on stage," where he "falls, gets up immediately, dusts himself, turns aside, reflects." When the whistle summons him again to the left, having learned a bruising lesson, he "hesitates, thinks better of it, halts, turns aside, reflects."

Thereafter, like a twentieth-century Tantalus, he suffers a series of fruitless temptations. A little tree descends from the flies. It has "a meagre tuft of palms casting at its foot a circle of shadow," a refuge from the pitiless heat associated with the dazzling light; but almost as soon as he thinks of taking shelter, the "palms close like a parasol, the shadow disappears." A "tiny carafe to which is attached a huge label inscribed WATER," another false promise from the flies, comes no lower than three yards from the ground. The label may be "huge," but the carafe itself is "tiny" and would provide only a tiny satisfaction. Still, he wants it. Although that deceitful heaven called the flies successively lowers a large cube, a smaller cube, and a smallest cube to clamber onto and bring him within reach of the carafe, he cannot contrive to make them serve him. Nor can he use a rope and a pair of tailor's scissors, more gifts from the flies, either by climbing to the flask up knots in the rope, which is "let out" from above to deposit him on the ground, or by cutting the rope with the scissors and trying to lasso the flask. He does not even get the opportunity to hang himself with the rope, because the tree's sole bough "folds down against trunk." Nor can he slit his throat with the scissors, which whisk back into the flies aboard one of the cubes. Before each distraction, he is studying his hands or else reflecting when the whistle from above or from either wing draws his attention to the latest torture to arrive from out of sight, apparently presenting him with the opportunity to take advantage of it but actually reinforcing the illusoriness of free choice.

Who is it enduring these merciless disappointments? An everyman? Of a sort. The playlet unavoidably points to the do-it-yourself frustrations in nearly every twitch of everyday life. In almost every instruction Beckett repeats that the man "reflects" or "continues to reflect." This author, who famously exploits words for their multiple meanings, does not say even once that the hero-victim "thinks" or, as in the partner play, "broods." He always reflects. Like the protagonist of *The Chairs,* he mirrors the spectators, reflects them and their travails back to themselves. At the same time the character will be more than an average person, for the role cries out for an acrobat, an adept clown. Spectators, recognizing themselves, can then laugh freely, as they did at the two most popular film clowns of the 1920s, Harold Lloyd and Buster Keaton, who excelled at unconsummated suicide routines, Lloyd in *Never Weaken* and Keaton in *Hard Luck*, both released in 1921, the opening of the leaping-out-of-windows decade. Beckett's incidents hark back to the early silent comics in another respect, but especially to Chaplin. Each time the mime is flung onstage or bowled over, let down, or otherwise humiliated, before he "reflects" he "dusts" or "brushes" himself, as if making a clean start, defying his shabby garb and reasserting a bathetic dignity.[8]

Finally, after the big cube "is pulled from under him" and he falls and "remains lying on his side," he "does not move." The whistle sounds, either from above or from the side, floating in from "the flies" or "the wings," heaven or earth, but he no longer responds to stimuli. The carafe teases him more mischievously than before as it "dangles and plays about his face." The leaves of the palm reopen to restore the morsel of shadow. As the play closes, "he looks at his hands" once more. Those tools, man's most versatile resource other than his brain, have proved unavailing. But they are, at least, not outside him or beyond his control. They take him back into himself as a refuge, but in this posture he looks more isolated than ever.

For *Act without Words II* Beckett calls for a *"frieze effect"*—a wide but shallow platform placed at "back of stage," that is to say, removed from the audience. The intervening gap, the forward area of the stage, becomes visually enlarged by keeping it dark, while the platform, "violently lit" behind the wide band of darkness, takes on the quality of a peninsula separated by the black inlet. Instead of one protagonist, we now have two, A and B, and instead of an everyman, we will observe two contrasting buffo types, hidden for the moment in two adjoining sacks, with a pile of clothing nearby. In the first mime playlet, the man needed above all a partner who could advise, help, reassure, hold the fugitive objects still so that he could benefit from them, however skimpily. This second playlet does have the two figures but not partners or even rivals. They perform at different times, reminiscent of the pair in John Maddison Morton's *Box and Cox* (1847) who occupied the same apartment at different times of the day and night.[9]

It takes two jabs of the goad to cause A's sack to show any movement, that is, to animate him. Beckett has ordained for him a string of activities. These include emerging from the sack, dressing, moving his and B's sacks from the right side of the platform to the center, undressing, and returning to his sack. B in his turn will carry out a corresponding function by dressing, moving the two sacks from the center to the left side of the platform, undressing, and returning to his sack. Where the two solos most markedly differ is in the pacing and punctuation Beckett wants for each. A "is slow, awkward (gags dressing and undressing), absent"—the "gags" will presumably involve putting on garments inside out, trying sleepily to cram two legs into a jacket sleeve, and so forth—while B's movements are "brisk, rapid, precise." A "broods" seven separate times between movements, prays twice, kneels once, swallows two pills. After taking off the clothes, he lethargically "lets them fall in an untidy heap."

Beckett notes that A's and B's "actions . . . though B has more to do than A, should have approximately the same duration." This being so, B's actions, coming second, will look all the more rushed and anal than A's. B needs only one jab to bring him to life. He checks his watch (ten times) and winds it (once), brushes his teeth, combs his hair, then brushes it and brushes his clothes, "inspects appearance" in a mirror, consults a map and compass, "does exercises . . . rubs scalp." After taking off the clothes (the same ones used by A, except that they both wear their own shirts), B "folds them in a neat pile." A keeps only his pills in the pocket of his shirt; B's shirt pocket holds his "large watch," toothbrush, and comb. B also plumbs the coat pocket for the clothes brush, map, and compass. A and B both reach into the coat pocket for a large carrot and take bites, although A "spits [his mouthful] out with disgust" whereas B "swallows with appetite." They both "crawl" in and out of their sacks; they are "bowed and staggering" as they each transport the sacks across the platform. They each carry out a cyclical stint, a day (a life in miniature), and in the same clothes. Have they, the fuddled and the frenetic, accomplished anything, separately or in sequence? If it can be rated an accomplishment, they have shifted the sacks and clothes from the right side of the platform to the left. And they have displayed themselves as ritual-bound reflexives, puppets.

Now what? Next time around will they shift sacks and clothes back from the left to the right? Will there be a next time? The goad assails A's sack again, and again it requires two pokes to get A to budge from the sack, after which he "halts, broods, prays," exactly as before, and the playlet ends so that we can deduce our own answer.

Like the whistle, tree, carafe, cubes, rope, and scissors in the other playlet, the goad operates from offstage. It enters from the right side. The first time it jabs at A's sack, it is said to be "strictly horizontal," without any support. When it jabs at B's sack, it enters "on wheeled support (one wheel)." For its third and last appearance, it enters on a two-wheeled support. Like the movement of the sacks from the right to the left of the platform, the goad's altered locomotion (what Ruby Cohn calls its "increased mechanization") denotes some (hardly any) change, comparable to the minute increments of change in other plays by Beckett that have led some scholars to deduce that he did not believe that human effort in life is futile.[10] Other scholars, seeing how paltry the changes are, imply that the best he has to offer is blighted hopes.[11] My own view is that it hardly matters on which side we come down in theory. Comic agony leaves an array of choices open, even in a dramatic world as tightly reined in as Beckett's. Rosette C. Lamont writes that "for Beckett tragedy and comedy interfuse and overlap" and that "Beckett's laugh, or that of his many clown-heroes, is a grimace, somewhere between soundless merriment and mute sobbing."[12] The proportions of comedy and agony we find in a staging will depend on whether it was tilted toward laughter, wonder, horror, pity, or some mixture, compromise, or novelty and on whether we saw it with a companion. From the published play our impressions will depend heavily on our own personalities.

As Beckett describes the goad's movements each time, it is cruel, relentless. It "stops a foot short of the sack" it is attacking; the point draws back, then "darts forward into sack," after which it waits to learn whether the sack will move. In the case of A's sack, its point draws back further the second time, then "darts forward again into sack," presumably with more force. The goad is a bully, the villain of the piece, yet without it the sacks would remain inert, much as the man in the other playlet would remain mired in his reflections if he were not provoked by the teasing from either side and above. However nervously, we do laugh at the prey of bullies.

The word *goad* seems to be, like the word *Godot*, a compromise between *god* and *goat*. The tragic ode, the *tragoedia*, from which Western drama is believed by some commentators to derive, is usually translated as a "goat song," and other commentators (as well as some of the same ones) have suggested that the horns, hooves, and tails of satyrs from the satyr plays that are said to have followed a tragic trilogy denote goats, rather than bulls or horses or other animals once taken to be fertility symbols. This mime play strews its allusions broadly and casts backward to well before the commedia dell'arte for its ancestors—to pre-Greek performance or, if there ever was such a thing, preverbal theatre. *Act without Words I* can be visualized as a condensed version of a single life, starting with the clown's being "flung backwards on stage." "When we are born," laments the distraught

Lear, "we cry that we are come / To this great stage of fools," a stage that offers no escape and on which there is only endurance at best, seasoned by unfulfillable temptations. *Act without Words II* executes two swift portraits in contrast while in apposition, two sets of involuntary reflexes, two days or lives that are pushed (by the goad) rather than pulled (by the whistle) and, to the extent that each moves the other's sack, interdependent.

So we come full circle to our opening, as chapters and essays are expected to do. Beckett's vision of life may not be heartening, but as the three figures in these mime pieces submit to their dazzlingly or violently lighted solitude, their minds, their sacks, their Beckett-fashioned traps, they strike chords of recognition that play on our sympathies the more they make us feel simultaneously amused and bemused.

FOR SEX AND EMPIRE
Cloud Nine, by Caryl Churchill

And in twenty years they all came back,
In twenty years or more
EDWARD LEAR, *"The Jumblies"*

The only mentions of "cloud 9," eleven of them, occur well into the second half of *Cloud Nine* (1979), in the course of a song lyric.[1] The lyric's last line, more or less a repetition of the one before, runs: "Upside down when you reach Cloud 9." The song's short verses deal, among other matters, with sex between two men, between two women, and between a bride of sixty-five and a groom of seventeen and with smoking "some dope on the playground swings / Higher and higher on true love's wings." Maybe these social irregularities, as they were taken to be not so long ago, are what is meant by "upside down." Will a spectator interpret cloud 9 as *up* exactly, a state of ecstasy, the way the term is generally understood?[2] Or down, as in a state of sin? or disappointment? or irony? or mockery, as in Aristophanes' *The Clouds*? Or is this cloud 9 up *and* down? Is it simply (or complicatedly) the act of sex? Is it the ultimate mirage? The instant of orgasm?[3]

The song belongs to Gerry, a youngish fellow from a working-class background, lavish with his sexual favors and persistent about his demands. As one of *Cloud Nine*'s parade of roles who reappear, sometimes transformed, usually enlarged, Gerry never lands on any cloud 9 in the action, though he claims he rises to it in the story, offstage. But then, nobody in the action rises (or falls) into the condition of a cloud 9—identified, but cloudily, only in the one song. The roles seem to yearn forward to it or glance nostalgically back at it or conceive of cloudscapes and dreamscapes, Cockaignes and Shangri-las that resemble it. The play conveys us well into the post-Ibsen theatre in which fantasy overlaps current affairs, history, and other ingredients of realism. Churchill plays hob with time, place, race, class, the sexes, the living and the remembered (or the nearly forgotten), the servers and the served. She tackles the progress of sexual liberation, its strivings against the odds and against many expectations. She yields to a feminist bias, which in places has a detectably masculine list. Because of its unorthodoxy, its sheer quirks, *Cloud Nine* opens out into one of the most impudent dramas since the start of the post-World War II revolutions in theatre.

As though to remind us of the disparity between the two eras in which it will live, *Cloud Nine*'s first act "takes place in a British colony in Africa in Victorian times." Its settings are described tersely: "Low bright sun. Verandah. Flagpole with Union Jack" (for scenes i, iv, and v); "an open space some distance from the house" (for scene ii); and "inside the house. . . . The blinds are down so the light isn't bright though it is day outside" (for scene iii). The decor has no more in common with a historically verifiable outpost of empire than with one of Hollywood's H. Rider Haggardish reconstructions of the 1930s inhabited by the likes of Sir C. Aubrey Smith, Allan Jeayes, Victor McLaglen, and Heather Angel or the Gaumont British musical adventure *Sanders of the River*.

The four members of the inner family at the heart of act I have significant names, three of them royal. The youngest, represented by a dummy, is Victoria. Her brother, who loves to take charge of Victoria's toy doll, is acted by a grown woman and called Edward, one of the two most popular names for English monarchs, the other being Henry. Their mother, played by a man, is Betty (one of the many diminutives of Elizabeth). Betty's lord and master, Clive, probably does not take his name from Clive Brook, a film actor once routinely allotted perpendicular-jawed, brilliantined, British heroes, but from Clive of India, 1725-74, the subjugator of three Indian provinces. The local equivalent of a consul and the play's nearest approach to a villain, Clive extols manliness, upholds colonialism, and keeps his family in line.[4] He calls his son Butterfingers during a game of catch and warns him, "You'll be no good at cricket."

BETTY: You've hurt Edward's feelings.
CLIVE: A boy has no business having feelings.

Of this domestic quartet Clive is the sole example of traditional casting. A reading of the play substitutes meagerly for the farcicality of a performance, in which Clive heads a household of intersecting opposites: a woman for a son, a man for a wife, and a dummy for a daughter. Clive announces, "I am the father to the natives here," and his personal family includes, by extension, Joshua, his African "boy" for the past eight years, played by a white actor; Ellen, Edward's gay governess; and Maud, Betty's prim mother, who taught her the formulas of self-suppression.

BETTY: I live for Clive. The whole aim of my life
    Is to be what he looks for in a wife.
    I am a man's creation as you see,
    And what men want is what I want to be.

The last couplet illustrates how the actors occasionally grow so knowing about their roles that they can step well outside them. Lines like these are author's "givens." They cannot be delivered with sincerity, hardly even with mock sincerity, and require tongues obtrusively bulging in cheeks.

Betty, despite her protestations of servitude to Clive, will soon be lured away from fidelity by Ellen and, at about the same time, by Clive's friend Harry, one of the household's two outsiders.[5] Harry drops in as a respite from the task to which he has dedicated his life, journeying up and down jungle rivers for murky purposes, nominally to fulfill his profession as an explorer and chart the rivers' courses but more plausibly to map the locations of male and female sex partners. Harry is what used to be called AC/DC. He not merely declares his love for Betty ("I need to go up rivers and know you are sitting here thinking of me") but also seduces young Edward (not for the first time) and issues a placid invitation to Joshua, "Shall we go in a barn and fuck? It's not an order." Joshua accepts.

The second outsider, a neighboring widow called Caroline Saunders, has fled from her home before what she thinks is a tribal uprising.[6] Clive, who eagerly grants her plea for sanctuary, keeps praising Mrs. Saunders's "amazing spirit" to his family. To her he proclaims that in addition to her amazing spirit she has an amazing smell. She terrifies him, he says. She is "dark like this continent. Mysterious. Treacherous." Since her arrival, he confesses to her, he has "had an erection twenty-four hours a day except for ten minutes after the time we had intercourse." His declaration goes on: if he ever found her "shot with poisoned arrows," he would make love to her corpse. But because she is alive and not kicking, he fondles her feet and legs, then vanishes under her skirt.

Joshua, the white black, plays the informer, as well as the butler.[7] To Clive he tattles about Betty with Ellen and Betty with Harry. He reports on protests among his fellow Africans, distinguishing himself from them, insisting he is white, like the actor in his role. He even takes a hand in flogging them and in other acts of vengeance regarded by Clive as punishment and by Joshua as "justice." These other Africans remain unseen elements in the story. Two of them happen to be Joshua's parents, but he tells Clive that he doesn't wish to mourn for them because they were "bad people." He says, "You are my father and mother."[8] Joshua has trained himself to be "whiter" than white. He has allowed Ellen to teach him to sing "In the Deep Midwinter," a favorite British carol at boys' and girls' schools and utterly inappropriate in an African milieu. He forswears what sounds like an African myth about creation that he has narrated to Edward, because it is "not true": "It's a bad story. Adam and Eve is true. God made man white like him and gave him the bad woman who liked the snake and gave us all this trouble." Nevertheless, Joshua, a devout spy and a traitor to his origins, likes to practice bits of token subversion within the family. He answers Betty back suggestively when she orders him to bring a book: "Fetch it yourself. You've got legs under that dress." When he sees Edward making a fuss of a doll that has fallen on the floor, Joshua murmurs, "Baby. Sissy. Girly." But when he divulges that Ellen "talks of love to your wife," Clive finally reprimands him: "Joshua, you go too far. Get out of my sight." Because of this rejection, in the last scene of act I Joshua's rebellion will break out openly. He cuts up Edward's doll, keeps "drinking steadily," and, at the curtain, levels his gun at Clive, who has just proposed a toast to "peace and joy and bliss." We may or may not hear the shot (the stage directions do not specify it), but we see Edward, who has just been cuffed by his father, doing "nothing to warn the others," as he "puts his hands over his ears," evidently to muffle the report.

Clive is about to be killed as the climax of a wedding. Earlier, after having learned about Harry's transgressions with his wife, he refuses to blame his friend. So does his wife.

BETTY: There is something so wicked in me. . . . I am bad, bad, bad—
CLIVE: You are thoughtless, Betty, that's all. Women can be treacherous and evil. They are darker and more dangerous than men.

These sentiments of Clive's—and especially selected adjectives (*dark, treacherous*), which came out during a scene with Mrs. Saunders, recur during Clive's conversation with Harry:

CLIVE: There is something dark about women, that threatens what is best in us. Between men that light burns brightly.
HARRY: I didn't know you felt like that.
CLIVE: Women are irrational, demanding, inconsistent, treacherous, lustful, and they smell different from us.

Harry, misinterpreting, "takes hold of Clive," presumably with some show of affection. Whereupon Clive, the misogynist, necrophiliac, and homophobe, is bewildered, thunderstruck by this "most revolting perversion. Rome fell, Harry, and this sin can destroy an empire." Poor empire: "My God, what a betrayal of the Queen. . . . I cannot keep a secret like this. Rivers will be named after you. . . . You must save yourself from depravity. You must get married." He recommends Caroline Saunders. Harry, in one of the many glints of comic agony that light up the roles, concedes, "I suppose getting married wouldn't be any worse than killing myself." Mrs. Saunders, however, lets him off the hook: "I could never be a wife again. There is only one thing about marriage that I like."[9] Whereupon gay Ellen is recruited to substitute for her as the face-saving bride.

HARRY: Ellen, I don't suppose you would marry me?
ELLEN: What if I said yes?
CLIVE: Run along now, you two want to be alone.

Do they? That settles that. We watch the wedding get under way.[10] We hear Ellen say, "Don't forget me, Betty," and recall her soap-operatic sentiments from not long before Harry's marriage proposal, in lines that reek of extreme comic agony: "Betty, Betty, I love you so much. I want to stay with you forever, my love for you is eternal, stronger than death. I'd rather die than leave you, Betty."

At the end of the act, two of the four women, the mother and daughter, remain locked in their Victorian pretenses. Betty sternly reminds Ellen, "You're not getting married to enjoy yourself," and Maud warns Ellen, "You don't cry at your own wedding, only at other people's." Of the other two women, Ellen bolts from the play (except for one fleeting return), sacrificed to Harry to insure impeccable reputations for them both, while Mrs. Saunders suffers a brutal dismissal from Clive. During the wedding nuptials, he impetuously kisses Mrs. Saunders, provoking his wife into the un-Victorian indignity of an attack on her guest, Mrs. Saunders. While the women wrestle on the ground, he cries, "I don't deserve this," and goes on to order Caroline out of the house, as though she had kissed him.

The five scenes of act I, set in 1880, harp on the untrustworthiness of appearances and on the metaphor of Africa as an unknowable, ravaged woman. Much of the second scene consists of a game of hide-and-seek, a synecdoche for that entire act, which evolves into a process of psychological seek and hide. Hide-and-seek here entails swift, unaccountable entrances and exits, rather like sudden births and deaths. In the nineteenth century's well-made drama, plotting decisions like these—materializing onstage and departing—required either satisfactory or nonsensical reasons, and they still do in the neatly plotted structures of Anouilh, Ayckbourn, and other recent dramatists. In Churchill's writing, however, there is rarely any justification for entrances and exits—no seams, neat or ragged, in the dramatic material. The action within each scene hops, skips, and leaps forward, unwilling to explain its movements in time and space. As a result, Churchill has mapped out a series of staccato miniscenes between two or three figures at a time, who, as often as not, seem to meet in order to take refuge from one another.

Something like the same, terrifically swift jolting forward of the action occurs in the four scenes that make up the second half of *Cloud Nine*, set in postcolonial England, circa 1980. The roles from act I, surviving the passage of a century, have miraculously aged by only twenty-five years. Victoria and Betty are now played by women, Edward by a man. Clive, Maud, Harry, Ellen, and Mrs. Saunders (the last two roles doubled) have given way to four newcomers: Victoria's husband Martin, Edward's promiscuous lover, Gerry, a young lesbian mother named Lin, and her small daughter, Cathy (performed by a male actor), who sings dirty skipping rhymes. Cathy's playmate, the small son of Victoria and

Martin, is heard about and yelled at but never seen; he exists in the story but never enters the action.

In her introduction describing the play's genesis, Churchill remarks that for *Cloud Nine*'s original production the Joint Stock Theatre Group formed a workshop and company of actors "considering their sexual as well as acting experience." This carefully ambiguous phrase could mean all kinds of things, including an odd (for this troupe) intention to cast to type. It implies that the several gay roles were assigned to gay (or occasionally gay) actors. The play started out, according to the playwright, as an exploration of the theme of sexual politics.[11] Later, "the idea of colonialism as a parallel to sexual oppression, which [Churchill] came across in Genet" and that "had been briefly touched on in the workshop" helped her resolve the setting and themes.

In act II the seeking and hiding of act I have been replaced by unrepentant confessing and revealing, which do call to mind the candor (though never the rococo style) of the dialogue in *The Maids*, *The Blacks*, *The Screens*, and, sporadically, *The Balcony*. There are further contrasts (virtual conflicts) between the two halves of this play. The verandah and clearing on the edge of the jungle give way to the jungle of cities—bits of a London park. The passage of the seasons, not a factor in equatorial act I, is stretched in temperate act II over the best part of a year.[12] From drums to humdrums: the exotic fauna in Churchill's nineteenth-century Africa have been supplanted by ordinary, baffled British souls who taste but can never fully digest their modern opportunities. Like the figures in *Uncle Vanya*, they are fatherless: nobody replaces Clive as the domineering (if ludicrous) presence. Are they true descendants of the *colons* from the days of imperial expansion? Or are they, as Jacob Bronowski might have had it, ascendants? The playwright's sympathetic portraits of them do not suggest that they fare better or worse than their predecessors. Liberation of one stripe and another in the late twentieth century may be desirable in itself, but it does not necessarily make life easier to cope with. And liberation comes, anyway, in allowances so controlled that the restrictions still in force seem to contradict the root meanings of the word.

Here we have Lin, a single mother. She walked out two years earlier on a husband who beat her. Like Mrs. Saunders, she could never marry again. She is a lesbian, as Ellen was, but whereas Ellen had no sexual experience with men, Lin has had enough to want to shun them.[13]

LIN: I just hate the bastards.
VICTORIA: Well, it's a point of view.

Lin is "grateful" that her husband let her keep Cathy, although raising the demanding child on her own drains her. She has let Cathy grow up between the sexes, wearing boys' clothes, playing with boys' toys, spouting blunt language, but the girl is also mad for jewelry and ornaments. In scene ii she enters "wearing a pink dress and carrying a rifle." Lin spends much of her day with an eye cocked on Cathy while conversing with Victoria, whom she "really fancies."

Much of the conversation runs one way. Victoria "reads while she talks." Not that she deigns to talk much. The role has gone from being a dummy—if not a model child, at least a passive one, never heard from, at the other end of childhood's scale from Cathy—to a bookish adult who feels itchily tormented by Betty ("Ten minutes talking to my mother and I have to spend two hours in a hot bath"). She doesn't "get on too well with [her] father" and in Martin has found a tolerant mate, who "helps with the washing up and everything" and urges Victoria to take a job up north in Manchester, even if doing that means abandoning him and their son for a time. Like Ayckbourn's Norman, Martin tells his wife, "I just want to make you happy." He personifies self-consciousness: he does not switch off his intellect during sex, and he experiences moral qualms: "I'm not like whatever percentage of American men have become impotent as a direct result of women's liberation, which I am totally in favour of. . . . My one aim is to give you rolling orgasms like I do other women. So why the hell don't you have them? My analysis for what it's worth is that despite all my efforts you still feel dominated by me." Anything but dominant, he confers those rolling orgasms on other women possibly to aid him in "writing a novel about women from the women's point of view." His determination to explicate Victoria's desires and abilities drives her into Lin's arms.

Grown-up Edward, now most of the way out of the closet, works on and off in the park as a gardener and plays housewife for Gerry, who either has grown tired of the arrangement or else never liked it. Gerry feels bored, trapped, and refuses to stay home.

GERRY: I don't want to be married.
EDWARD: I do.
GERRY: Well I'm divorcing you.
EDWARD: I wouldn't want to keep a man who wants his freedom. . . .
GERRY: I'll collect my stuff from the flat in the morning.

Gerry has already recited a soliloquy in which he tells how he picked up a male partner on the commuter train and they managed a reciprocal orgasm during a six-minute ride between stations, and then he avoided seeing the man again. Later, Gerry returns to the park in search of whoever is on tap. "There's never any trouble finding someone. I can have sex any time." (The play was written and performed a couple of years before the first news about AIDS.) He finds what a stage direction calls "Edward from act I," and they talk fondly, as if nothing had gone wrong between them, as if this were a meeting from long ago wrenched out of its time slot. It is now that Gerry sings the song "Cloud Nine." In that position in the play it seems to exude pathos rather than the defiance it suggests as an isolated lyric.

The Edward from act II, disillusioned with men, turns for consolation to his sister, first holding hands with her, then touching her breasts and saying he would rather be a woman.

VICTORIA: I think I should warn you I'm enjoying this.
EDWARD: I'm sick of men.
VICTORIA: I'm sick of men.
EDWARD: I think I'm a lesbian.

In the following scene the pair of them join Lin in a ritual to summon the original mother goddess of creation, of fertility, in the hopes that she will "make us the women we can't be" and that for good measure she will throw in an orgy of sex and cruelty. But all they succeed in calling up is, first, Martin, who was out looking for them without the help of the goddess and tells them, "You're all pissed out of your minds," and then Lin's dead brother, Bill. Killed shortly before in Ireland, a remnant of the empire on which the sun at one time never set, Bill appears briefly. He rattles off a monologue, every line of which has two or three sexual oaths that typify a soldier who tries to sound threatening and virile but who robs the magic word of its sultry glamour by overworking it: "I got so I fucking wanted to kill someone and I got fucking killed myself and I want a fuck."

The Lin-Victoria-Edward ménage swings into operation with Martin as a vaguely attached loose end. It is a momentary expedient only, for Victoria has decided to take the job in Manchester, while the others remain in London, and they have no idea how they will cope and whether they will grate against one another. For the time being, Edward and Martin share the child-sitting and housework while the two women go out to work.

Betty, observing this new, fragile reconciliation, sets about shedding her Victorian fears and neuroses in order to transform herself. She has already left Clive, who evidently did not get shot after all or not fatally wounded. She takes a job as a doctor's receptionist, pays tribute to the formation of the ménage, even lightly envies its members: "You do seem to have such fun all of you." Tentatively she offers to join them and to provide the money for a house where they can all live together. She also strikes up a sexless (or is it?) friendship with Edward's former lover, the amorously gay, freewheeling Gerry. As the strongest dramatic tie between the two acts and the two eras, Betty signifies that she now accepts herself as an independent being, "a separate person," when she burbles her way through a soliloquy about the delights of unashamed masturbation, an improvement over sex with Clive in the old days—or, more commonly, the absence of sex with Clive. She is prompted into these reflections by curt visitations from her mother, Maud, and from Ellen, who once loved her.

The return of these roles—as literal revenants or as living persons garbed as in act I—is left to the discretion of the director. The playwright gives no clues. Nor does she particularize Clive, who strolls back onstage in the last couple of moments to reproach Betty mildly and to regret the passing of the empire as he follows it by passing on into the wings of time. Is he a new old man? Or the Clive of act I, possibly gussied up with ghostly lighting or other trickery? His five lines are clearly meant to be eclipsed, though, by the return of "Betty from Act I" (the male actor), who embraces Betty's older, more resolutely relaxed self. This final moment composes a pact between the Betty who was and the Betty who is, and thus a temporizing of the differences between the old imperial Britain and the new one with its fresh sets of fears and raw, vulnerable spots. It skids briefly into the narcissistic vein of how-I-learned-to-love-myself commercialism but is one of the rare falsely imposed touches in the satire.

One might have expected at least a few "straight" people and many hypocrites who are latter-day Clives to consider the behavior in *Cloud Nine* offensive, warped, or unfortunate, depending on whether they resorted to the language of shock or of pity or therapy. Would these be the same people who sop up fights and shoot-outs and torture in films, theatre, and television shows?[14] Very likely. The author must have meant to scandalize right-thinkers. But her play is satiric, and so she does not judge the roles, their afflictions and addictions; she merely sets them down without disapproval for our inspection. By chance (not imaginably by design) *Cloud Nine* captivated audiences and critics in Devonshire and then in London and went on to welcomes all over the world, even in some of the more puritanical corners of the United States. Critics mostly took exception, if any, only to the harmless age jump of twenty-five years for the roles, coeval with a jump of one hundred years in the action. Detonating a blast of indignation over sexual mores seemed much harder to accomplish in the 1970s and 1980s than it was seventy to one hundred years earlier, when experimental dramatists came in for the sort of public abuse generally reserved for a pimp, a prime minister, or Jack the Ripper.[15]

I have no explanation, watertight or waterlogged, for the cheery reception accorded *Cloud Nine*. It is certainly an outspoken play but just as certainly a farcical play, which trades not only on the innovations of dramatic content introduced by playwrights like Ibsen, Shaw, Wedekind, and Genet but also on the innovations of form practiced by Apollinaire, Beckett, Vian, Ionesco, Pinter, and others. Perhaps the farce keeps the roles at enough of a distance from the spectators to discourage identification: people enjoy a riot of laughs; nobody in the audience feels threatened. Perhaps the juggling of roles, the doubling and tripling, are so ingenious that they soften the hard edges of the material. Perhaps the play's good-natured banter and its warm appreciation of the difference between one temperament and another sugarcoat (even mute) the unmistakable satire. Perhaps the theatregoing public is more selective or specialized than it was a century ago, owing to smaller playhouses and season subscriptions. One picks a company or play that dovetails with one's position on the political spectrum. Perhaps nobody regrets the loss of the empire any longer because today it would be "too much of a handful." ("And Africa," laments the revivified Clive at the close of act II, "is to be communist, I suppose.") Perhaps so many performances of one kind or another, so many distractions, have competed in the past quarter of a century for the chance to fray our sensibilities that nobody notices the trees for the other trees.

Trees, yes. Whatever the play's reception in the future, its two settings invite comparisons and contrasts with outdoor spectacles of the past, specifically with the music- and verse-drenched pastorals of the Renaissance and Baroque periods. Some of these extravaganzas went far beyond the romances between ringleted shepherdesses and their piping swains, the Corios and Silvias with their alternating outbursts of frantic devotion and tart jealousy, into reconstructions of mythical stories. Other writings took on a satiric flavor, like that of *Love's Labor's Lost*, which unwinds in an imaginary version of Navarre, a landlocked island realm between Spain and France, or of Molière's *The Princess of Elis*, set in a Greek valley of antiquity, or the same author's *Comic Pastoral*, a lavish segment of the *Ballet of the Muses*, the huge entertainment concocted for Louis XIV. Thomas McFarland, among other authors, has drawn attention to the range of literary yearnings in history for pastorals, arcadias, Edenic fancies, and utopias, which are linked to dreams of eternal youth.[16] They are probably also connected to embellished memories of unspoiled childhoods. In both acts of *Cloud Nine* the comic pastoral has gone to seed—first, during what some patriots considered a golden age of empire, now seen as leaden, and a century later, back at home, in the "motherland," in what serves townspeople as a pitiable contraction of the vanished open forest and grassland, the realms of green, where miracles might have happened.

SUMMARY
Farcical Overlay

The word *tragifarce* is a relative newcomer to the critical vocabulary. Tragedy and farce, long regarded as extremities of literature and drama, fulfill our yearning, when united, for an ideal wholeness and our beliefs that opposites attract—but more, that extremes can and often do adjoin and spill over into each other. I would broadly separate a tragifarce from a melodramatic farce by stressing that, in a tragifarce, the roles seem to bring trouble on themselves as they head inexorably toward what they also wish most strongly to avoid, whereas in a "melofarce" trouble happens by chance, that is, at the will of the playwright. The roles are buffeted rather than perversely purposeful. I propose a distinction between tragifarce and tragicomedy much like the one between farce and comedy: the comic components are intellectual, depending on wit, that is, deliberate intentions to amuse on the part of the witty roles, while the farcical components depend on the roles' unintentional funniness, which is mainly knockabout and may even be anti-intellectual.

In this segment of the book I have pulled tragifarce under the aegis of comic agony. Anybody who maintains that the book's title should be "Comic and Farcical Agonies" is correct. But there are plenty of borderline cases. Like exceptions that disprove rules, they defensibly belong on both sides. If one insists on a resolution, under which rubric, comedy or farce, does *The Importance of Being Earnest* most happily sit? I see no reason, though, to hew to a resolution other than the off-chance that it will aid our appreciation of the play as written or performed. For other purposes the choice is likely to be arbitrary.[1]

The composition of this third and final segment smacks of bias: four of the five plays it examines started life in France. They do not support a willfully Francophile plan; they fell into place because they felt to me like inevitable choices. During this century Paris has offered a wider and more variegated drama than other national theatre centers because it has been the most venturesome and the most playful. Paris has also been uncommonly hospitable to foreign artists, and of the four authors working in French, one was born in Russia, another in Romania, another in Ireland, and Apollinaire, born in Rome, had a Russian *émigrée* for a mother and an unknown father.[2] Comic agony is not a movement and not quite a genre, but it has enjoyed an international inspiration.

Plays that seem to me to fall into this third segment include Arden's *Live Like Pigs*; most of Peter Barnes's work, especially *Red Noses, The Ruling Class,* and *Laughter!*; most of Kenneth Bernard's plays, including *How We Danced While We*

Burned; Brecht's *Arturo Ui*; Fo's *Accidental Death of an Anarchist*; García Lorca's *The Shoemaker's Prodigious Wife*; Giraudoux's *The Madwoman of Chaillot*; Mrozek's *Out at Sea* and *Charlie*; O'Casey's *Purple Dust*; Shaw's *Shewing Up of Blanco Posnet*; Shepard's *Fool for Love* and *The Tooth of Crime*; Stoppard's *Jumpers* and *Travesties*; Synge's *Tinker's Wedding*; Pirandello's *Tonight We Improvise*; and that astonishing, premodern by birth (1822) but otherwise indisputably modern precursor by a prodigy, Grabbe's *Jest, Satire, Irony, and Deeper Significance*, a title that is an extended synonym for comic agony.

CONCLUSION
The Playful End

In equal scale, weighing delight and dole.
CLAUDIUS, IN *Hamlet*

Not really *equal* scale. Seldom equal in print. Just about never equal in performance, not even in two performances of the same production. Delight and dole as variables make the plays discussed in the preceding chapters all the more eligible as topics for disagreement, a word that is a harsh synonym for dialogue. Disagreement, arising from dialectical clashes between delight and dole, will keep stirring up these and other plays, stop them from settling peacefully, like turtles, in the mud of cultural consciousness. Disagreement will also give one healthy airing after another to their themes; and among those themes comic agony harps on two that are perennial, mortality and sexuality.

Mortality, not death. Authors working the vein of comic agony return over and over, squarely and glancingly, to their and our worries about making the most of our span, which a large proportion of us do not accept as a firm allotment. Into many of these plays the questions of suicide enter directly and indirectly—indirectly when the roles seem bent on betraying their own best interests.

And sexuality, not love. Drama's forms seem never to have become as apposite for love stories as the novel's proved to be, whether in the supreme fictions of the nineteenth century—Tolstoy, Flaubert, Hardy—or such later prose recountings of love's demands and obsessions as Italo Svevo's *As a Man Grows Older* (La Senilitá) and García Márquez's recent *Love in the Time of Cholera.* Plays nearly always pull love into collision with some other force, rather than finding it a topic to explore wholly, by itself. In the past century, playwrights have turned gratefully to sexuality as a substitute topic that their stages can handle justly. And, at first, reticently: Ibsen serves as the model of discretion in *Ghosts, Hedda Gabler, The Lady from the Sea, The Master Builder, Little Eyolf,* and *When We Dead Awaken* in dropping hints of illicit, irregular, and ferocious sex. He got mixed results. Both Ibsen and Shaw (following dissemination of the three "Plays Unpleasant") had to contend with battalions of prudes and hypocrites who succeeded in banning their plays in some places while unwittingly promoting them in others. Wedekind waited almost a decade and a half for the first production of his gelded *Spring's Awakening* and did not live to see it and his pair of Lulu plays performed intact. He missed the second of them, *Pandora's Box,* in Pabst's durable film version (1929) by eleven years.[1] But several decades later in the United States, despite the code in Hollywood and flaccid controversies over such works as *The Moon Is Blue* and *The Seven-Year Itch*, the commercial theatre, like theatre and movies elsewhere, needed hardly any prodding from fringe productions to confirm what it had always known: that S-E-X can spell capital box office. *The Balcony* ran off-Broadway in 1960 with a cast of some of the finest younger actors in the country and under the directorship of José Quintero, whose O'Neill productions had made him a culture hero. Many commentators who welcomed or resented Genet's tirades about the sale of sex kinks reckoned with his poetry and his courage (or impudence) but hardly (or not) at all with his comic gifts.

Some directors have since come to rely on sexuality not as a stand-in for love but for its peepshow aspects—love*making*. (Why should movies, especially the porn variety, shovel up all the bucks?) Their stagings celebrate the visual and auditory and faintly provocative meetings of bodies pushing and pulling at each other accompanied by roars, sighs, and labored fugal music, a spectacle that is so manifestly not the real experience that they often play it for easy chortles. Bumping, humping, groping, masturbating, and oral pastimes have grown popular—required—among inferior deconstructors and those who ape them. When they flatten the inherent drama in a play, ironing out the folds and tucks of conflict contrived by the playwright in order to replace them with their own wrinkles, they reduce different plays to the same measly assortment of physical clichés and exorbitance.[2] An argument or even a debate turns into a scrap. Flirtation turns into extended copulative feats. Deconstruction turns into destruction.

In the Introduction I mentioned that the three subdivisions add up to a quantitative breakdown of comic agony, by degree or by amounts of the opposed ingredients and the extent to which they, the serious and the laughable, interplay. For those readers who like their distinctions less soggy, I append a slightly more rigorous breakdown, which is qualitative. In dramatic writings that rely on comic agony we find one or more of the following four types of interweaving or mingling or fighting-it-out between unlike genres: within scenes (a comic or farcical role plays opposite a tragic or pathetic role, e.g., Jean and Julie in *Miss Julie*); within roles (characteristics in a single part are simultaneously serious and funny, pathetic and laughable, e.g., both Vanya and Waffles in *Uncle Vanya* or Hjalmar and his father in *The Wild Duck*);[3] in the overall structure of a play-within-a-play, a sample of theatricalism (an outer and an inner play conflict; one of them is comic, the other not, e.g., Pirandello's theatre-in-the-theatre trilogy, *Poor Bitos*, and some other plays by Anouilh, such as *The Rehearsal*); and between speech and behavior, dialogue and stage directions (roles established as comic or partially comic or farcical and lines that are plaintive or agonized, e.g., those of Ann in *Man and Superman* or of Marchbanks in *Candida* or of any role in Beckett's longer plays).

Two halves of a work, or even of a scene, may come into funny-serious conflict. We then confront not interweaving but alternation, not comic agony but tragicomedy.[4] Sometimes this will be the happy ending tacked on to a threatening dramatic situation, that is, a tragic or melodramatic ending averted or smoothed over, as in *The Comedy of Errors, The Tempest, The Winter's Tale,* and *Measure for Measure,* as well as O'Neill's *"Anna Christie"* and Bergman's film *Ansiktet* (known in English as *The Face* or *The Magician*). In other instances the tragicomedy will be the obverse, a troubling end imposed on a lighthearted situation, as in Chaplin's late picture *A King in New York*.

Of the plays discussed in this book I admire some more than others and for a variety of reasons. I hope, though, that the chapters do not anywhere suggest that I rate comic agony superior to tragicomedy or other genres. Nor do I claim that it is always as easy as words imply to distinguish alternation from interweaving. A new name for a bundling together of accepted works is bound to be difficult to accommodate mentally, at least for a time. If these fifteen plays exhibit common characteristics, between them as artifacts there also gape divergences, much as we find divergences between different works by the same artist and between different productions of the same work or different performances of the same production, caused by directors' reconceptualizing or by casting or by accident. There are a number of further plays I could have put forward as examples of comic agony. A representative sampling once seemed like an enticing possibility—from diverse countries, religious sensibilities, centuries or decades, ethnic sources, positions on the economic treadmill, from men, women, gay and lesbian authors—a testimonial to this writer's political and literary liberality. A number of those plays excited me, and I actually wrote about them. I withheld the results, though, when rereading the chapters released more dole than delight. For consolation I listed some of them in the three Summary sections.

The plays' initial and continued appeal to me arose from one common feature, their irrepressible playfulness. By "playfulness" I do not mean mere whimsy, anymore than I believe that by itself playfulness is always worth attention. Rather, these authors' refusal to take themselves altogether seriously, even while coping with a maelstrom of agonizing material, inspires my respect and affection. Being playful bespeaks modesty and at the same time the most overweening artistic desire: to monopolize clashing interpretations of an idea or a feeling. It's also chancy. Playwrights who range over the terrain of comic agony pit themselves against themselves; they endanger their reception; they strain the goodwill and reputations of accomplished collaborators; they risk baffling audiences with a plethora of theatre, knowing that most audiences want to understand everything and miss nothing and will let out their irritation when those two conditions go unfulfilled. For the playwright who longs above all else for acceptance, Dryden's question retains its sting: "Are not mirth and compassion things incompatible?" What can a playwright hope to gain from delving into the doublenesses of comic agony? Perhaps an impulse to record life more accurately than a film can (even a documentary) or a novel or one of those popular treatises on philosophy or religion or sociology that pledges straightforward answers—life with its live actors and impromptus and quivering impurities. But perhaps the playwright has an aptitude for transposing the mixed impressions life constantly shoots at us, what Dr. Johnson called "the real state of sublunary nature." Today that "real state" seems unreal. So many contradictions does it flaunt (suburban living with its open spaces, such as toxic lawns; cars that cannot move along their "expressways"; cities in which summer heat is aggravated by the spewings of air conditioners; poor, grudging medical attention, if any, for those who are most sick; the worst food sold to those most in need of good nourishment) that identifying a sprinkling of them seems like callous disregard for the countless remainder.

Justifying at more length this—what is it? taste? whim? aspiration? pressure?—this playwriting ambition to dramatize the comic agonies of life might be a stimulating exercise, but concluding chapters, like concluding scenes, should come to a brisk end. For now I will put the ambition down to ornery temperaments of playwrights and their impatience with the unimportance of being earnest—with the self-puffery that has taken over the language of teachers, newspaper columnists, politicos, and other moving mouths on television, the expanding vacuity that threatens to invade, maybe swamp, all critical writings on the arts.[5]

In the realm of comic agony the best works I know consist of substantial content molded by playful forms. The pain remains, but it has been transcended, triumphed over. The creating artists step outside their agony and make toys of it, put it through hoops and somersaults, racket it around on unprecedented landscapes. They seek more effectual and, if they are fortunate, more durable ways to convey it than by whining or pleading or weeping.

Their playfulness, a species of poetry, becomes their claim to remembrance.

NOTES

Introduction

1. John Dryden, "An Essay of Dramatic Poesy," 1668, in Bernard F. Dukore, ed., *Dramatic Theory and Criticism* (New York, 1974), 325.

2. Samuel Johnson, preface to *The Plays of Shakespeare*, in W. K. Wimsatt, Jr., ed., *Samuel Johnson on Shakespeare* (New York, 1960), 23 ff.

3. See Harriett Hawkins, "What Neoclassical Criticism Tells Us about What Shakespeare Does Not Do," in Maurice Charney, ed., *Shakespearean Comedy* (New York, 1980), 37-46. Hawkins writes about Johnson on Shakespeare, among other matters, which include remarks on the wavering (not to say, hospitable) boundaries of comedy. The essays collected by Charney form a series of useful correctives to dogmatic theory.

4. "Just as Greek tragedy retained and developed the satyr-play, so Elizabethan tragedy retained a satyric counterpoint in its clown scenes and the farcical underplots of *Faustus* and many later tragedies. The same element provides those superb episodes of the Porter in *Macbeth*, the grave-diggers in *Hamlet*, and the serpent bearer in *Antony and Cleopatra*, which so baffled Classically-minded critics who had forgotten about the satyr-play." Northrop Frye, *Anatomy of Criticism* (New York, 1968), 292.

More than twenty years before Marlowe wrote *Dr. Faustus*, Thomas Preston had subtitled his *Cambyses* "a lamentable Tragedie, mixed full of plesant mirth." The medieval and still popular *Second Shepherd's Play* perfectly fits the definition of tragicomedy as it evolves from rural knockabout humor to Christmas piety.

5. Archibald Henderson, *George Bernard Shaw: Man of the Century* (New York, 1956), 471.

6. Eric Bentley, *The Life of the Drama* (New York, 1964), 353. *The Life of the Drama* did give new life to the dramatic genres and to the components of theatre that Aristotle originally discerned. Bentley reformulates them so that they apply to modern plays and apply afresh to older ones.

7. Bernard Shaw, review of *The Wild Duck,* by Henrik Ibsen, 17 May 1897, in *Our Theatre of the Nineties,* vol. 3 (London, 1932), 136-37.

8. In acting classes teachers will sometimes ask students to play a scene of unrelieved tragedy as farce or to do the opposite. Directors also like to loosen up their actors in similar fashion. Now and then I have invited graduate students to conceive a contrary reinterpretation of a tragedy, melodrama, or farce with no alteration of the dialogue or stage directions. Some of the more imaginative results enlivened the task of reading term papers well beyond my expectations. But these exercises took the plays in question altogether into the comic or the agonized. They did not constitute comic agony.

9. Later "Antigones" have tended toward the self-aggrandizing heroine or hero, such as Ibsen's Dr. Stockmann or Miller's John Proctor.

10. George Thomson, *Aeschylus and Athens* (New York, 1968), 156-58.

11. William Arrowsmith, "A Greek Theatre of Ideas," in *Classical Tragedy: Greek and Roman*, ed. Robert W. Corrigan (New York, 1990), 358.

Virgin Sacrifice

1. The translations quoted in this chapter come from Rolf Fjelde, trans., *Ibsen: The Complete Major Prose Plays* (New York, 1978), 391-490.

2. The plays include *Brand, Ghosts, The Lady from the Sea*, and *Little Eyolf*. Hedda Gabler dies pregnant—her child is never born—but she burns the manuscript that she may have unwittingly "mothered." In *When We Dead Awaken* Irene the model accuses Rubek the sculptor of having sacrificed their "child" by altering his sculpture.

3. In *Iphigenia at Aulis*, so that the Greek fleet may secure a wind to sail it to Troy, Iphigenia embraces her fate as a victim of Artemis. Like her, Polyxena in *Hecuba* goes purposefully to her death at the hands of the Greeks: she will govern her own destiny, not submit passively to murder. In *The Heracleidae* Makaria, the daughter of Heracles, offers up her life to ensure sanctuary in Athens for her brothers and sisters. All three of these young women are virgins, as is Antigone. In choosing death they explicitly renounce marriage and children of their own. They become "brides" of Hades.

4. In an earlier draft of the play the room was not a study but a billiard room, in which the greenness would have been more obtrusive.

5. Were Ekdal and Werle actually guilty of illegal tree-felling? Werle says his former partner was irresponsible and foolish; Ekdal should have recognized and respected the boundaries of the private property. Gregers, however, now believes his father let an innocent Ekdal take the rap. The play does not corroborate either stand. Werle does seem conscience-stricken, like his son, trying to make up for the Ekdal family's misfortunes by the aid he gives. He also welcomes Gregers back to Christiania warmly and offers to let him manage the firm. One gets the impression that he is attempting to buy Gregers's silence. But Werle might equally be doing his paternal duty by his son, as he sees it, and he may have helped the Ekdals because he feels honestly sorry about the tarnishing of their name. Further, Old Ekdal does seem woolly minded in the action, much as Werle describes him as having been in the story.

6. An affair at one time between Gina and Gregers might make Gregers and his father former rivals for Gina and exacerbate the bitter feelings between them. It would also clarify his sudden departure for Hoidal, which took place, according to him, longer ago than Hjalmar remembers, that is, before Hedvig was born. Could Gregers have been sent away by his father, who then took advantage of his absence to become Gina's lover? These and other speculations receive no support from the critical figure, the most enigmatic role in the play: that of Gina.

7. Mary McCarthy, "The Will and Testament of Ibsen," originally published in *Partisan Review*, reprinted in Mary McCarthy, *Sights and Spectacles* (New York, 1956), and in several anthologies of Ibsen criticism.

8. Gregers is a bachelor at thirty-five or so, and we catch no hint of his ever having been close to any woman but his mother. According to Thompson, Hjalmar is "clearly impotent—married fifteen years and Hedvig not his daughter." Alan Reynolds Thompson, "Ibsen as Psychoanatomist," *Educational Theatre Journal* 3, no.1 (March 1951): 37.

9. Ingjald Nissen, *Sjelelige Kriser i Mennesekets Liv: Henrik Ibsen og den Modern Psykologi* (Spiritual crises in people's lives: Henrik Ibsen and modern psychology), (Oslo, 1931). Dounia B. Christiani expands on Nissen's theory; see Christiani, ed., *The Wild Duck: A Norton Critical Edition* (New York, 1968), 211.

10. Hermann Weigand, *The Modern Ibsen* (1925; New York, 1960), 158.

11. James Walter McFarlane, ed. and trans., *Ibsen: An Enemy of the People, The Wild Duck, Rosmersholm* (New York, 1961), 440.

12. We have no proof from the play that Werle did indulge in affairs during his marriage—the business with Gina came later—but his wife told Gregers so and Gregers believed her.

13. The varied items were deposited in the attic long ago by an old sea captain known as the Flying Dutchman, although he was not Dutch. In Wagner's opera, it will be recalled, the Dutchman anchors his ship off the Norwegian coast and is finally saved from the curse of having to sail the seas by the sacrifice of Senta, the daughter of a Norwegian sea captain. Senta had fallen in love with a portrait of the Dutchman's double, a Spanish nobleman. It would be challenging to explicate this mention of the Dutchman in various ways—as a reference to the sea, to Norway, to legendary heroes and heroines, to Wagner, even to Nietzsche—but I cravenly avoid the challenge.

14. Hjalmar blames his daughter's weak eyes on heredity: his mother evidently had "bad eyes" too. When Hjalmar later learns that Werle's sight is also failing, he (and the others) will assume that Hedvig is Werle's daughter. But the play does not resolve the paternity one way or the other. Otto Reinert eloquently draws attention to the flow of Ibsen's images that deal with seeing and blindness in "Sight Imagery in *The Wild Duck*," in *Journal of English and Germanic Philology* 15, no. 3 (July 1956): 457-62, reprinted in Christiani, *Wild Duck*. Other critics and directors have drawn attention to the play's subtheme of photography, which might be fraught with implications about "seeing": seeing realism, seeing through the eyes (and artistry) of others, the selection of a viewpoint and focus, and so on.

15. In the course of the scene Mrs. Sørby offers Hjalmar financial assistance from her husband-to-be, which he and Gina promptly refuse; mentions that Werle will soon be blind, "helpless," and dependent on her; brings a deed of gift that confers a monthly income of one hundred crowns on Ekdal for the rest of his life, with the sum to pass on after he dies to Hedvig; hints to Gina that a woman should tell her husband-to-be everything doubtful about herself—she has been frank with Werle, she says, and has let him know "every last scrap of gossip about me" (in saying this she goes against Relling's advice to bury any truth that may jeopardize one's happiness, and she confirms Gregers's advice to bring the truth to light); and says that for most of his life Werle has had to listen to "sermons on his sins," delivered, we assume, by the first Mrs. Werle and repeated in the play by Gregers—she adds that "generally those sermons were aimed at the most imaginary failings."

On the strength of this last matter, I take it that Werle is no more assuredly Hedvig's father than Mrs. Sørby is her mother. Before or after Werle "had his way" with Gina, Mrs. Sørby might have been his mistress and become the mother of his illegitimate child. In this case they could have hit on the idea of promoting a home for their daughter by arranging for Gina to marry Hjalmar. Gina would naturally know about this arrangement and accept the payments for the child's upkeep in the form of a generous salary for Old Ekdal's copying work. Gina would still love the child she had raised. Between the second and third drafts of the play Ibsen deleted a line of Gina's that ran: "I brought her into the world." See "Second Draft of *The Wild Duck*," in McFarlane, *Ibsen*, 282.

Both Hedvig and Hjalmar vaguely entertain the possibility that Hedvig does not belong to Hjalmar and Gina. Hedvig conjectures to Gregers that her mother could have found her: like the wild duck, she may have come into the house as a "gift." And Hjalmar, who gripes that Gina and Mrs. Sørby often "whisper and gossip" together, says that Mrs. Sørby "always cared a lot for Hedvig" and that she and Werle could take the girl away from him "any time they liked." Mrs. Sørby does bring Hedvig a present for every birthday. When she appears in her big scene, she is put out to find Hjalmar, Relling, and Gregers there. She wanted, she says, a private talk with Gina.

All these points are circumstantial. Hedvig's true parentage is a fascinating and unresolved but ultimately incidental question.

16. Hjalmar, it's true, is fond of hyperbole, and when he breaks out with these epithets he is in spiritual turmoil: incensed with Relling for having led him to think he is capable of a great invention; incensed with Hedvig for not being his daughter, as he believes or fears to believe; and annoyed at himself for having announced that he is walking out on his family and home when he does not want to (and subsequently does not do so).

Hjalmar never expresses any anger toward Gregers. This reticence may be one reason why Gregers plies his ideal so industriously for Hjalmar's benefit. That ideal has been rejected over and over. Hjalmar is the first person we know of who listens sympathetically to Gregers. He feels that Gregers needs "a friend's watchful eye on him." Later he seems to relish Gregers's respect for him as a man of extraordinary potential.

17. Aesculapius (or Asklepios), the first physician and son of Apollo, was so skilled in the medical arts that Zeus, fearing that he might cure all illness and make men immortal, killed him off and banished him "downstairs" to Hades. Thanks to his good works below and to nepotistic pressure by his father, he was later taken up to Olympus to become the god of medicine. His nickname was the Leech.

There are two references to leeches in *The Wild Duck*. Hedvig tells Gregers that she taught herself to say prayers "when Daddy was sick and had leeches on his neck, and then he said he was in the jaws of death." The leeches must have been applied by Relling. Relling subsequently mentions that he made Molvik "demonic" by creating a fontanelle on his neck to draw out the poison. (Translations usually omit the word *fontanelle* in favor of some more conversational modern equivalent.) A fontanelle is a medically induced blister or ulcer for withdrawing bodily fluid—blood, pus, or, in Molvik's case, a flow of unhealthy ideas—from the head. Its use is an obsolete form of surgery (although liable to return under some new medical pretext). A fontanelle, then, is an artificial leech.

18. In addition to the duck-and-dog coupling, there are other kinds of pairing and cross-pairing between the roles. We have two fathers, two sons, two former housekeepers merging into wives, and a doctor and a theologian to minister blunderingly to body and soul. There are even two servants of Werle's who get the play started, a pair of customers who insist that Gina photograph them "as a couple," and, for some reason, "two separate chimney shafts" in the attic.

In the cross-pairing, Ekdal and Hjalmar are both hunters (one with a rifle, the other with the pistol that kills Hedvig) and both "copiers" (one with a pen, the other with a camera), and both have frustrated careers. The Werles, father and son, try in their contrasting ways to improve the lot of the Ekdal family. Hedvig and Gregers are both fantasizers, and they behave like only children, whether they are or not. Relling and Gregers are apostles. Gina does photographic retouching, while Relling spreads vital lies. At the end the two fathers, Werle and Ekdal, both retreat to the forest, the one actually, the other symbolically. (It is also possible to work out a number of threesomes or triads, but the play is then liable to seem less like a series of peopled events than a string of algebraic equations.) The pairings of opposites and "resemblers" seem to me to enhance the unification of the roles.

19. Brian W. Downs says that it "does not seem to me an expression at all consonant with his usual speech and is either farcically inappropriate or else cloudily portentous." Downs, *A Study of Six Plays by Ibsen* (New York, 1950), 155.

20. There is at least one other dramatic connection between Ekdal and Hedvig. At the end of the second act Ekdal has fallen asleep. Gina and Hjalmar lift him and carry him out. At the end of the fifth act they will similarly carry out Hedvig's corpse.

21. The imprecision of a word like *nature* has critical advantages if it emphasizes the degree to which this play draws on the combined poetry of myth, history, visual and verbal symbols, and theatrical enactment. But the whole work does not exist on different "levels" or in separable "dimensions." The play is itself, all of itself, at the same time. Realistic conflicts, myth, historical analogy, and supernaturalism interpenetrate. Ibsen's poetry—all poetry—is indivisible.

22. Rolf Fjelde, foreword to the original publication of his translation of *The Wild Duck*, in *Ibsen: Four Major Plays* (New York, 1965), xxviii-xxix.

23. The sea's inexplicable appeal is one of the subjects of Ibsen's later play *The Lady from the Sea*. Its heroine, Ellida Wangel, says, "I believe that, if only mankind had adapted itself from the start to life on the sea—or perhaps *in* the sea—then we would have become something much different and more advanced than we are now. Both better—and happier." She adds that man's regret at having become a land animal "is the deepest source of all [his] melancholy." From Fjelde's translation in *Ibsen: The Complete Major Prose Plays*.

Ibsen's use of the metaphor of a drowned world does not mean that he believed man had once actually dwelt in a Rousseauistic state of nature, nor that life in the modern era is less "free" and "open." He is dealing with an instinctual *desire* to live close to nature and with fears that there has been a rupture between man and his original environment.

24. A few examples include: "My home is down in ruins around me." "How could I go on here and have my heart shattered every hour of the day?" "There's this horrible doubt—maybe Hedvig never really, truly has loved me." "The joys of life *I* have to renounce are higher than rabbits."

Frosty Spring

1. The translation of *Spring's Awakening* quoted in this chapter is by Eric Bentley and taken from Eric Bentley, ed., *The Modern Theatre*, vol. 6 (New York, 1960), reissued in Eric Bentley, ed. and trans., *Before Brecht: Four German Plays* (New York, 1989). Some recent translations, such as one performed (and copyrighted in 1989) but not yet published by Douglas Langworthy, prefer the title *Spring Awakening*.

2. Story filed by Ralph Blumenthal, *New York Times*, 22 Dec. 1968.

3. *New York Times*, 13 April 1970.

4. In the mid-1980s the Monty Python team's film *The Meaning of Life* featured a

sketch in which a teacher, played by John Cleese, earnestly tried to instruct a class of schoolboys in the details of the sex act by demonstrating on a bed at the front of the classroom, using his wife as partner. The boys yawned, dozed, and gazed out of the windows, consumed by apathy.

5. Francis J. Ziegler, introduction to *The Awakening of Spring*, trans. Francis J. Ziegler (Philadelphia, 1912). H. F. Garten, *Modern German Drama* (New York, 1962). Similar intentions ascribed to Wedekind of striking home a message have continued to greet almost every production of the play in the United States and in Britain. See, for example, Benedict Nightingale's review of a production at the National Theatre in the *New Statesman*, 7 June 1974. I did not see the production. Like other stagings, it may have invited harsh critical strictures by compelling the text to "speak out."

6. In a review of a W. E. Yuill's translation of Wedekind's *Diary of an Erotic Life,* John Simon says that in the untranslated autobiography of Wedekind's wife, she "correctly sized up the phenomenon that fascinated her husband, 'that tragic events flip over into the grotesque.'" *New York Times Book Review*, 18 Nov. 1990, p. 13.

7. Wedekind's apparently arbitrary plotting, with its broken-off scenes, is worked out with care. Act I has five scenes. Wendla appears in the first and third, while Melchior alternates by appearing in the second and fourth. The fifth scene brings them together in their most significant encounter. The pattern is all the more elegant for being unobtrusive.

In synopsizing the action here, I follow each of the three main roles through his or her scenes, in order to emphasize the interdependence of the roles. The plotting grows fairly complex. There is a double main plot, Wendla-Melchior and Moritz-Melchior, which puts Melchior at the center of the action, but Wendla and Moritz are involved in secondary plots that involve their relationships with their families, schoolfellows, and other people.

8. I have not been able to discover whether the broken lines were inserted through caution on Wedekind's part or, more likely, owing to the nervousness of his original publisher. This is the only enacted coition in the action, but the broken lines break in at subsequent places when there is masturbation onstage.

9. Most of the children in the play feel unworthy of their parents. In another scene Martha says her father and mother "would feel something was missing if they didn't have a little mess like me for a daughter."

10. The question of whether the man or the woman derives more satisfaction out of the sexual act relates to the causes of Tiresias's blindness and prophetic gifts. See the chapter on *The Breasts of Tiresias*.

11. The cold comfort of Frau Gabor's if-everybody argument points up how little Wedekind's play has dated. Unusual acts or words, from the most experimental and rash to the barely unorthodox, still give rise to absurd fears of setting "new precedents" for "everybody."

12. Wedekind must have felt pleased with this line about the Pyramids. He used it in a later play, *King Nicolo*.

13. Hänschen, inflamed by his Palma Vecchio print, thinks of developing a crooked back, lackluster eyes, and marrowless bones. Moritz, brooding about Fräulein Snandulia the seductress and Ilse the plaything of artists, cries, "It saps my strength." We smile at

such sentiments today, yet some seventy years after the play was written "a pamphlet addressed to boys and issued by the U.S. Public Health Service [said] auto-erotism (which it [called] 'self abuse') 'may seriously hinder a boy's progress toward vigorous manhood.'" Fredric Wertham, introduction to *Auto-Erotism* by Wilhelm Stekel (New York, 1961), 6.

Sireless in Russia

1. In practice, clumsy staging can obscure the complexity of the moment. Amid the hubbub of movement and cries from the five actors present, a director eager for simplified, suspenseful, un-Chekhovian results may allow the noise and the firing of the pistol to drown the word "Bang!"

2. I am quoting here and subsequently from the translation by Ann Dunnigan in *Chekhov: The Major Plays* (New York, 1964).

3. In *The Wood Demon* Vanya's first name is George (Gyorgy). An English version of the play appears in S.S. Koteliansky, trans., *Plays and Stories: Anton Tchekhov* (London, 1937). The later play diverges from this earlier one—is, one might say, liberated from it— especially in its two outer acts, I and IV, in other respects, some of which are mentioned later in the chapter, but most obviously in the refashioning of the roles. Eric Bentley's *In Search of Theatre* (New York, 1953), 322-43, traces the artistry deployed by Chekhov in transforming one play into the other.

4. The subtitle, however, *Scenes from Country Life*, seems to lighten the emphasis on Vanya and to hint that the play gives a partial portrait of contemporary conditions.

5. Debts to Dostoevsky are plentiful in Chekhov's writings. As an extreme example, consider two lines of verse from *The Possessed* as an inspiration for the theme of *The Cherry Orchard*: "The peasant with his axe is coming, / Something terrible will happen." Fyodor Dostoevsky, *The Possessed*, trans. Constance Garnett (New York, 1963), 32.

6. David Magarshack deduces that the "evil" Elena "represents bodily beauty" and goes out of her way to steal Astrov from the "good" Sonya, who "represents spiritual beauty," but that Elena never intends to have an affair with Astrov or to forsake the safety of her marriage. Such an interpretation is theatrically workable, but the moral distinction this critic insists on between Elena and Sonya strikes me as being too schematic for a play by Chekhov. Magarshack states that "the line of demarcation between the two [women's roles] is drawn with unmistakable clarity by Chekhov." See Magarshack, *Chekhov the Dramatist* (New York, 1960), 260-62.

7. Eric Bentley remarks a propos of Vanya's intentions: "If missing his aim at such close quarters be an accident, it is surely one of those unconsciously willed accidents that Freud wrote of. Vanya is no murderer" (*In Search of Theatre*, 325).

8. A television documentary made during the first flush of *perestroika* and dealing with the history of a Miss U.S.S.R. contest showed at one point a poster on a wall with a motto in English: "It's so boring to be beautiful."

9. In *Contradictory Characters* (New York, 1973), 75-104, I argued that Natasha in *Three Sisters*, who is typically portrayed in stagings and criticism as an out-and-out villain, is as much a victim as are the sisters and Andrei.

10. Vanya is forty-seven during the action. If Vera was his older sister, then Sonya might be over thirty and thus older than Elena, who is twenty-seven.

11. In his closing speech, shortly before he lies down to die (along with, presumably,

Old Russia), Firs does mention that his strength is sapped, but his final moments are given over to chastising himself for not running after his master, Gayev, in case the latter has forgotten to put on his fur coat.

12. One of Telegin's outworn, dimly perceived ideals is what he calls pride, or what we might call doing the wrong thing for the right reason. He explains (not without further pride in the telling) that he gave financial support to his wife, who ran off with her lover the day after Telegin married her, and that he went on to provide for the education of her illegitimate children.

Some of Chekhov's disjunct figures who succeed Telegin include Solyony and Chebutykin in *Three Sisters* and Charlotta, Varya, and Epikhodov in *The Cherry Orchard*. In the latter play the disjunct Lopakhin even makes a stab at filling the fatherly role in the family. In doing so, he unintentionally wrecks the family.

13. The pitiful hanger-on appears strikingly in several of Pinter's plays, from the kidnapped Stanley in *The Birthday Party* to Davies in *The Caretaker* and Sam in *The Homecoming*.

14. V. Yermilov saw "the main theme" of *Uncle Vanya* as "beauty and its destruction," introduced lightly in the first scene when Marina remarks on how Astrov's looks have deteriorated over the previous eleven years. The theme is sustained by Astrov's denunciation of negligence over the forests, by the running-down of the estate, and by the indolence, the uselessness, of Elena. Yermilov's original chapter in a 1948 book about Chekhov's dramaturgy provides an illuminating study of the play. This theme of beauty wasted also applies to several other Chekhov plays. A condensed version of the essay, translated by Elizabeth Henderson, appears in Robert Louis Jackson, ed., *Chekhov: A Collection of Critical Essays* (Englewood Cliffs, N.J., 1967), 112-20.

15. English translations offer different stage directions preceding this speech. Ann Dunnigan and Elisaveta Fen: "with bravado"; Stark Young: "with false nonchalance"; Ronald Hingley: "inwardly fuming." The last one seems closest to the literal Russian which says "sulking" or "sullenly" (the archaic word *budiruya*).

16. An ironic interpretation usually comes about after a play has had many showings and has grown familiar. The director and actors not only present a "new concept" but also mean it to be assessed in contrast to the earlier interpretations. They thereby toy with the significance of the act of performance.

17. Whatever the meaning of the glasses worn by all the Company of Toga actors, the parasols invoked memories of Winnie in Beckett's *Happy Days*.

18. In *The Sea Gull* young Treplev, who ultimately shoots himself, is, like Voinitsky of *The Wood Demon*, a modern Russian Hamlet of sorts. His mother, Arkadina, plays a Gertrude, his uncle, Sorin, a benevolent Claudius, and his beloved, Nina, an Ophelia; but the father figure, the Hamlet senior, is missing. Act I of *Three Sisters* tells us that the father of the Prozorov family, the General, died a year before. During the rest of the play the sisters and their brother will grieve that they cannot return to Moscow—but to the Moscow of their childhood when the General lived and took care of them and the property. The owner of the house and estate in *The Cherry Orchard*, Ranevskaya, whose husband died, cannot be persuaded to stay home and discharge her obligations to the house, land, servants, and family. She runs off to her selfish lover in Paris and squanders what remains of her income on him. As a result of her being unable to stand in for the father-manager, the

estate is bought out from under her.

Inward Journey

1. Of the many translations of this play in and out of print, I have found three of the most easily available to be the most useful: Harry G. Carlson's in *Strindberg: Five Plays* (Berkeley, Calif., 1983); Elizabeth Sprigge's in *Six Plays of Strindberg* (New York, 1955); and Evert Sprinchorn's in *August Strindberg: Selected Plays,* vol. 2 (Minneapolis, 1986). The citations in this chapter are taken from all three translations.

2. Many artists before Strindberg consciously (so to speak) dipped into their unconscious for inspiration, but Strindberg devised the term *automatic art*. See his essay "The New Arts; or, The Role of Chance in Artistic Creation," trans. Albert Bermel, in *Inferno, Alone and Other Writings*, ed. Evert Sprinchorn (New York, 1968), 97-103.

3. Harry G. Carlson, *Strindberg and the Poetry of Myth* (Berkeley, Calif., 1982), 191-213.

4. Evert Sprinchorn, *Strindberg as Dramatist* (New Haven, Conn., 1982). The three figures are Buddha, of whom there is a statue in scene iii; Christ, a savior, as Arkenholz is a savior, with a Sunday child's vision; and Siegfried in Wagner's *Ring* cycle, especially *Die Walküre*.

5. In Sprinchorn's Wagnerian interpretation Hummel plays Wotan, and Adele is a Brünnhilde who is not rescued from an equivalent of the ring of fire. One might add the Colonel as a rough equivalent of Alberich the dwarf, who has to surrender the ring to Wotan, as the Colonel does to Hummel in scene ii.

6. Strindberg, like most Europeans, remained highly conscious of class rank, a topic that permeates most of his drama.

7. Transformations became an acting technique in the United States in the early 1960s, arising from improvisations practiced by the Second City companies and by the Open Theatre. Before long they were taken up all over the country and abroad as a practice for training actors and for rehearsing scenes. Some American playwrights like Megan Terry and Jean-Claude Van Itallie used them repeatedly in their playscripts. Strindberg, like Wagner, Gozzi, Shakespeare, and other dramatists, saw and took advantage of the inherent theatricality of transformations.

8. Hummel anticipates Alfred Hitchcock's movie shots in which the camera moves like a spirit through windows. In *High Anxiety* Mel Brooks sends a Hitchcockian camera through a window—and smashes it.

9. "Cryptology is all," whispers Kenneth Burke parenthetically during a discussion of secrets in tragedy (in a context I have lost).

10. The infection at the core suggests either cancer or venereal disease, as a number of critics have noticed, and this explanation might also be compatible with Arkenholz's remark about the most beautiful flowers being the most poisonous.

11. I do not mean to imply by this string of contrasts that there are not also similarities between Julie and Jean. But Strindberg implies that they are drawn together, fascinated, by their differences.

12. The version cited here is Horace Gregory, trans., *Ovid: The Metamorphoses*, (New York, 1958), 278-80.

13. Apollo decreed that the sounds of grief, "Ai, Ai," to commemorate the death of

Hyacinthus, would also begin the name of the hero to come, Aias (Ajax).

14. For this amalgam of opposites I prefer the mythical *hermaphrodite,* with its Olympian allusions, to the more physiological word *androgyne.*

15. Arvid Paulson, trans., *Letters of August Strindberg to Harriet Bosse* (New York, 1959), 16n13. See also Carla Waal, *Harriet Bosse: Strindberg's Muse and Interpreter* (Carbondale, Ill., 1990).

16. Writing about "a strain in the comic tradition" that "presents a pattern of freeing the woman from bondage to an infertile (incestuous) lover," W. Thomas MacCary applies that tradition to Shakespeare's "pattern of action in the Persephone myth from the male point of view." Shakespeare continues "to associate the young girl with freshness, fertility, and innocence (she is herself a flower), to emphasize her fascination with the penis (the hyacinth or narcissus) and therefore to see in her the potential for the insatiable demands of mature women, i.e., mothers." MacCary, *Friends and Lovers: The Phenomenology of Desire in Shakespearean Comedy* (New York, 1984), 42. It may be worth adding that Wagner's Siegfried repeatedly bewails the loss of his mother, Sieglinde, who died giving birth to him, and that he associates Brünnhilde, almost as soon as he sets eyes on her, with his dead mother. That Valkyrie is, too, a mother figure of sorts, or at least the mature woman-lover, since she protected Sieglinde for a time, slept for however long it took Siegfried to be born and grow up and discover her inside her encircling fire, and was a stepsister to Siegfried's mother and father and is therefore now his aunt-beloved. The function of a Valkyrie in Norse and Gothic mythology—returning the souls of slain warriors to Valhalla—both emphasizes and transcends sexual distinctions. (I do not share MacCary's view of mature women.)

17. See Evert Sprinchorn and Seabury Quinn, Jr., trans., *The Chamber Plays* (New York, 1962), 228n.17. In this note Sprinchorn mentions that Strindberg wanted a subtitle with the picture, the quotation from the Apocalypse (21:4) that includes "And death shall be no more."

18. Hummel's name may derive from the second half of the team of William F. Howe and Abraham H. Hummel, crooked lawyers who defended many notorious underworld figures in New York during the last three decades of the nineteenth century. The team was dissolved by the district attorney in 1907, the year when Strindberg wrote *The Ghost Sonata.* See Richard H. Rovere, *The True and Scandalous History of Howe & Hummel* (New York, 1947).

Playing the Role for Real

1. I retain the Italian title and the name of the protagonist to avoid confusion with other Henrys, Henris, Heinrichs, and as a reminder that the play has an Italian (not to say Italianate) origin and viewpoint.

2. The translation cited in this chapter is Eric Bentley's *Emperor Henry* in *Pirandello's Major Plays* (Evanston, Ill.), 1991.

3. I say "aptly" Germanic because northern Italians were, and possibly still are, predominantly descended from the Germanic Lombards.

4. The hereditary situation of Enrico and his sister is reminiscent of that of Madame Ranevskaya and her brother, Gayev, in *The Cherry Orchard.* In both cases the female child of the family owns the property.

5. Albert Bermel, "Jean Vilar: Unadorned Theatre for the Greatest Number," *Tulane Drama Review* 10 (Winter 1960): 24-43.

Summary: Comedy in Hiding

1. Film "genres" multiply. *Thelma and Louise* (1991) was designated the first female buddy picture.

2. Irving Howe, introduction to *Short Shorts: An Anthology of the Shortest Stories,* ed. Irving Howe and Ilana Weiner Howe (New York, 1983), xiv-xv.

Jest and Superjest

1. Bernard Shaw, *Complete Plays with Prefaces,* vol. 3 (New York: 1963) is the standard edition. The play was first published in 1906. Citations from it in this chapter are taken from the initial paperback printing (London, 1946).

2. G. Wilson Knight, *The Golden Labyrinth* (New York: 1962), 352. Martin Meisel observes in *Shaw and the Nineteenth-Century Theatre* (Princeton, N.J., 1963), 183, that in *Man and Superman* "the Comedy becomes a parable for a Philosophy."

3. According to the postscript, "The evolutionary theme of the third act of Man and Superman was resumed by me twenty years later in the preface to Back to Methuselah, where it is developed as the basis of the religion of the near future." If this were H. G. Wells or Paul Claudel writing, the words might mean exactly what they say. But not Bernard Shaw—not with that giveaway word *near* tucked in.

4. The main plot of *Man and Superman* deals with such a love-versus-honor conflict, although Shaw, with a typical subverting of tradition, resolves his play in favor of love.

5. Morris, it might be said, was also a Communist by artistic choice, as his *News from Nowhere* (1891) implies in promoting belief in an utopian community of craftsmen living together, a fraternity and sorority in harmony with its own goodness and beauty, populated by William Morrises and their female counterparts. Morris gave his life to beauty; designed his home after he married—his own furniture, kitchenware, wallpaper; printed his own books on a hand press; wove his own curtains; and founded the Society for the Protection of Ancient Buildings in Britain. He was the Communist Citizen Most Likely to Succeed before *Communist* became a term of abuse (and long before the Soviets and Chinese took to evasively calling themselves socialists), because he was so bent on self-sufficiency and self-improvement as to be selfless. Morris's communism belonged, says St. John Ervine, "not to the age of Karl Marx, but to the ages of the Icelandic Sagas." He was wealthy and could afford to keep up a house in Hammersmith (not far from the one in the play at Richmond) and another in Gloucestershire. Shaw may have Morris in mind when he has Tanner write in his "Revolutionist's Handbook" that "a genuine communist" is "roughly definable as an intensely proud person who proposes to enrich the common fund instead of to sponge on it." Tanner also mentions John Noyes, who founded the Oneida community in America, made up of polygamous craftsmen and their multiple families. I do not mean—far from it—to equate Tanner as a personality with Morris or Noyes. In the preface to *The Apple Cart*, however, Shaw quotes the aphorism of Morris: "No man is good enough to be another man's master." This is a fair summary of what Morris apparently understood by communism. Tanner's communism has an inevitable aristocratic tinge to it. He accepts his position as a "master" in English society, and his advocacy of

the Superman as an ideal means that he goes along with something like Nietzsche's "master morality."

6. Ramsden might be compared in our time to a board member of Freedom House, perhaps a former socialist or Communist, later a "liberal-with-a-small-*l*" who fought the Communist conspiracy twenty-four hours a day until communism foundered in Eastern Europe without his help or opposition.

7. The three unmarried men in the play have sisters: Octavius and Violet, Ramsden and Miss Ramsden, Straker and Louisa. (The older Malone is a widower.) This array of sisters may be a coincidence, but it probably is not.

8. When Tanner attributes a quotation to Voltaire, Straker corrects him: it was from "Bow-Mar-Shay."

9. It seems to me plausible that Shaw derived the idea of Mendoza's band of squabbling idealists from the outlaws ("Know then that some of us are gentlemen") who elect the exile Valentine their leader in *The Two Gentlemen of Verona*, IV. i. One critic wrote, "Neither before nor after *The Two Gentlemen of Verona* has dramatic literature known a band of outlaws like these—except once: there are the pirates of Penzance: but then Gilbert meant his to be funny." H. B. Charlton, *Shakespearian Comedy* (New York, 1938). So did Shaw. Another critic was subsequently "reminded of W. S. Gilbert's pirates, that other band of unterrifying desperadoes who inform us that they 'are all gentlemen gone wrong.'" Berners A. W. Jackson, ed., *The Complete Pelican Shakespeare* (London, 1969), 188. Shaw must have been familiar with *The Pirates of Penzance* (1880), but knew *The Two Gentlemen* intimately as he proves in his celebrated putdown of Augustin Daly's adaptation of that play in 1895 in *Our Theatre of the Nineties*.

10. A number of critics, including Margery Morgan, Louis Crompton, and Charles A. Carpenter, interpret the last embrace—accompanying dialogue and stage directions—as a not-so-covert version of a sex act onstage between Ann and Jack. Carpenter writes: "In Elizabethan drama the terms 'kill' and 'die' [which occur in the text] readily evoke the crescendo of the sex act, mutual orgasm. Given Shaw's highly suggestive context, with Ann panting (though not like a Great Dane, of course) and moaning, 'It is lasting longer than I thought,' the sexual implication of Jack's 'Let it kill us' is impossible to fend off. Seconds before, Ann has said: 'If anyone comes while we are like this, you will have to marry me' (try accenting *comes, this*, and *marry*)." Charles A. Carpenter, "Sex Play Shaw's Way," *Shaw Review* 18, no. 2 (May 1975): 70–74.

11. Tanner is a more complicated version of Charteris in Shaw's early play *The Philanderer,* while Ann and Violet divide and share some of the characteristics of Julia and Grace, the two women who compete for Charteris and by whom he claims to be pursued. The last stage direction of *The Philanderer* is a shocker. Charteris, a playboy by profession, goes to congratulate Julia, whom he has palmed off on a man she does not love. At the end of this bright sex comedy, the stage direction says, "Charteris, amused and untouched, shakes his head laughingly. The rest look at Julia with concern, and even a little awe, feeling for the first time the presence of a keen sorrow." Julia has not only got the wrong man, but Charteris, the "right" man, adds to her misery with his amused and unfelt congratulations. The play's ending broadens into something quite different from comedy, as do, say, Molière's *The Forced Marriage* and *The Misanthrope*. Shaw lightened the agony of this scene—which makes us look back more intently at the rest of the play—by adding a

fourth, reflective act; but he restored the agony by excluding the fourth act from the published and performed versions of *The Philanderer*.

12. Arthur Ganz alludes to "the sadly desperate breeding projects in Section X of The Revolutionist's Handbook." Ganz, *George Bernard Shaw* (New York, 1983), 147.

13. Fredric Berg's doctoral dissertation, "Shaw and Superman: The Development of a Dramatic Structure to Serve the Presentation of a Philosophical Concept" (City University of New York, 1990) traces the genesis of the Superman in Shaw's earlier plays.

14. Shaw goes on: "This may puzzle the people who believe that there is such a thing as an absolutely right point of view, usually their own. It may seem to them that nobody who doubts this can be in a state of grace. However that may be, it is certainly true that nobody who agrees with them can possibly be a dramatist, or indeed anything else that turns upon a knowledge of mankind. Hence it has been pointed out that Shakespear had no conscience. Neither have I, in that sense."

15. To illustrate further this distinction between satire and a picture of a desirable course of events to come, let me cite as an example of the latter Edward Bellamy's *Looking Backward* (1888), a classic that is sometimes said to have influenced the young Shaw. In this novel the hero, Julian West, has crossed a time bridge of 113 years: he was put to sleep by hypnosis in 1887 and awakens in the year 2000, still only thirty years old. West finds himself in the marvelous, peaceful, egalitarian society (a new Boston complete with "credit cards") that has replaced the old, greedy capitalism of the nineteenth (and twentieth) century.

16. For a discussion of Joan's fallibility as a human being, readers are referred to my *Contradictory Characters* (New York,1973), 185–206.

17. A drily comic irony similar to Shaw's is found in Samuel Butler's novels. One sentence from chapter 14 of *Erewhon,* for example, anticipates Shaw's attitude to the improvement of the mind. The narrator, a self-styled missionary and the son of a clergyman, hopes to convert the nation of Erewhon to nineteenth-century Protestantism: "Was there nothing which I could say to make [the Erewhonians] feel that the constitution of a person's body was a thing over which he or she had at any rate no initial control whatever, while the mind was a perfectly different thing and capable of being created anew and directed according to the pleasure of its possessor?"

Dependence Day

1. The production of *Our Town* directed at Lincoln Center by Gregory Mosher subtly let the play's less cheerful notes reverberate.

2. Citations in this chapter come from *Ah, Wilderness!* in O'Neill, *The Plays of Eugene O'Neill* (New York, 1955).

3. Sid historically precedes two other dramatic figures who are at their best when drunk: the millionaire played by Harry Myers in Chaplin's *City Lights* (1935) and Brecht's Herr Puntila (1941).

Society as a Brothel

1. Jean Genet, *The Balcony*, trans. Bernard Frechtman (New York, 1958). All quotations in this chapter come from this first English edition.

2. *The Balcony* happens to be the first play that presented a brothel, its employees,

and its patrons without trying to win a maudlin sympathy for them.

3. Wilhelm Stekel, *Sexual Aberrations*, trans. S. Parker, 2 vols. (New York, 1964). In this connection see especially vol. 2, pp. 343-48.

4. Theodor Reik, *Masochism in Sex and Society*, trans. Margaret H. Beigel and Gertrud M. Kurth (New York, 1962). This title, a commercial come-on, is a lumpish translation of Reik's title in German, *Aus Leiden Freuden,* which means literally "Out of Suffering, Joy" and is borrowed from a letter written by Beethoven. See especially part 7, "Social Forms."

5. In *Danton's Death*, when Danton hears that one of Robespierre's cronies wants all masks torn off, he replies that the faces will be torn away with the masks. The same might be said of the kinkies in *The Balcony*.

6. I argue in favor of the search for an audience at some length in my *Contradictory Characters* (New York, 1973), 122-43.

7. Once we look at it this way, *The Balcony* is a directly political work. Allan Francovich writes, "As Genet points out in his preface to *The Balcony*, directors have often forced a political interpretation on his works. Had they understood the dynamics of any of the plays they might not have felt so free. They might have realized that a truly organic view of politics was already implicit in the structure of the work." Frankovich, "Genet's Theatre of Possession," *The Drama Review* T-45, pp. 25-45. See also Lucien Goldmann, "Une pièce réaliste: le Balcon," *Les Temps modernes* (June 1960).

8. Genet pulls a crafty trick in the Beggar's studio (scene iv), just before we see Irma's room. The three panels of the screen, which were red, brown, or green previously, are now mirrors. The Beggar's reflected gestures move in each of these three mirrors; he multiplies himself fourfold, another apparent act of power. But these are false mirrors. Genet calls for three actors to play the reflections. He wants real-looking reflections, it seems, not silvered surfaces, and realizes that only an accomplished designer could bring off the desired effect. Three mirrors set up as a screen might reflect the chandelier he calls for in each scene so blindingly that the spectators could not hold their gaze on the proscenium.

9. For a discussion of the "nothingness" or "absence" in *The Balcony* see Josephine Jacobsen and William R. Mueller, *Ionesco and Genet: Playwrights of Silence* (New York, 1968). The authors make much of the Bishop's line about heading toward absence but pay little attention to the end of the line, which has to do with death and God and the possibility of transfiguration. Their book dubs as "playwrights of silence" two of the most voluble writers and most conscious stylists of the postwar theatre.

10. According to Richard N. Coe, *The Balcony* has an epic structure like that of a play by Brecht. Coe goes on to say: "The Brechtian theatre insists on a conventionally positive attitude in the dramatist, and Genet has done his best to conform—but only with partial success." Coe, *The Vision of Jean Genet* (New York, 1968), 257. This opinion rests on three misunderstandings. First, if Coe means Brecht when he personifies "the Brechtian theatre," he is wrong in arguing that Brecht has a "conventionally positive attitude" as a dramatist: Brecht has a highly unconventional, anything-but-affirmative attitude as a dramatist. Second, Genet does not seem to be remotely trying to do "his best" to "conform" with such an attitude, which sounds closer to softhearted Broadway than to either Genet or Brecht. Third, *The Balcony* does not have an epic structure but, appropriately, the structure of a *Grand Hotel* sort of play. Irma, at the brothel's center, resembles the

goddess in a Greek tragedy who governs the action from the sidelines (prologue and/or epilogue). Tom F. Driver identifies her with the author: "Irma is Genet. As playwright, he is the mistress of these illusions, the theater his bordello, we his paying customers." See Driver, *Jean Genet* (New York, 1966), 37.

11. Especially in the chapter called "The Primitive Phase" in *The Origin of the Theatre* (1955; New York, 1961), Benjamin Hunningher applies to the theatre the theories developed by Johan Huizinga in his classic work *Homo Ludens: A Study of the Play Element in Culture* (Boston, 1955). Huizinga deals with the nature of games, their social implications as playing, their mimetic properties, their rules and conventions and forms. He discusses such solemn activities as warfare, the law, and philosophy (as well as art) as they are affected by their "play elements."

Dionysos in Sussex

1. Citations in this chapter are taken from Alan Ayckbourn, *The Norman Conquests* (New York, 1979).

2. Ayckbourn mentions the theatrical interdependence of time and space in his introduction to *Absent Friends*: "The stage action matched real time almost second for second," and its "time span had the intended consequence of making the play far more claustrophobic [than the trilogy, which it followed], almost oppressive." Alan Ayckbourn, *Three Plays* (New York, 1979), 8. Ayckbourn also theatricalizes time and space in *Taking Steps*, in the course of which the characters march horizontally onstage, pretending to ascend and descend flights of stairs. Several floors of a dwelling, as well as the steps themselves, coexist on the same stage level.

3. The televised version of the trilogy showed a model of the house and garden, and as the opening credits rolled past, the camera descended slowly into the reproduction of the roofless dining room or sitting room or into the garden until the shot of the model dissolved into that of the life-sized setting.

4. In the West End production, which I did not see, Felicity Kendal played Annie; in the videotaped version, Penelope Wilton did. Both have winning personalities, although I would say Kendal tends to be slightly more detached, more amused, as a performer. In the West End the other actors were Tom Courtenay as Norman, Michael Gambon as Tom, Mark Kingston as Reg, Bridget Turner as Ruth, and Penelope Keith as Sarah. Keith repeated Sarah on television. The television production had Tom Conti as Norman, David Troughton as Tom, Fiona Walker as Ruth, and Richard Briers as Reg. The TV six conspired in their acting as devoutly as a rep team, responding to one another's delicate inflections of tones, lips, eyes, brows, and even, it seemed, noses.

5. East Grinstead is one of those place-names that make Britons crack a reflexive smile, and not because there is any West, North, South, Upper, or Nether Grinstead. It is not coastal, like Hastings, not picturesque, not historic, not conceivably romantic.

6. At another moment, Tom says with staid aptness, "Your cat's gone up a tree, Annie." This is a literal statement and also a metaphorical image of Annie's plight.

7. Sarah may not wear the pants in her household, but she does keep an eye on them. In *Round and Round the Garden*, she warns Reg, "Put an apron on . . . otherwise you'll ruin those trousers." As it turns out, Ruth accidentally tips wine on Reg's trousers.

8. The balky chair is one example of how the farceur in Ayckbourn introduces

objects into a number of scenes in the trilogy: brambles that stab Norman, pajamas he has bought for his East Grinstead weekend, food (including spilt wine and the tin of water biscuits that Sarah hurls at Reg), and elusive fuse wire.

9. Ayckbourn's time scheme allows for a nine-hour lacuna on Sunday. The author gives no explanation for this hole in the action, nor is there any reason why he should. As far as I can tell, no significant happenings in this time period affect the action.

10. As Sidney Howard White puts it, Annie "desperately wants to believe what the playful Norman is already convinced of, that there is still romance in the world—despite 'the cynics and liberationists'—and that he is the *one* person who can bring it into their lives." White, *Alan Ayckbourn* (Boston, 1984), 65.

11. He lies, for instance, when he tells Annie he left a note for Ruth saying that their marriage is over. Or else he lies when he then denies that he wrote and left it. He tells Ruth that she looks "fabulous" and, almost immediately after, that she looks "a dreadful mess." He also tells her that he "thought better of" the weekend, when in truth Annie withdrew from it under pressure from Sarah.

12. Norman echoes the repeated line "On such a night" in the scene between the gratified Lorenzo and the suspicious, despondent Jessica (*Merchant of Venice* V.i. 1-22).

13. A similar, rejected Dionysos impersonation is invited into a later Ayckbourn comedy, *Season's Greetings*. Clive Morris, a writer, takes part in a Christmas celebration and becomes the love object for three of the women in the family. Morris, who achieved a modicum of fame with his first and only book, is humbled more rudely than Norman is and becomes, indeed, a sacrificial victim when a macho member of the family shoots and almost kills him.

Summary: Pain in Hiding

1. As might have been predicted, at least one critical work has associated Shaw with tragicomedy: C. D. Sidhu, *The Pattern of Tragicomedy in Bernard Shaw* (Delhi, 1979).

Male Heroine

1. The translation by Louis Simpson is published in Michael Benedikt and George E. Wellwarth, eds., *Modern French Theatre* (New York, 1964).

2. A chamber pot and a basin adorned most hotel rooms in the days before room sinks and individual bathrooms. The urinal might occur to Thérèse (and Apollinaire) as a symbol of her newfound masculinity. All three are at least slightly connected by being lavatorial. But the Husband's association of a butter dish with a piano and a violin strains the imagination. Very likely that is what it was meant to do.

3. European history books used to say that Napoleon killed off the youth of France by invading Russia. France did have a laggardly population growth during the nineteenth century, more so than that of any other big European nation. The country also lost hundreds of thousands more of its young men during World War I, while others who survived the war suffered from shell shock for many years or walked about with shrapnel still lodged or afloat in their bodies. Yet others, Apollinaire among them, later died from their wounds. France's low productivity in manufacturing and agriculture up until about 1960 is often ascribed to its relatively aged population mean.

4. Whereas Aristophanes' heroine persuades the women of Greece to withhold their bodies from their husbands until peace is declared between Athens and Sparta, Apollinaire's heroine replaces her husband—she goes off to fight his wars for him—until experience teaches her that war is futile. Apollinaire states in his preface that he wrote his play "above all for the French as Aristophanes composed his comedies for the Athenians."

5. The word *surrealism*, as Apollinaire uses it, needs to be distinguished from its usage in the 1920s, when a number of playwrights took the name from Apollinaire but their inspiration from "psychic automatism," as publicized by André Breton, the self-appointed mentor of the movement. According to Breton, psychic automatism would "express the real functioning of thought . . . without any control of reason." Strindberg had come up with the same notion thirty years earlier and called it automatic art. But there can be little doubt that Breton guessed at the possibilities inherent in automatic writing from Apollinaire's play.

6. The balloons on their strings may be an answer to Gide's famous essay, "The Evolution of the Theatre," written the same year as Apollinaire's first draft of his play, 1903. (For the performance in 1917 Apollinaire added only the prologue and the last scene.) Gide the classicist says, "Art is always the result of constraint. To believe that it rises higher as it becomes freer is to believe that what keeps a kite from rising is its string. . . . Art, like Kant's dove, must be supported by resistance in order to rise." André Gide, *My Theatre: Five Plays and an Essay* (New York, 1952).

7. Joseph Campbell, *The Hero with a Thousand Faces,* 2d ed.(Princeton, N.J., 1968), 154.

Timid Exhibitionist

1. Albert Bermel, "Adamov in New York—and Out Again," *Tulane Drama Review* T-5 (Autumn 1959): 104-7.

2. The Malagrida quotation serves as the epigraph to book 1, chapter 22, of Stendhal's *The Red and the Black.*

3. The English version of *Taranne,* translated by Albert Bermel, is published in *Four Modern French Comedies,* with an introduction by Wallace Fowlie (New York, 1960).

4. Arthur Adamov, *Strindberg* (Paris, 1955), 8. In the first chapter of this book, Adamov writes, "It was Strindberg, or, more exactly, *A Dream Play,* that incited me to write for the theatre." Adamov's Taranne is reminiscent of Indra's Daughter in *A Dream Play,* as well as the student Arkenholz in *The Ghost Sonata* or the Stranger in *To Damascus*: Taranne is a psychologically convincing figure who seems "real" enough but moves through a succession of unreal settings.

5. The solo speech recalls Chekhov's playlet *On the Harmfulness of Tobacco,* in which the monologist Nyukhin, who is supposed to be delivering a public lecture, scurries about from unfinished bits of narrative and family gossip to the fears that hide behind everything he says: fears of his wife and daughters, fears about his ineffectuality.

6. In production, the Manageress's set change ought to be matter-of-fact, not weird or conspiratorial. This particular dream exists almost on the plane of naturalness, so that the protagonist is misled into expecting a train of real, everyday events. The play's dreamlike atmosphere is much closer to that created by Kafka in *The Trial* than to Orson Welles's distortions and exaggerations in his striking film adaptation.

7. Taranne is listed at the head of the dramatis personae, Jeanne at the foot, following the order of appearance, but of the fourteen roles, only these two have names. The other twelve have titles, such as Chief Inspector, Lady Journalist, Old Employee, Manageress.

8. Adamov's extraordinary discussion of his own exhibitionism, an article written in 1939, was published as "part of a psychoanalytic journal" called *L'Aveu* (The confession) in 1946 and published in an English translation by Richard Howard in *Evergreen Review* 2, no. 8 (Spring 1959): 64-95.

9. Philip Weissman, *Creativity in the Theatre* (New York, 1965), 12-13. When he deals with exhibitionists in general, Weissman seems sound enough in a fairly obvious way. But in his later references to actors (see especially 18 et. seq.) he would enrage an existential psychologist because he does not cope with the individual personality. He uses infantile and childhood fears to account for a person's subsequent choice of profession, rather than showing those fears to be some (among many) determinants of later psychological turmoil.

10. "The absence (or lack) of communication" has served honorably and now deserves a friendly burial, along with such other soporific collections of words as "the crisis of identity," "the alienation of man (of youth, of workers, of intellectuals)," "the unreality of reality," "the loss of (family) values," "man's inhumanity to man," and "the degeneration of language."

Anything but Absurd

1. In a medieval farce called *Le Cuvier* (The washtub) one of the two principals, a peasant, is named Jaquinot (Jimmy), and his mother-in-law, Jaquette. His wife has no name.

2. The quotations in this chapter are taken from the original translations by Donald M. Allen of *Jacques* (entitled *Jack*) and *The Chairs* in *Four Plays by Eugène Ionesco* (New York, 1958).

3. In French, *cat* and *sex* are both four-letter words.

4. Ionesco follows a similar pattern, much more explicitly, in a later, longer play, *Exit the King* (Le Roi se meurt). I recall hearing a radio play many years ago on the same theme, Tyrone Guthrie's *The Flowers Are Not for You to Pick*. A surge of memories passes through the consciousness of a young clergyman in the last few seconds before he drowns, as he "comes up for the third time."

5. Shakespearean nonsense:

DOGBERRY: Marry, sir, they have committed false report; moreover, they have spoken untruths; secondarily, they are slanders; sixth and lastly, they have belied a lady; thirdly, they have verified unjust things; and to conclude, they are lying knaves. (*Much Ado About Nothing* V.i.210-14)

HOLOFERNES: Most barbarous intimation! yet a kind of insinuation, as it were, *in via,* in way, of explication; *facere,* as it were replication, or, rather, *ostentare,* to show, as it were, his inclination—after his undressed, unpolished, uneducated, unpruned, untrained, or, rather, unlettered, or, ratherest, unconformed fashion. (*Love's Labor's Lost* IV.ii.13-18)

BOTTOM: The eye of man hath not heard, the ear of man hath not seen, man's hand is not able to taste, his tongue to conceive, nor his heart to report, what my dream was. (*A Midsummer Night's Dream* IV.i.209-12)

6. A figure in Alan Ayckbourn's *Taking Steps* puts his listeners into a snooze as soon as he starts to speak.

7. The repeating of words or mutilated bits of words until they acquire a preliterate sound, or distinct "sound values," was taken up by a number of postwar playwrights, among them Ann Jellicoe (especially in *The Sport of My Mad Mother*) in Britain and Megan Terry in the United States.

Almighty Goad

1. The two *actes sans paroles*, a "mime for one player" and a "mime for two players," translated from the French by Beckett, appear in Samuel Beckett, *Krapp's Last Tape and Other Dramatic Pieces* (New York, 1960), 123-41.

2. Charles R. Lyons writes, "While his plays have become briefer and more cryptic through the years, this brevity and intensification do not reveal an increasingly esoteric and private theatrical imagination. On the contrary, they demonstrate Beckett's increasing faith in the communicative resources of the theatre." Lyons, *Samuel Beckett* (New York, 1983), 171.

3. Linda Ben-Zvi, "Phonetic Structure in Beckett: From Mag to Gnaw," in *Beckett Translating / Translating Beckett*, ed. A. W. Friedman, Charles Rossman, and Dina Sherzer (University Park, Pa., 1987), 155-64.

4. *Film* similarly includes a reduction to the essentials of pure moviemaking, and by *pure* here I mean freed of dialogue. Its eight and a half (before Fellini) pages of screenplay supplemented by five pages of notes veer in and out of a peremptory tone akin to that of the stage directions in Beckett's plays.

5. Alan Schneider, *Entrances: An American Director's Journey* (New York, 1986), 354.

6. Alan Schneider, "Working with Beckett," in *On Beckett: Essays and Criticism*, ed. S. E. Gontarski (New York, 1986), 243.

7. Ruby Cohn, *Back to Beckett* (Princeton, N.J., 1973), 188.

8. When he wrote the repeated stage direction, "falls, gets up immediately, dusts himself," was Beckett thinking of the 1936 movie *Swing Time,* in which Fred Astaire and Ginger Rogers, in the number by Jerome Kern and Dorothy Fields, kept urging audiences to "pick yourself up, dust yourself off, start all over again"?

9. Jane W. Stedman remarks: "Morton's 'Romance of Real Life,' as its subtitle described it, is an almost perfect example of that form of Victorian farce which consists of placing a pair of characters with antithetical interests, habits, or occupations, in an eccentric situation which demands ingenuity, often of a wildly inventive kind, and which is frequently resolved arbitrarily—the forced ending being part of the fun." Stedman also notes that Morton "had adapted his play from two French farces: *Une Chambre aux Deux Lits* (A Room with Two Beds) and *Frisette*." Stedman, *Gilbert Before Sullivan* (Chicago, Ill., 1967), 18. Beckett was almost surely familiar with, or aware of, the British play and one of its antecedents. Whether Neil Simon knew of the play or of the principle of mismatched partners, he used it in something like the traditional fashion in *The Odd Couple.*

10. Cohn, *Back to Beckett*, 177. Perhaps the goad needs the "increased mechaniza-

tion" to travel more distance as the sacks are shifted farther from the right wing.

11. In an introductory essay, Gerald Rabkin finds in Kenneth Bernard's drama "a post-Beckettian universe without God, justice, reason, order." See *Two Plays by Kenneth Bernard* (Santa Maria, Calif., 1990), i. The term *post-Beckettian* may mean Bernard has gone beyond Beckett in some respect(s), which is not true, or that Beckett has made the world look terrible for those in the theatre who followed him. But in many of his plays Beckett certainly posits both a god and order—so much order that the inanimate roles, such as objects, oppress the human (or humanoid) roles.

12. Rosette C. Lamont, "To Speak the Words of 'The Tribe': The Wordlessness of Samuel Beckett's Metaphysical Clowns," in *Myth and Ritual in the Plays of Samuel Beckett*, ed. Katherine H. Burkman (Cranbury, N.J., 1987), 58, 63.

For Sex and Empire

1. As a twelfth mention, the song has a title, which in Brechtian style prefaces the lyric and in which the word *nine* is, for the only time in the text itself, spelled out in letters. The play appears in several anthologies, in whole and in part. The original edition was published by Pluto Press, London, in 1979. That edition is the one quoted in this chapter.

2. According to one source, the words *cloud nine* date back at least to 1965. Eric Partridge, *Dictionary of Catch Phrases*, rev. Paul Beale (Westchester, N.Y., 1986). Other slang dictionaries interpret it as "the very pinnacle of bliss," "the height of euphoria," "paradise." Beale suggests that it compares with "over the moon" and is a numerical advance on the earlier "cloud lucky seven," though other authorities refer to the shorter "cloud seven."

3. In an interview Churchill related that an older woman who had had a "very violent and unhappy marriage, with no pleasure from sex at all . . . remarried." With her new husband, she said, "when we have our organisms [*sic*], we're on cloud nine." From Judith Thurman, "Caryl Churchill: The Playwright Who Makes You Laugh About Orgasm, Racism, Class Struggle, Homophobia, Woman-Hating, the British Empire, and the Irrepressible Strangeness of the Human Heart," *Ms.*, May 1982, p. 57.

4. There is an eternal topicality in Clive's defense of "pacifying" the local community: "It's all over now. Everything is under control. . . .We did a certain amount, set a village on fire and so forth." When asked if the raid was necessary, he replies, "Obviously, it was necessary . . . or it wouldn't have happened."

5. Harry, as a reminder, is the familiar form of Henry, the other most popular name for an English king.

6. *Caroline*, the adjective applied to the years in which Charles I and Charles II reigned, especially the latter, has additional bearing here. Elin Diamond points out (with some exaggeration) that "the celebrated first scene [of *Cloud Nine*] presents a cast of characters made familiar in *The Widow Ranter*," a play by a woman lately looked on as a matriarch of feminism, Aphra Behn, who lived 1640-89, almost entirely in the reign of Charles II, and whom Diamond compares with Caryl Churchill in "Closing No Gaps: Aphra Behn, Caryl Churchill, and Empire," in *Caryl Churchill: A Casebook,* ed. Phyllis R. Randall (New York, 1988), 161-74.

7. Judith Thurman quotes the playwright: "The white actor plays a black, and men play women, because the black man and the women are unreal to themselves, they have no

sense of their own value—they have both taken on the identity given to them by a white man." But in addition, "there was no way I could suddenly get hold of a black actor" ("Caryl Churchill," 57). This is another instance of nontraditional casting or unorthodox design or some other experimental quirk of production caused by making the best of circumstances, rather than by artistic choice. A famous example is the Mercury Theatre *Julius Caesar* of Orson Welles and John Houseman in 1937, costumed in contemporary gangsters' clothing because money ran short.

8. Every time Joshua's parents are mentioned, they are called his "father and mother," in that order.

9. If Caroline had accepted Harry's offer and accompanied him on his trips, she would have been entitled to call herself Mrs. Saunders of the Rivers.

10. This wedding between Harry and Ellen, writes John M. Clum, "provides the ironic and fitting climax to Act I of *Cloud 9*. It is the triumph of appearance over reality, heterosexual order over polymorphous perversity." Clum, "'The Work of Culture': *Cloud 9* and Sex/Gender Theory," in *Caryl Churchill: A Casebook*, ed. Randall, 102.

11. Kate Millett's book of that title had been published in 1970.

12. Technically the four scenes take place on a winter afternoon, in spring, on a summer night, and "in late summer."

13. ELLEN: Betty, what happens with a man? I don't know what to do.
    BETTY: You just keep still.
    ELLEN: And what does he do?
    BETTY: Harry will know what to do.

14. In 1990 the MTV organization declined to broadcast a video called "Justify My Love," made by the rock performer Madonna, on the grounds that it showed the "erotic fantasies of the star and a lover, portrayed by Madonna's boy friend, Tony Ward, during an assignation in a Paris Hotel. The fantasies [involved] voyeurism, female and male bisexuality, cross-dressing, mild sadomasochism and multiple partners." Protesting the cancellation, "Madonna asked, 'Why is it that people are willing to go to a movie and watch someone get blown to bits for no reason and nobody wants to see two girls kissing or two men snuggling. I think the video is romantic and loving and has humor in it.'" Story filed by Stephen Holden, *New York Times,* 28 Nov. 1990, p. C13.

15. I say "seemed," and not "was," much harder for two reasons: Christopher Durang's *Sister Mary Ignatius Explains It All for You* ran into local censorship in many communities at about the same time; and in 1990, by which time plays and films had become studded with epithets, verbs, and adjectives that would have been rated obscenely unacceptable only thirty years before, the head of the National Endowment for the Arts caved in to the roars of a number of cultural cavemen by inserting a censorship clause into acceptance contracts of the Endowment's awards, provoking many artists and groups into public statements rejecting the awards until the clause was removed for 1991 and thereafter.

16. *Shakespeare's Pastoral Comedy* (Chapel Hill, N.C., 1972). See especially "Comedy and Its Pastoral Extension," 20-48.

Summary: Farcical Overlay

1. A trapper who built a cabin right on the 49th Parallel was compelled to decide

whether to pay taxes to Canada or the United States. He elected to join the United States, because, he said, "I hear them Canadian winters is fearful cold."

2. The opening words of Francis Steegmuller's biography read: "Nobody knows to this day, for a certainty, who the father of Guglielmo de Kostrowitzky was, and some people think that even when Kostrowitzky grew to manhood and was known as Guillaume Apollinaire he himself may never have been sure. At various times he hinted at being the son of an eminent personage—a noble, a prince of the blood, a heretic, a prelate, or even a pope. Perhaps it is in celebration of one of those references that Picasso made his drawing of Apollinaire on the throne of St. Peter, wearing the tiara—and a wrist watch." Steegmuller, *Apollinaire: Poet among the Painters* (New York, 1963), 3.

Conclusion

1. Some of Wedekind's plays remain in print in bowdlerized versions, such as in *Five Tragedies of Sex* (London, 1952), although translated (by Stephen Spender and Frances Fawcett) and published under admirable auspices.

2. I recently saw productions of a seventeenth-century comedy by Molière and a twentieth-century Russian drama about the life of Molière on successive days. In each case the director scorned the original drama and interposed scenes of humping and sex, so that a pair of unlike, unconnected plays became forced step-siblings, losing their individuality and reminding a spectator of uncounted other productions.

3. This type of interweaving is not the same as the contrast between viewing a comic or farcical role from without (funny and hapless) and from within (put upon, desperate, pitiful). It presupposes a simultaneously amused and compassionate attitude on the part of spectators, allowing for unfathomable vagaries in those attitudes. A famous cartoon by Charles Addams showed an auditorium packed with spectators whose expressions denoted the utmost horror, save for one face screwed up in sadistic glee.

4. An unusual example of tragicomedy (alternation), which in places slips into tragifarce, is the opera *The Ghosts of Versailles* (1992) by William Hoffman and John Corigliano. Operas from the nineteenth Century and earlier generally adhere closely to a pure genre like tragedy, melodrama, or comedy, although Mozart's are notable exceptions. The scenes in *Versailles* alternate briskly between farce and camp on the one side, acute pathos on the other.

5. Here are a few samples of talk-show fustian that keep sneaking into print: *strategy, agenda, concern, empowerment, resonate, ongoing, to be supportive of, to be hopeful that, basically, in depth, discourse* (noun and verb), *thrust, gravitate toward, proactive, reactive, fundamentally, essentially, catalyst* (for "cause"), *to power, to fuel, to stem (from), to spark, to spawn, more (or equally) importantly, very real, key* (as an adjective), *savvy, there is a sense that, in a very real sense, we have* (or *one has*) *the sense that, downsize, to dialogue, to impact, marginalize, in context, share with* (for "tell"), *problem, solution, non-solution, it is interesting to note that, in terms of* (for "in" or "of" or "for"), *as far as . . . is concerned, subconscious, more* (or *less*) *central to.*

Other offenders, as Henry IV says, we will pause upon.

INDEX

Adamov, Arthur, 191; *Professor Taranne*, 1, 153–60, 212–13; *All Against All*, 153; *The Big and the Little Maneuver*, 153; *The Invasion*, 153; *The Parody*, 153; *Ping Pong*, 153; "The Confession," 214 n. 8
Addams, Charles, 218 n. 3
Adler, Alfred, 10
Adrian, Max, 56
Aeschylus: *The Oresteia*, 10, 156; *Prometheus Bound*, 7, 156; *Seven Against Thebes*, 151
Aesculapius, "the leech," 200 n. 17
Akalaitis, JoAnne, 175
Allen, Donald M., 214 n. 2
Angel, Heather, 182
Anouilh, Jean, 185; *Poor Bitos*, 81, 194; *The Rehearsal*, 194; *Ring Round the Moon*, 139
Apollinaire, Guillaume, 189, 191; *The Breasts of Tiresias*, 143–52, 202 n. 10
Apollo, 66, 205 n. 13
Arden, John: *Live Like Pigs*, 191
Ardhanarisha (myth: Shiva and Shakti), 151
Aristophanes: *The Clouds*, 181; *Lysistrata*, 211 n. 4
Aristotle, 3, 197 n. 6
Arrowsmith, William, 7–8, 197 n. 11
Augustine, Saint, 99
Axelrod, George: *The Seven-Year Itch*, 194
Ayckbourn, Alan, 10, 185; *Absent Friends*, 211 n. 2; *Absurd Person Singular*, 125; *The Norman Conquests*, 124–38, 187; *Season's Greetings*, 212 n. 13; *Taking Steps*, 211 n. 2, 215 n. 6

Babel, Isaac: *Sunset*, 81
Balzac, Honoré: *The Human Comedy*, 122
Barnes, Peter: *Red Noses*, 191; *The Ruling Class*, 191; *Laughter!*, 191
Beauvoir, Simone de, 153
Beckett, Samuel, 189, 191, 194–95; *Acts Without Words, I and II*, 174–80; *Eh Joe*, 175; *Embers*, 174; *Krapp's Last Tape*, 174–75; *Rockaby*, 175; *Endgame*, 175; *Film*, 175, 215 n. 4; *Happy Days*, 102, 174, 204 n. 17; *Play*, 174–75; *Waiting for Godot*, 153, 166, 174, 179
Behn, Aphra: *The Widow Ranter*, 216 n. 6
Benavente, Jacinto: *The Bonds of Interest*, 139
Bentley, Eric: *In Search of Theatre*, 203 nn. 3,

7; *The Life of the Drama*, 4, 197 n. 6; *Stage 2*, 139
Ben–Zvi, Linda, 174
Berghof, Herbert, 79
Bergman, Ingmar: *Ansiktet*, 195
Bernard, Kenneth, 216 n. 11; *How We Danced while We Burned*, 191–92, 216 n. 11
Bismarck, Otto, 96
Blin, Roger, 153
Blumenthal, Ralph, 30
Boadicea, queen of Britain, 143
Böcklin, Arnold: "The Isle of the Dead," 60, 61, 67
Bosse, Harriet, 67
Brecht, Bertolt, 139; *Arturo Ui*, 192; *The Caucasian Chalk Circle*, 2; *Galileo*, 81; *Puntila and his Serf Matti*, 209 n. 3
Breton, André, 213 n. 5
Briers, Richard, 211 n. 4
Bright, John, 89
Bronowski, Jacob, 186
Brook, Clive, 182
Brook, Peter, 127
Brooks, Mel: *High Anxiety*, 205 n. 8
Büchner, Georg, 153; *Danton's Death*, 210 n. 5
Burge, Stuart, 56
Burke, Kenneth, 205 n. 9

Campbell, Joseph, 151
Camus, Albert, 153
Carlyle, Thomas, 96
Carlson, Harry G., 59
Casson, Lewis, 56
Chaplin, Charles, 2; *City Lights*, 209 n. 3; *A King in New York*, 195
Chekhov, Anton, 6, 80, 153; *The Cherry Orchard*, 48, 50, 51, 52, 203 n. 11, 204 nn. 12, 18, 206 n. 4; *On the Harmfulness of Tobacco*, 213 n. 5; *The Sea Gull*, 204 n. 18; *Three Sisters*, 55, 203 n. 9, 204 n. 17; *Uncle Vanya*, 44–57, 160, 186, 194; *The Wood Demon*, 47, 49, 52–53, 203 n. 3, 204 n. 18
Chopin, Frédéric, 163
Christ, 97, 99, 123
Christiani, Dounia B., 198 n. 9
Christie, Julie, 51
Churchill, Caryl: *Cloud Nine*, 181–90
Churchill, Winston, 97